In *Canada's National System of Innovation,* Jorge Niosi discusses the theoretical underpinnings of the concept of innovation, examining the works of Charles Edquist, Christopher Freeman, Bengt-Ake Lundvall, Richard Nelson, and others around the world. He argues that the concept is particularly useful in analysing science and technology policy and related institutions.

Niosi looks at the history of Canada's national system of innovation (NSI), particularly during the post-war period, illuminating the fact that during and after World War II Canadians developed over 30 research universities, 150 government laboratories, and dozens of government policies aimed at nurturing innovation in private firms, academe, and government organizations. He uses data obtained through questionnaires sent to all the large research and development organizations in Canada to analyse Canada's domestic system of innovation, and he finds increasing collaboration between universities, government laboratories, and private firms.

He concludes that Canada has been quite successful in creating a national system of innovation and that the federal government, through its initiatives and innovative techniques, has been the main factor in the creation of this system.

JORGE NIOSI is professor of administration at l'Université du Québec à Montréal.

Canada's National System of Innovation

JORGE NIOSI

with
ANDRÉ MANSEAU
and
BENOÎT GODIN

McGill-Queen's University Press
Montreal and Kingston · London · Ithaca

Legal deposit first quarter 2000
Bibliothèque nationale du Québec

Printed in Canada on acid-free paper

McGill-Queen's University Press acknowledges the
financial support of the Government of Canada through
the Book Publishing Industry Development Program
(BPIDP) for its publishing program. It also acknowledges
the support of the Canada Council for the Arts for its
publishing program.

Canadian Cataloguing in Publication Data

Niosi, Jorge, 1945–
    Canada's national system of innovation
    Includes bibliographical references and index.
    ISBN 0-7735-2012-0
    1. Research – Canada. I. Godin, Benoît II. Manseau,
    André III. Title.
    T177.C2N55 2000   507'.2071   C99-901198-7

This book was typeset by Typo Litho Composition Inc.
in 10/12 Baskerville.

Contents

Tables, Figures, and Insets   vii

Preface   xv

1 Introduction: The NSI and R&D   3

PART I: THE NSI WITHIN CANADA'S BORDERS

2 Canada's R&D System   31

3 Canada's Domestic R&D System   76

4 Linking the Units: Technology Transfer   98

5 The Rise of Cooperative R&D   112

PART II: THE INTERNATIONALIZATION
OF CANADA'S NSI

6 Towards a North American System of Innovation?   131

7 Canadian R&D Abroad. The Patent Record   145

8 Canadian R&D Abroad. Management Practices   167

9 Conclusion. Canada's NSI Today   193

References   205

Index   219

Tables, Figures, and Insets

TABLES

1.1 Percentage of gross expenditure in R&D (GERD) performed by each sector in G7 countries, 1995 / 12

1.2 Percentage of GERD financed by each sector in G7 countries, 1995 / 12

1.3 R&D expenditures in G7 countries, 1995 / 13

2.1 Canada's R&D in 1938 / 33

2.2 Business R&D, by industry, 1955 / 35

2.3 Major Canadian corporations with R&D capabilities, 1969 / 36

2.4 Federal government R&D organizations, 1969 / 43

2.5 Provincial research organizations, 1969 / 44

2.6 Largest Canadian research universities, 1969 / 46

2.7 R&D-active companies: figures from Revenue Canada and Statistics Canada, 1992 / 56

2.8 Concentration of industrial R&D, 1973 and 1995 / 58

2.9 Top twenty-five industrial performers of R&D in Canada, 1995 / 59

2.10 BERD by industry, R&D expenditure intentions, 1995 / 60

2.11 Technology transfer activities, selected Canadian universities, 1992 / 62

2.12 Federal organizations performing R&D, 1995–96 / 64

2.13 Revealed technological advantages (RTAs) of Canadian industry, 1988–91 / 69

2.14 Canadian trade balance in advanced technology products, 1994 / 70

2.15 Venture capital in Canada, 1996 / 72

2.16 Convergence of GERD/GDP in industrial countries, selected years, 1961–95 / 74

3.1 Target population, number of valid responses, and response rate, 1993 / 78

3.2 Regional distribution of Canadian laboratories with twenty-five or more employees, 1993 / 78

3.3 Some characteristics of laboratories sampled, 1992 / 79

3.4 Major laboratories' missions / 81

3.5 Sources of funds for laboratories, 1992 / 81

3.6 Distribution of industrial R&D funds in laboratories, 1992 / 83

3.7 Research outputs in laboratories, 1992 / 83

3.8 Motives for technology transfer / 85

3.9 Major or single most important benefits to laboratories of technology transfer / 86

3.10 Major and most important problems engendered in laboratories by technology transfer / 86

3.11 Number of laboratories patenting and licensing, 1990–92 / 88

3.12 Cooperative agreements, 1992 / 88

3.13 Main motives for cooperation by laboratories / 89

3.14 Laboratories declaring important difficulties (%) / 91

3.15 Position of laboratories within the parent
      organization / 91

3.16 Central versus divisional laboratories / 92

3.17 Industrial laboratories with/without government
      contracts / 92

3.18 Total R&D budgets in central and divisional government
      laboratories, 1992 / 92

3.19 Organization within government laboratories, 1992 / 93

3.20 Patents in central and divisional government laboratories,
      1992 / 93

3.21 Total R&D budgets in university laboratories, 1992 / 93

3.22 Internal organization of university laboratories,
      1993 / 94

3.23 Effectiveness criteria, 1993 / 94

 4.1 Technology transfer in Canadian laboratories,
      1990–92 / 101

 4.2 Motives for technology transfer / 102

 4.3 Strategies used by laboratories for promoting technology
      transfer / 103

 4.4 Benefits obtained by laboratories from technology
      transfer / 105

 4.5 Problems with technology transfer / 105

 4.6 Levels of success in technology transfer / 106

 4.7 Commercial impact of technology transfer / 106

 4.8 Characteristics of industrial laboratories involved in
      technology transfer / 107

 4.9 Characteristics of government laboratories involved in
      technology transfer / 109

4.10 Characteristics of university laboratories involved in
      technology transfer / 111

 5.1 Technological cooperation by Canadian R&D
      laboratories / 114

5.2   Main motives for cooperation / 115

5.3   Main area in which technological cooperation assisted research, 1990–92 / 116

5.4   Problems experienced in cooperation by laboratories, 1990–92 / 116

5.5   Characteristics of industrial laboratories involved in cooperative R&D / 118

5.6   Size of industrial laboratories and cooperative agreements / 118

5.7   Government laboratories with cooperative R&D / 119

5.8   Types of government laboratories according to main partners / 120

5.9   University laboratories involved in cooperation / 121

5.10 Results of licences and cooperation, 1990–92 / 122

5.11 Laboratories' total budgets, 1990–92 / 123

5.12 The rise of government licensing revenues / 123

5.13 Sources of income in government laboratories, 1990–92 / 125

5.14 Sources of income in industrial laboratories, 1990–92 / 125

6.1   The North American NSIs compared, 1993 / 135

6.2   Foreign R&D expenditures in the United States, 1977–96 / 139

6.3   R&D expenditures by majority-owned foreign affiliates of U.S. parent companies, by country, 1982–95 / 140

6.4   Distribution of strategic alliances among economic blocs, 1985–89 / 143

6.5   Canadian international alliances in various economic blocs, 1992 / 143

7.1   Foreign R&D expenditures in the United States and at home, by country, 1990 / 151

7.2   U.S. patents of large Canadian MNCs, granted to their U.S. subsidiaries, 1992–94 / 154

7.3 U.S. patents of Canadian SMEs, granted to their U.S. subsidiaries, 1992–94 / 156

7.4 U.S. patents of Canadian firms, granted to their European subsidiaries, 1992–94 / 157

7.5 Patents granted in the United States to Canadian-owned and -controlled corporations operating abroad, and patents granted to Canadian inventor resident in Canada, 1992–94 / 158

7.6 Patents from foreign R&D obtained by Canadian MNCs, 1992–94 / 159

7.7 Rank correlation between foreign patents and RTA of Canadian firms / 160

7.8 Correlation coefficients and factorial analysis for location determinants of Canadian R&D in the United States / 162

8.1 Geographical distribution of foreign R&D activities in the sample / 176

8.2 Missions of overseas R&D laboratories / 178

8.3 Reasons for establishing R&D abroad / 179

8.4 Budget allocation in laboratories, by mission / 181

8.5 Types of R&D establishment and main R&D activity, as per budget / 181

8.6 Outputs of foreign R&D / 183

8.7 How R&D projects are determined / 184

8.8 Origins of R&D initiatives / 185

8.9 Difficulties of foreign R&D units / 185

8.10 Related diversifiers / 187

8.11 Vertically integrated firms / 188

8.12 The global corporation / 189

9.1 The evolution of Canada's NSI, 1955–97 / 196

9.2 Share of patent applications in manufacturing in Canada, by industrial sector, 1975 and 1990 / 198

FIGURES

2.1   Canada's R&D units: four types, by activity / 48

2.2   Canada's R&D units: four types, by research output / 48

2.3   GERD, by performing sector, 1963–97 / 55

2.4   GERD, by funding sector, 1963–97 / 56

6.1   Canadian merchandise exports to the United States, 1988–96 / 136

6.2   Canadian merchandise imports from the United States, 1988–96 / 136

6.3   Canadian merchandise exports to Mexico, 1988–96 / 137

6.4   Canadian merchandise imports from Mexico, 1988–96 / 137

6.5   U.S. direct investment in Canada, 1988–96 / 138

6.6   Mexican direct investments in Canada, 1988–96 / 139

6.7   Canadian direct investment in Mexico, 1988–96 / 140

6.8   Canadian direct investment in the United States, 1988–96 / 141

7.1   Canadian direct investment abroad, 1994, and Canadian patents abroad, 1992–94 / 153

9.1   Main high-tech industries in Canada, as % of BERD, 1977–97 / 199

9.2   Canada's NSI: money flows / 200

INSETS

1   Entering the Production of Satellites / 42

2   Public Support for Aeronautical Innovation / 44

3   The Evolution of Tax Incentives for R&D, 1960–92 / 50

4   Promoting Biotechnology / 51

5   Basic and Applied Public Research: NRC's Plant Biotechnology Institute / 95

6   Newbridge Networks' R&D / 97

7 Technology Transfer from Industry: IBM Canada / 107

8 Technology Transfer from Universities and Government Labs: Performance Plants Inc. / 108

9 PAPRICAN: Pulp and Paper Research / 126

10 PRECARN and IRIS: Intelligent Systems / 127

11 Primary Metals: Alcan Aluminium and Inco Ltd / 163

12 Northern Telecom / 164

13 Bombardier / 164

Preface

As Canada enters the twenty-first century, it faces several major challenges. One is the consolidation of its national system of innovation (NSI) – that is, the system composed of its innovating firms, universities, and public laboratories, together with the institutions (public and private) that finance innovation. This system developed slowly after Confederation and during the first four decades of the twentieth century, and it has experienced rapid growth in the last sixty years. It may suffer from several gaps and inefficiencies, including overlapping of governmental jurisdictions, duplication of some corporate efforts, missing elements, and some lack of coordination. Nevertheless, it has been a major contributor to Canada's prosperity in the postwar period and may become the most decisive factor of its prosperity in the future. It is now challenged by governments' budgetary priorities.

This book is a tentative portrait of the state of the system of innovation in the mid-1990s. Its first goal is to identify its major strengths and weaknesses and its core elements. Its second, theoretical goal is to develop, refine, and apply the concept of NSI, which seems key to the understanding of present and future trends in economic development. I try to link the concept with theories of endogenous growth, competence perspectives, and evolutionary economics. Chapter 1 is thus devoted to theory about NSIs. In part I, chapter 2 traces the origins and evolution of Canada's NSI, and chapters 3–5 study its domestic system of research and development (R&D). In part II, chapters 6–8 analyse the internationalization of Canadian R&D and inquire into the possible eventual development of a North American supranational system of innovation. Chapter 9 draws the main lessons from the past and suggests possible future paths.

This book is partially the result of my own work, and partially the outcome of research collaboration. In 1992–93, I conducted a massive study on R&D laboratories across Canada with the help of Dr André Manseau, at that time my PhD student in business administration at the Université du Québec à Montréal, and now working with the National Research Council. Several chapters (3–5) of this book summarize the main results of that study and are co-authored. This national study was made possible by the collaboration of Professors Barry Bozeman (director, School of Public Policy, Georgia Institute of Technology, Atlanta) and Michael Crow (professor, Department of International Studies, Columbia University, New York), who kindly shared with me their research methods in laboratories' management. I wish here to acknowledge my gratitude for their generous help. In 1995–96, I conducted a survey of Canadian laboratories abroad, with the help of Professor Benoît Godin, of the Institut national de la recherche scientifique in Montreal. Chapter 8 is the result of that survey. Both the domestic and the international studies were supported by the Social Sciences and Humanities Research Council of Canada (SSHRC) and the Fonds FCAR (Quebec). The international study was also supported by the Fulbright Program, of which I was a fellow in 1995–96, during my sabbatical year at Stanford University as a visiting scholar. I also wish to acknowledge my debt to these institutions for their help during these research projects. Finally, the two anonymous readers of the manuscript made many useful and generous comments, which helped me to improve the book.

Canada's National System of Innovation

1 Introduction: The NSI and R&D

It has become standard knowledge today that technical progress – whether embodied in new capital goods, in the skills of the labour force, or in management and organization – is the engine of economic growth. Developed and developing countries differ basically in their gross stock of capital, in the average duration and quality of workers' education, in their expenditures on research and development (R&D), and thus in their ability to produce and assimilate technological and organizational innovations (Maddison, 1994). The theory of national systems of innovation (NSIs) tries to explain different growth rates in various countries on the basis of national performances in production and adoption of innovation. National performance depends not only on the amounts spent on R&D but also on the institutions, competencies and learning processes through which innovation takes place.

The theory of technological innovation, which started with the concept of the heroic and isolated entrepreneur presented in the writings of Schumpeter (1934), has progressively integrated larger organizations and become a systemic perspective with four major components. First, for technological innovation to occur, actual – or at least potential – markets are essential; these are usually, but not necessarily, domestic in nature. Second, most innovations have taken place within the research departments of established corporations and, in a few cases, within government or university laboratories or within entrepreneurial firms. Third, governments have to provide innovating companies with some financial support in order to share the risks of both the research process and the market reaction to the novelty; they also have to provide highly qualified workers (technicians, managers, engineers, and scientists) who will create the innovation and move it towards the market. Governments also provide the regulatory framework (standards and protection of intellectual property through patents and trademarks) required to stimulate innovation. As well, they create competence (through the education system) and usually intervene in creating the networks of innovators through which positive externalities occur among the different agents of the innovation systems. Finally, innovations appear not in isolation, but most frequently in clusters: for example, new materials or new products require new processes and spur the creation of new machines. These clusters point to the existence of underlying flows of knowledge among innovating organizations. New products usually appear in a number of designs to serve different markets, thus increasing the systemic nature of the process.

Innovation is basically a geographically located phenomenon, at both national and regional levels. Only some twenty countries possess the markets, technological infrastructure, financial institutions, and qualified personnel required to create industrial novelty. Within these nations, a few urban regions concentrate most innovative activities, such as Silicon Valley and Route 128 in the United States, Paris in France, and the M4 Corridor in Britain. But these countries and regions differ in the way in which they conduct innovation: in institutions, in the role of the state, in openness to foreign ideas, in the links among innovating regions, and in the relative weight of universities, government laboratories, and private firms. The concept of national system of innovation (NSI), created in the late 1980s, tends to include all these systemic aspects of the innovative process. I therefore start this chapter by defining the concepts of innovation and NSIs and then look at issues of international convergence and international flows of technological knowledge and personnel and financial support, as well as regional as opposed to national flows. I conclude by stressing the importance and the continued relevance of NSIs.

WHAT IS TECHNOLOGICAL INNOVATION?

Innovation is technical novelty – new or improved products and processes – successfully taken to the market. This activity usually takes place within private firms. Government laboratories and universities often participate in the "upstream" phases of the innovative activities, such as fundamental or applied research. Most frequently, however, private companies gather ideas from users, from the public sector, or from their own employees in marketing, manufacturing, or R&D and apply these ideas to develop new or improved products or processes.

Technology is knowledge about production. It may be incorporated in blue-prints, manuals, books, articles, machines, or equipment, or it may consist only of expertise embodied in technical personnel and thus be tacit, uncodified experience, more difficult to transfer and communicate.

Technological innovation is different from what may be called social, institutional, or organizational innovation. The adoption of new processes, new materials, new products, or new machines often requires changes in the way in which workers and technicians are organized: redefinition of jobs, retraining of employees, new hierarchies or the abolition of existing ones, and other novelties within the firm. Organizational innovation usually accompanies technological innovation. Sometimes the change starts with social innovation, and this sort of change then requires new equipment; the adoption of total quality control, for example, may necessitate new scanning machines, microscopes, or other instrumentation. Conversely, sometimes new technology propels organizational novelty. As Perez (1983) and Nelson (1994), among others, have emphasized, technological and organizational innovations within the firm and within larger, macro-institutions, such as public policy and governmental organizations, also tend to evolve with technological change. For analytical purposes, nevertheless, it is useful to differentiate technological novelty from organizational innovation.

THE CONCEPT OF NSI

The idea that countries differ in the way in which they conduct technological innovation was first proposed by Bengt-A. Lundvall (1988, 1992), Richard R. Nelson (1988, 1993) and Christopher Freeman (1987, 1988, 1995). These authors have produced somewhat varying definitions. Lundvall emphasizes the knowledge dimensions and the interactive character of the learning processes taking place between users and producers within the nation-state. Freeman stresses the way in which private institutions support innovation, as in corporate R&D, in-house training, and industry–university cooperation. Nelson puts more accent on the public institutions that regulate, finance, and keep the innovative process alive. The three writers distinguish between the *narrow* definition (encompassing only the institutions active in R&D, and the public regulatory agencies) and the *broad* sense (including also supporting private institutions, such as banks, and public ones, such as government infrastructure and education systems). Despite differing emphases and some theoretical differences (Nelson is a committed evolutionist, unlike Lundvall and Freeman), the three are writing about the same phenomenon and use similar arguments.

This book is about the NSIs as defined in the restricted way. For this purpose, I have elsewhere helped elaborate the following definition: "A national system of innovation (or national R&D system) is a system of interacting private and public firms, universities and government laboratories, aiming at the production and use of science and technology within national borders. Interaction among these units may be technical, commercial, legal, social and financial, inasmuch as the goal of the interaction is the development, protection, financing or regulation of new science and technology" (Niosi, Saviotti, Bellon, and Crow, 1993).

The most important of the institutions active in the NSI is the corporation, especially one with R&D capabilities, that takes innovation to markets. The NSI also involves government laboratories and universities as well as public agencies with funding mandates for scientific and technical development or with regulatory powers.

Linking these institutions are technical and scientific ideas and data flowing in all directions (among firms, as well as between firms, universities, and public or non-profit laboratories), public money funding innovation in business, and people moving from university to industry and government laboratories, but also from industry to government research centres and between companies. There are also regulatory flows from government to industry regarding intellectual property, standards, coordination, and direction of the system. All these flows can be measured, and many have been, both at the national and at the international level. The concept of NSI presupposes that national flows are more abundant than international flows: shorter distances and a similar culture, legal system, and system of public regulation confer unity on the NSI. Also, flows of people, ideas, and public money are more abundant within borders than across them.

Nevertheless, in the last twenty years international flows have grown rapidly, and they represent an increasing share of the total flows. In particular, smaller countries such as Canada, Sweden, and Switzerland have proportionally more international linkages than do larger countries such as the United States and Japan – more international alliances and more international scientific cooperation. Also, a higher proportion of large companies with head offices in small and medium-sized industrial countries own expatriate R&D laboratories in other industrial countries. The search for economies of scale, the improvement of telecommunication and transportation systems, and the internationalization of production help explain the increasing interconnection between NSIs (Niosi and Bellon, 1994). Internationalization thus complicates the picture without distorting the basic pattern.

MICRO- AND MACRO-DETERMINANTS OF SYSTEMIC LINKS

The quality and quantity of the links that exist among independent institutions in an NSI depend on the internal routines of these institutions and on public policies. These two factors are the micro- and macro-determinants, respectively, of the density of links among organizations within a national system.

Internal Routines and Systemic Links

Organizational routines within business firms are responses to environmental pressures. As Nelson and Winter (1982) have suggested, routines are the "genes" of organizations. Routines survive if they bestow on the organization some competitive advantage over competitors. Organizations vary in the emphasis that they place on networking routines, which link the business firm to other, independent firms, universities, and other organizations. For firms to adopt these routines, networking must bring them some competitive advantage – for example, the sharing of some rare resource, such as skilled managers or researchers, funding, complementary information, or even space (Niosi, 1995). Japanese companies are supposed to have discovered the advantages of cooperation because of their desperate shortage in all the above-mentioned resources during the postwar period.

Internal organization is usually coherent with the strategy for relationships with other organizations. Thus if a government laboratory has chosen the publishing of scientific papers as a major mission, it will relate with independent organizations mostly through flows of scientific information; its effectiveness will be measured through the number of papers published, the quality of the journals in which they are published and the number of citations that they receive. Conversely, if its mission is to transfer technology to industry, it will probably develop quite different criteria for assessing effectiveness: these may include the number of successful technology transfers, the amount of revenue received through these transfers, and their economic impact in terms of employment created in the transferee's institutions. Firms trying to collect some essential resources from their environment will probably emphasize networking and will develop rules and routines governing intellectual property, effectiveness, and organization in order to ensure that cooperation with external organizations reduces the internal shortage.

Macro-determinants

Governments influence the links between firms and other organizations within the NSI by laying out the rules and regulations under which these institutions operate (Lazonick, 1991). These rules and regulations will affect the institutions' missions and modify their effectiveness criteria. Rigid anti-trust laws, such as those in the United States before passage of the National Cooperative Research Act in 1984, will deter cooperation among firms. Conversely, governmental programs aimed at nurturing cooperative industrial development (such as Europe's Airbus and Arianespace) or fostering technological development (such as ESPRIT, EUREKA, and RACE in the European Union and Japan's Fifth Generation Computer Project) will have the opposite effect, fostering cooperation and encouraging a more organized market system.

The role of governments in organizing the form of markets is particularly crucial in the technological field. Governments fund, directly or indirectly, somewhere between 40 per cent and 50 per cent of each industrial country's total R&D; therefore they have a say in the missions and routines of at least some institutions and research projects. This is most obviously the case in government-owned and -controlled institutions, such as public laboratories and universities; governments usually prescribe their missions, rules on intellectual property, and evaluation criteria.

However, private R&D laboratories and private universities are also, under governmental influence through public funding of R&D; governments may, and often do, attach conditions to publicly funded programs for R&D. These conditions may specify whether public funds will support individual companies or groups of collaborative firms conducting R&D and whether individual researchers or cooperative teams employed by different institutions may or may not apply for funds. Also, the granting authorities can measure the success of R&D programs or projects by looking at either independent results (such as a unit's publishing or patenting) or collaborative results (such as joint patenting or publishing); only this latter method promotes cooperation. In order to obtain these public funds, research organizations will have to adapt their internal routines to the requirements of the government programs. The analysis of public programs and internal routines of the institutions is thus key to understanding their systemic links.

Also, governments intervene in the creation of new technological systems – that is, "networks of agents interacting in a specific technology area under a particular institutional infrastructure to generate, diffuse and utilize technology" (Carlsson and Jacobsson, 1997). Public authorities usually provide the funds and the institutional framework needed to create entire new technological fields. We see below the key role of the Canadian state in the creation of the aircraft, aerospace, and nuclear industries and biotechnology during the Second World War and later (chapter 2). This role of governments in the development of new technologies can be explained by the "infant industry" argument that has been put forward by writers from John Stuart Mill to Paul Krugman as a rationale for industrial public policy.

THE NATIONAL R&D SYSTEM AND THE NATIONAL FINANCING OF INNOVATION

As shown above, NSIs in the broad sense include two major, somewhat different elements: the R&D laboratories and public regulatory system and the supporting system for financing innovation. The R&D system (or the NSI, defined narrowly) has basically three sectors: private and public corporations with innovating capabilities (usually with R&D centres or laboratories), research universities, and government laboratories. First, most of the industrial firms conducting R&D have permanent and regular R&D capabilities, but others run temporary and project-based research. Most public and private corporations undertake principally applied R&D, and a few also conduct some fundamental and basic research. Their ultimate output is new and improved products and processes, but intermediary products include research reports, prototypes, pilot plants, blue-prints, and operating manuals.

Second, the R&D system also includes government laboratories, which are active mostly in applied research and also conduct some fundamental R&D. Their outputs are mostly publications and patents but also include some prototypes, some pilot plants, and algorithms.

Third, the R&D system also includes universities, which are especially busy in fundamental research and training. Their output consists of publications, graduate students, and patents. They provide the NSI with skilled personnel and new ideas about the external world, including physical, chemical, and biological characteristics of materials, organisms, and phenomena.

The other major component of the NSI in the broad sense is the financial system of innovation. It is composed of institutions that do not conduct R&D but are key to the continuous sustainability of the system: they are the private and public funding agencies. Two very different types of institutional systems provide financial support to innovation. In the Anglo-Saxon world (in the United States, the United Kingdom,

Canada, Australia, and New Zealand), venture capital firms provide new companies with investment funds, for start-up, development, merger, or reorganization. Governments finance innovation projects linked to national missions, as in defence, environment, and health. Still, international comparisons suggest that, even within the Anglo-Saxon tradition, national systems for financing innovation differ. All the above-mentioned countries seem to exhibit regional disparities in the supply of investments, with disproportionate concentration in some regions and short supply in others (M. Green, 1991). Also, new technology enterprises have received support of different intensity from venture capital firms in different countries.

In continental Europe and East Asia, the commercial banking systems are involved more in supporting industrial investment and innovation. Within this model, national differences are striking, even among industrial countries. Aoki (1990, 1994) has argued that the continuous relationship between industrial firms and their main banks in Japan has reduced critical asymmetries in technical information between the former and the latter and allowed the main banks better to select promising new firms and projects in established firms. The 1997–98 crisis in East Asia may indicate that this was not the case and that complacency was a more dangerous obstacle to the screening of industrial and technical projects by banks than information asymmetries. Among western European financial systems, the German is probably closest to the Japanese. In France, conversely, both the state and the large commercial banks jointly support the financial burdens of innovation.

WHY DO COUNTRIES DIFFER, AND HOW DOES IT MATTER?

The idea behind the concept of NSI is that countries differ in the way in which they conduct innovation and that these differences affect economic performance. Governments support the bulk of technological innovation in all advanced countries. A good proportion of the national differences is attributable to differing national missions and public-sector efficiency. In the words of Paul Krugman (1993: 71/2): "Nations matter ... because they have governments whose policies affect the movements of goods and factors." Thus "mission-oriented" countries (for example, those with a strong defence establishment, such as France, Russia, the United Kingdom, and the United States) have produced more novelty in aerospace, advanced materials, telecommunication, and related industries with military applications. Conversely, commercially oriented countries (such as Canada, Denmark, Finland, Germany, and Japan) have emphasized civilian technologies with market applications.

Also, the United Kingdom and the United States have a more re-search-oriented innovation system, with better scientific universities but a less advanced corporate training system and production organizations that are less oriented to the market. In these countries – the world's technological leaders of the last two centuries – scientific and technological achievements have been numerous, but some firms, habituated to "cost-plus" military contracting, have seemed less able to adapt technology to commercial markets or to adopt and modify existing technical knowledge from overseas sources.

Industrial countries vary substantially in terms of the relative share of financing and execution of R&D undertaken in the three main sectors of the R&D system – industry, government, and university (see Tables 1.1 and 1.2). Canada is the G7 country in which industry executes and finances the smallest percentage of gross expenditures in R&D (GERD) and university the highest.

In absolute terms, the United States spends almost as much as all the other G7 countries put together, which are also the next largest performers (Table 1.3). In relative terms, Japan and Germany, with 3.0 per cent and 2.8 per cent, respectively, of their gross domestic product (GDP) spent in R&D have outpaced the United States, at only 2.6 per cent. When defence expenditures are subtracted in each country, U.S. dominance is less noticeable: the US share of G7 R&D expenditures recedes from 45.9 per cent of total G7 GERD to 39.9 per cent of civilian expenditures.

The differences among national R&D systems go far beyond amounts spent, institutions that execute or fund innovation, and even types and intensity of flows between R&D units – I next consider seven differences. As well, the mandates, internal routines, and performances of research institutions differ among industrial nations. Data on patents show that technological capabilities are nation-specific and cumulative and tend to persist over time (Patel and Pavitt, 1991; Archibugi and Pianta, 1992).

First, countries differ in the size and characteristics of their resource base. Some, such as Australia, Canada, and the United States, have extensive mineral, energy, and agricultural resources; they thus conduct relatively more R&D and achieve more innovation in areas such as agriculture, energy, and metallurgy. Other nations, lacking such a resource base, probably concentrate more on knowledge-intensive consumer and industrial goods – Germany, Japan, and South Korea, for example. Also, these latter countries have tended to devote at least some of their research efforts to overcoming these resource scarcities: Germany's chemical R&D has been, for more than a century, a fabulously successful effort to produce dyestuffs, fuels, and pharmaceutical products in the laboratory (Haber, 1971); hence the continued dominance of its chemical industry in world markets.

Table 1.1
Percentage of gross expenditure in R&D (GERD) performed by each sector
in G7 countries, 1995

	Business enterprises (%)	Government (%)	Higher education (%)	Non-profit (%)	Total
Canada	60.0	15.8	22.9	1.3	100
France	61.6	20.9	16.2	1.3	100
Germany	66.2	14.7	19.0	n.d.	100
Italy	57.1	20.1	22.9	n.d.	100
Japan	65.2	9.6	20.7	4.4	100
United Kingdom	65.5	14.5	18.8	4.2	100
United States	71.8	9.5	15.2	3.4	100

Source: OECD, *Main Science and Technology Indicators* (Paris 1997).

Table 1.2
Percentage of GERD financed by each sector in G7 countries, 1995

	Business enterprises (%)	Government sector (%)	Other national sources (%)	Abroad (%)	Total
Canada	46.7	37.7	5.1	10.5	100
France*	48.7	41.6	1.4	8.3	100
Germany	60.9	37.1	0.3	1.7	100
Italy	48.7	47.4	n.d.	3.9	100
Japan	67.1	22.4	10.4	0.1	100
United Kingdom	48.0	33.3	4.3	14.3	100
United States	59.9	36.1	4.0	n.d.	100

Source: As Table 1.1.
*1994 data.

Second, size matters. Large industrial countries, such as Germany, Japan, the United Kingdom, and the United States, have a more diversified innovation system than smaller countries, such as Canada, Denmark, Sweden, and Switzerland. The latter focus innovation activities in a few areas – for instance, aerospace and telecommunications in

Table 1.3
R&D expenditures in G7 countries, 1995

	United States	Japan	Germany	France	United Kingdom	Italy	Canada
Total ($bn)*	179.1	82.0	38.1	27.1	21.3	12.7	10.0
% of GDP	2.58	3.0	2.28	2.34	2.05	1.14	1.61
Per capita ($)	680.9	654.5	466.6	466.1	364.8	221.6	338.1

Source: As Table 1.1.
* Current purchasing parity power U.S. dollars.

Canada, agriculture in Denmark, telecommunications and mechanical industries in Sweden, and pharmaceuticals and electrical machinery in Switzerland.

Third, government intervention in innovation goes far beyond defence or other missions. Governmental priorities are many, and they substantially affect the areas picked for innovation and the organization of innovative activities. Even in non–defence-oriented countries, some governments have picked winning industries: in Canada, energy, regional aircraft, and telecommunication equipment; in Denmark, agriculture and small and medium-sized industry; and in Italy, electronics and aerospace. Governments have also affected market structures: western European authorities have given priority to national champions; Japan has promoted national oligopolies.

Fourth, university systems also differ. Germany and the United States have public and private universities that have for more than a century encouraged industry–university collaboration. The result has been a more continuous stream of ideas from the university to production and a steady flow of funds from industry to higher education. Conversely, in France and Italy public academic institutions have no private counterpart, and fewer links have traditionally existed between research universities and private corporations. Universities there have probably been less responsive to private-sector demands.

Fifth, countries vary in the significance and missions of government laboratories. Canada, France, the United Kingdom, and the United States have a large number of public laboratories, many of which are quasi-universities: they conduct a substantial proportion of the country's basic and applied research, supported by government funds.

Until the 1980s, technology transfer to industry was not among their most important missions. Conversely, the large Japanese public laboratories are fewer, and their main goal is to help industry to conduct research and to monitor, adapt, and apply existing technology. In 1990, the Japanese national laboratory system consisted of some 105 institutes that employed some 13,200 full-time researchers and had budgets totalling slightly over U.S.$6 billion, representing some 6 per cent of Japan's total R&D expenditure (Schatz and Mowery, 1994). Japanese national laboratories act as memory, support, and source of preliminary research for large national projects in which industry, academe, and government cooperate, but they are not the promoters or even the primary sites of these projects, which remain industry-oriented and -executed. Parallel to these institutions, Japan has close to six hundred local and fairly small research institutes with nearly U.S.$2 billion in total budget for promotion of local and regional economies. All government laboratories taken together represent some 10 per cent of Japan's total R&D expenditure. By contrast, in 1993, while American government-owned and -operated laboratories represented a similar percentage of U.S. R&D expenditure ($16.6 billion, or some 10 per cent of total domestic expenditure on R&D), government-owned, contractor-operated, and government-funded non-profit laboratories represented another $6.6 billion. This U.S. system includes some seven hundred establishments and some 13.8 per cent of total R&D expenditure. Moreover, the U.S. system is working on a substantially different basis from the Japanese. Most of these American laboratories work for the federal departments of Defense, Energy, Health, or Transportation that fund them. (The Canadian system, as we see below, was built along the American model.)

Sixth, national financial systems also differ. In countries such as Germany, Japan, and South Korea, universal banks and industrial financial conglomerates supposedly reduce the information asymmetries between financiers and industry. The latest financial crisis in Southeast Asia has shown that complacency in the lending policies of the banks was also frequent. Conversely, in countries with commercial banks and open, competitive capital markets, such as Australia, Canada, the United Kingdom, and the United States, there may be weaker links between innovative industry and finance. Technological novelty needs other financial institutions in such a system.

Seventh and finally, countries differ in the amount of resources that they invest in R&D. Some, such as Japan, Sweden, Switzerland, and the United States, spend nearly 3 per cent of their GDP on R&D. Others, such as Australia and Canada, spend about 1.5 per cent. These national gaps are only slowly reduced over time (Patel and Pavitt, 1994).

Despite these and probably other sources of national differences, some fifteen industrialized countries have tended, since 1945 and at least till 1990, towards an obvious convergence in terms of productivity and per capita revenue (Baumol and Nelson, 1994; Abramovitz and David, 1996). The convergence does not, however, include most of the other less developed countries. Hence one may wonder whether NSIs really matter. In this book, I argue that they do. Convergence is confined to fifteen or twenty countries, if one includes the most advanced Asian newly industrialized countries (NICs) in the postwar period and omits most other nations. Also, the technological specialisation of industrial nations remain constant in the long run (Archibugi and Pianta, 1992).

Additionally, once the basic forces of convergence (imitation and technology transfer) have been exhausted, the forces of divergence may reappear (Abramovitz, 1988). More specifically, once the possibility of catching up by adopting foreign technology and organization has disappeared because of complete convergence, each country will have to produce its own development path. It is far from evident that the national paths will be similar, as each country will rely on its own, different natural and human resources.

Productivity levels among the less R&D-committed industrial countries may in the future depend on several factors. First, they may adopt other countries' R&D results, either through foreign ownership and control of domestic industry (Australia and Canada) or through massive knowledge imports from the technological leaders (the case of Japan). Second, some late-industrializing countries may sustain their prosperity and productivity through technological imports paid for by the export of natural resources (Argentina in the twentieth century). This kind of prosperity may well be ephemeral, as many of these resources are non-renewable. Third, less-committed countries may specialize in industries with low R&D intensity; this may be the case of Italy (with an edge in industries such as clothing and furniture) and Denmark (highly competitive in agricultural products). These explanations are probably complementary, but the second in particular points to short-lived factors of convergence.

Also, the present productivity convergence may have already nearly exhausted itself. New industrial leaders may be emerging on the basis of new and more efficient productive organization, such as Japan, or on the basis of market size, such as the enlarged European Union. The United States may also regain much of the ground it lost in the last three decades, by allocating more resources to civilian R&D and fewer to basic science and military research. Inasmuch as national differences in the institutions supporting innovation remain significant, so

will differences in economic performance, and even part of the productivity convergence may disappear. The sudden and recent removal
of the former Soviet Union from the group of advanced industrial nations may illustrate the importance of institutions and the volatility of
convergence.

ARE NATIONAL DIFFERENCES IN INSTITUTIONS DISAPPEARING?

National institutions supporting innovation differ, but some of their
differences may also disappear in the coming years. There are at least
four sources of institutional convergence.

First, countries tend to copy successful institutional innovations
from elsewhere. This is true at both the firm and the national levels.
For instance, some characteristics of the organization of the Japanese
firm – such as just-in-time manufacturing, concurrent engineering,
and total quality control – are being adopted by Western firms. After
1945, Japanese managers went to the United States to study scientific
management and adopted and improved American practices. Later,
u.s. managers came to adopt some of these revamped institutional innovations (Nelson, 1992).

Also, successful public programs and the organization of the public
sector can be copied. For instance, Canada, the European Union, and
the United States have been promoting industrial cooperation among
domestic firms, as Japan did in the postwar period (Niosi, 1995). Also,
governments in all advanced countries are creating incentives for public laboratories to collaborate with industry (Bozeman, Papadakis and
Cohen, 1995).

However, it is too early to assess how valuable the institutional bor-
rowings will be in the long run. Organizational imitation is much less
complete and precise than technological copying. Organizations are
far more complex and difficult to observe than technologies, and cultural traits and local contracts that affect organizations cannot be
erased overnight. Hybrid forms of institutions are likely to emerge
from most attempts at organizational borrowing (Abo, 1994; Niosi,
1998).

Second, there is an across-the-board trend towards decreasing intervention by the state in economic development and towards financial
deregulation. Both tendencies may blur some national differences in
the institutional infrastructure.

Third, the blurring of national differences may prove elusive; for instance, it seems that some forms of direct government intervention,
such as public corporations, are fading, while other forms, such as

public financing of technological cooperation, are increasing. These technology policies also show national idiosyncrasies (Patel and Pavitt, 1994). Similarly, the deregulation of national financial systems is probably affecting some activities, such as commercial banking, less than others, such as venture capital, which are closer to the NSI.

Fourth and finally, there are many debates about the internationalization of technological activities. The growth of international alliances, the internationalization of R&D, and other related trends seem to indicate that technology flows more freely than it previously did and that national borders have become more porous. While these trends are crucial, some of them may reinforce, rather than reduce, national differences. Thus if all industrial corporations operating in a given industry concentrate all their R&D activities in a few countries because of their better natural or human resources, this factor may have the effect of strengthening national differences, instead of re ducing them. Technology transfer will centralize technical capabilities in countries – or regions within those countries – that are more efficient. Of course, in some industries the effect of foreign R&D or international technological alliances may be just the opposite – one of international diffusion and convergence. Paul Krugman (1993) has already explored this issue.

DIFFERENT PATHS: AN INTRODUCTION TO MULTI-DYNAMICS AND MULTI-STABILITY

The creation of Canada's NSI has preceded by two decades that of the Southeast Asian NICs (Taiwan and South Korea) and followed the latecomers in the G7 (Italy and Japan) by one decade. Differences between the Canadian catching-up effort and that of the countries mentioned above appear to involve not simply time; it is also a matter of institutions developed, industries chosen, and the relative weight of the policy instruments used to attain them. The Canadian path towards development of an NSI may display some general traits, which one can find in the development of other NSIs: strong public intervention, including the creation of government laboratories, research universities, and policy inducements for industrial R&D. Various countries, however, used at least some different policy instruments and institutions, or another combination of them, to nurture the development of their NSI.

South Korea

In the 1960s, in its efforts to industrialize, the South Korean government nationalized the banks, in order to provide capital to local firms to support their entry into mature, capital-intensive activities, such as steel production, shipbuilding, heavy chemicals, and car manufacturing. It also promoted development of a particular type of enterprise – the local conglomerate (*chaebol*) – with the purpose of attaining the scale economies inherent to these activities (Kim, 1997). Import protection and export promotion were also key measures in the process of industrial catching up. Later on, in order to foster the development of new, high-technology industries, such as telecommunication equipment and computers, the government relied again on the same chaebols. Also, it restricted inward foreign direct investment in order to ensure that the "winners" of the local competition would be domestic firms. South Korea did not rely on small and medium-sized enterprises (SMEs), as Canada did in software and biotechnology, and did not stimulate university research, as Canada has done with success since the 1960s. The result has been a highly concentrated Korean industrial structure, dominated by a dozen or so large domestic conglomerates.

Conversely, in Canada, some of the public efforts have resulted in the development of large local corporations (such as Bombardier in aircraft, CAE in flight simulators, and Nortel Networks in telecommunication equipment) but also resulted in the entry of large foreign corporations (such as IBM and Compaq in computers, Merck Frosst in pharmaceuticals, and Pratt & Whitney Canada in aircraft engines), which thrived on public-policy inducements. Few public policies have operated in Canada to deter large foreign firms from participating in domestic industry or taking advantage of public-policy inducements. At the same time, thousands of local firms have been created in Canada in software, and hundreds in biotechnology. However, in both Canada and South Korea, the government conducted and financed most R&D efforts in the early stages (1940s and 1950s in Canada, 1960s and 1970s in South Korea), until private industry used the public direct and indirect incentives to conduct R&D and became more R&D-intensive.

Taiwan

The Taiwanese started catching up in the 1950s and 1960s, and manufacturing exports played, as in South Korea, a major role, together with imported technology. However, contrary to South Korea, Taiwan invited foreign capital to participate in the industrialization effort and relied more on small local firms and public laboratories for new technologies and on state corporations for heavy industries (Deyo, 1987). The Taiwanese model, like Canada's, also kept the banks independent from industrial firms – a policy that would hamper development of large local private corporations but, in the late 1990s, would provide the foundation of a much more solid financial system than South Korea's.

In the first thirty years, the Taiwanese government was the primary source of funding for R&D; the trend changed in 1989, when private industry for the first time funded slightly over half of total gross expenditure on R&D (GERD), estimated at U.S.$4.94 billion in 1994 (Fang and Yang, 1997). A large part of the Taiwanese R&D effort, however, still takes place in public laboratories, such as the Industrial Technology Research Institute (ITRI), with over 5,000 researchers, and state corporations (Wade, 1990; Yang, 1998). Also, in the 1990s, public-sector agencies and research institutes played a coordinating role in the development of a large number of domestic technological alliances linking small and large firms with public research laboratories to foster innovation in advanced, high-technology industries.

Italy

Italy developed its heavy and high-technology industries in the 1930s and 1940s, usually under state control, mainly within the IRI group (Institute for Industrial Reconstruction), founded in 1933 to save the Italian banking system from collapse. IRI was used to launch the manufacturing of aircraft engines before the Second World War (through the Alfa-Romeo subsidiary, later sold to Fiat), together with shipbuilding and steel manufacturing. After the war, IRI nurtured production of telecommunication equipment and computers (through its STET subsidiary) (Posner and Woolf, 1967; Holland, 1972; Bonnelli, 1994). Thus most high-tech industries grew, unlike the situation in Canada, under government ownership. Related to this characteristic is the extremely high corporate concentration of Italian R&D activities: as late as 1985, the seven largest R&D-active firms performed 52 per cent of all Italian BERD. Finally, no university development equivalent to Canada's occurred in Italy after 1945. The Italian university system is characterized by very low mobility of scientists and engineers to industry and a limited amount of applied and interdisciplinary R&D (Malerba, 1992). Italy is responsible for a disproportionaltely small share of the world's scientific publications, and the networks between industry and university are tenuous. As a result, its science-based industries are the least developed among the G7 countries. In the 1990s, Italy's high technology showed signs of stagnation, of which the very low (and declining) ratio of GERD to GDP is only one (Balcet, 1995).

INTERNATIONALIZATION OF TECHNOLOGY AND NSIs

Technology is "going global" through many different channels, including overseas R&D, international technological alliances, and international technology transfers. Several taxonomies have been suggested to classify global technological activities. In one of the latest and neatest, Archibugi and Michie (1995) suggest distinguishing among "global exploitation" of existing technologies, "global collaboration" for the production of new technology, through international technological alliances, and "global generation" of technology through expatriate R&D within multinational corporations (MNCs). In all three cases, some technological flows cross borders.

First, global exploitation of technology can, up to a certain level, be measured through international payments for technology within national trade accounts, through patenting abroad, and through international trade in high-tech products. The first indicator offers the most precise measurement of real technological flows, as patents are usually requested by non-residents not to exploit a technology internationally but to prevent competitors from imitating or copying it.

Second, the measurement of global collaboration, or international technological alliances, is still in its infancy. Despite an abundant literature, no precise method has emerged to compare the share of international collaboration to that of purely national collaborations or to the domestic R&D effort of business enterprises in any industrial country. Also, technological collaboration is a fast-changing phenomenon and is one of the more strategic, and thus confidential, issues of the corporation. Thus figures are not readily disclosed by business enterprises.

Third, global generation of technological activities seems the easiest element to quantify, given the available data on R&D expenditures by foreign enterprises in most industrialized nations and on patenting through overseas subsidiaries. Foreign manufacturing activities normally represent extensions of domestic manufacturing. Companies produce abroad similar or complementary products to those produced at home. Also, research operations abroad usually constitute extensions of domestic R&D. Today, the concept of NSI includes only R&D activities carried out within national borders, although a few authors have from the start pointed out that international R&D activities limited the usefulness of the present concept of NSI (Chesnais, 1992). This delimitation is the result of both conceptual and methodological factors. From a conceptual point of view, the intellectual weight of neoclassical economics may be crucial: within this framework, production takes place only within national borders. Multinational corporations are still not an integral part of the standard theory. Also, the NSI concept is rooted in the German economist Friederich List's notion of national production systems; in the mid-nineteenth century, when List wrote his influential book on this subject, national and domestic economic activities were virtually the same. Today, we distinguish between gross domestic product (GDP – that is, what is produced within national borders) and gross national product (GNP – that is, GDP plus the revenues obtained by national factors abroad).

I would argue for a similar distinction within the concept of NSI. We should distinguish between the *national* and the *domestic* systems of innovation. In the first, we include the innovation conducted by national factors (i.e., Canadian-owned and -controlled firms, whether they produce it in Canada or not) and subtract innovation conducted by foreign firms in Canada. The second concept should be left to account for innovation within Canadian borders, regardless of the ownership and control of the innovating organization.

From a methodological point of view, there is a major obstacle to the integration of overseas research activities of national firms into the NSI concept. Very few countries – the most notable exception being the United States – collect and publish figures on both overseas R&D by national firms and foreign R&D conducted by overseas firms in the national territory. Canada collects only figures on foreign R&D performed within its frontiers. Nevertheless, it seems useful to integrate the foreign R&D activities of national firms into the concept of NSI. In this book, I use "NSI" to designate both the national and the domestic systems; only in chapter 6 do I try to evaluate the relative scale of innovation conducted abroad by Canadian firms.

REGIONAL VERSUS NATIONAL SYSTEMS

Within national boundaries, innovation is not distributed homogeneously. In fact, it is usually concentrated within a small number of urban districts: in the United States much has been written about Route 128 around Boston, Massachusetts, and Silicon Valley in California (Hall and Markusen, 1985); in England, about Cambridge and the M4 Corridor between West London and Bristol (Breheny, Cheshier, and Langridge, 1985), and in Canada, about Toronto, Montreal, and Ottawa (Amesse, Lamy and Tahmi, 1989). The relevance of the regions and local clustering within NSIs does not need to be demonstrated any more (Swan, Prevezer, and Stout, 1998).

Within this literature, it has been argued that most technological learning and externalities take place within specific industrial districts (Storper, 1992). Other authors have also postulated that the most useful perspective is not national, but regional or local (De la Mothe and Paquet, 1996). Personal proximity and confidence and trust are deemed to facilitate appropriate flows of knowledge, and they tend to occur locally, not nationally or internationally.

The regional perspective seems, however, somewhat more useful for infant industries and proprietary capitalism. Managerial capitalism and large firms are not regional or local in any possible sense, with the Silicon Valleys of this world probably the best possible environment for the development of new industries such as microelectronics and software in the last decades or biotechnology today. However, once large firms operate in the national or the global market, they gain externalities from across the country, and often even from their international operations.

This book argues that the two perspectives – the regional and the national – are not opposed and exclusive, but rather complementary. From a historical point of view, geography and physical proximity have been important factors in the diffusion of technological and organizational knowledge; this was the theme of Alfred Marshall's concept of industrial districts, where most externalities took place in the late nineteenth and early twentieth centuries. Still today, pools of talent and skills are often found in some regions more than others. Even today, labour is the least mobile of productive factors, and this fact explains much of the significance of regions within national systems. However, national communication and transportation infrastructures, national policies for technological development, and nation-wide corporations have for several decades undermined the relative role of industrial districts: today national technological alliances, cross-regional financial flows, and informational links transcend regions (Freeman, 1991). Industrial districts have not disappeared, but large corporations are moving knowledge and organization from one district to others. These flows do not annihilate regions, but they do explain the creation of new regional centres within national borders and the rapid expansion of some centres.

Also, local diseconomies develop, and they may partially offset regional advantages. New regional poles appear to offer regional advantages. Space has become expensive in Silicon Valley and even in California generally; therefore many high-tech companies have been moving plants and sometimes headquarters to districts in other states, such as Austin in Texas, Phoenix in Arizona, and Portland in Oregon.

NSI AND TECHNOLOGY POLICY

NSI theory best fits into the evolutionary approach to technology policy. The evolutionary explanation of technology policy and its normative conclusions differ substantially from the neoclassical ones. The main neoclassical rationale for the existence of technology policy re-volves around market imperfections: technological knowledge being essentially a public good, companies tend to invest too little in its pro-duction, thus leading to a sub-optimal welfare outcome. In the neo-classical model, however, firms are perfectly rational entities, and information is not technological knowledge but price information about capital labour and outputs (Smith, 1991). In this perspective, the economy is a deterministic system, which adapts perfectly to exoge-nous changes (including technological change), instead of being a complex system that produces technological changes by itself. In the neoclassical approach, market failure precludes optimal resource allo-cation, and the role of policy is to prevent market failure. However, this model does not explain what makes public policy fail or the dy-namic effects of this government intervention.

The evolutionary perspective of technology policy rests on its bounded-rationality micro-foundation and on its corollaries of variety in organizational strategy and ubiquity of learning processes. It also rests on the concept of routines as the "genes," or main structural characteristics, of firms. Technology policy may have, on this basis, dif-ferent goals (Metcalfe, 1995; Carlsson and Jacobsson, 1997), perhaps four in number.

First, governments may aim at increasing technological innovation and economic growth by promoting across-the-board adoption of R&D routines in private firms. Hence horizontal policies such as R&D tax credits, non-targeted subsidies for R&D, and tax deferrals.

Second, governments may seek to increase variety (of firms, strate-gies, products, or processes in the economy) by nurturing new indus-trial activities, new processes or new products within existing firms, or the creation of new firms. This is usually what happens when technol-ogy policy aims at diversification of the industrial base of a country or a region. The case of the creation of new technological systems is one of increasing diversity and variety.

Third, governments may try to prevent diffusion of inferior technol-ogies locked in by historical events (David, 1985; Arthur, 1989) or, conversely, to promote diffusion of competing technologies locked out but exhibiting long-run potential.

Fourth, increasing returns and dynamic cumulative effects – which seem pervasive in information-intensive industries – suggest that govern-ments may be interested in promoting the early entrance of national firms into an emerging industry exhibiting these characteristics in order to reap the growth benefits of these activities. This family of models was inspired by Arrow's "learning-by-doing" (Arrow, 1962), in which increas-ing returns arise within the production process. Drawing also from

Myrdal's principle of cumulative and circular causation, Kaldor (1981) argued that, in industries with increasing returns, first movers have the advantage of declining costs as markets and scale of production develop. In the "endogenous growth" theory of Paul Romer (1986, 1994), long-run growth is driven by the accumulation of knowledge – a basic form of capital that exhibits increasing returns. Knowledge can grow without limit, and externalities diffuse, first within the knowledge-creating nation and then within other nations with similar per-capita revenue.

The last element of the model is diminishing returns in the production of new knowledge within individual investments – a condition that is required to ensure that consumption and utility do not grow too fast. Paul Krugman (1986) and W. Brian Arthur (1994) followed the same direction as the previous authors and tried to model situations in which policies on strategic trade and on industry and technology may benefit the nations that implement them. In some of these models, long-run economic growth is a function not always of free trade, but sometimes of strategic advantage created by government policy, fostering creation of knowledge-intensive industries through an adequate mix of industrial, technology, and trade interventions. Industries with rapid rates of growth, increasing returns in the application of knowledge, first-mover advantages, and export markets are the most suitable areas of application of these models. Technology policy is a logical consequence of these models.

While none of the revisionist authors of the new trade and policy models has endorsed the concept of NSIs, the two approaches are evidently complementary. Policy on trade and on industry and technology falls within national jurisdiction and is closely linked to the NSI. The Southeast Asian industrial nations (Japan, Singapore, and South Korea, as well China and Taiwan) have exhibited high industrial growth and seem to be implementing specific versions of these models. Learning, knowledge, and cumulative processes are key in both the NSI theory and the new trade theories. History and early institution building matter in both models because of increasing returns. Finally, as Pack (1994) has argued, direct support for endogenous growth models is weak, but there is an increasing sense that productivity growth is determined as much by organization as by pure and simple investments in technology and R&D (Stiglitz, 1988).

TOWARDS A COMPETENCE THEORY
OF NATIONS

The NSI perspective, the knowledge approach, and evolutionary economics converge with the most recent theories of the firm (Barney,

1991; Hamel and Prahalad, 1994; Foss and Knudsen, 1996). In the new theory of the firm, which brings together the competence and the evolutionary approaches, firms differ in their specific endowment of resources, as well as in the routines they have developed to increase and renew their specific stock of resources. This perspective starts from the assumption that resources are heterogenously distributed among firms and that they are imperfectly mobile. Consequently, firms exhibit long-term differences in their rates of return, as they manage or not to build sustainable competitive advantages. This approach can be used to build a competence theory of nations that draws from the concept of the knowledge economy, the NSI, and evolutionary economics.

One may hypothesize that what characterizes different national economies is the particular, idiosyncratic mix of assets and resources (including human resources) as well as the institutional routines that nations have developed in order to increase or maintain those resources. Nations differ in the way they are able to discover, exploit, and conserve natural resources and in the way they produce, attract, and retain human resources through a complex set of institutions and incentives, including business enterprises, universities, and government laboratories and policies. The competence theory of the firm postulates that the specific set of assets and routines that constitutes the competitive advantage of firms is difficult to observe and, consequently, to imitate, because of causal ambiguity. Similarly, the specific mix of national institutions that makes up the competitive advantage of nations is difficult to imitate. Thus developing nations have faced enormous obstacles to understanding and imitating the institutional mix that has rendered a handful of developed countries the repository of so much of the world's industry and technology. I suggest here that the NSI perspective is the central element of the now-unfolding competence theory of nations.

EFFICIENCY, EFFECTIVENESS, AND NSIs

National systems of innovation, like many other biological and human systems, are "x-efficient" (Leibenstein, 1976; Niosi, 1999b). By this, I mean that their efficiency (as well as their effectiveness) is variable. Standard economic theory tends to assume that firms and other organizations are perfectly efficient; that institutions are neutral in efficiency terms because, under conditions of perfect knowledge, every organization purchases its inputs and uses them efficiently; and that all possible inefficiencies come only from distortions in price and quantity.

In evolutionary and institutional theory, as in management science, institutions display variable levels of efficiency and effectiveness. Both criteria can be assessed at the levels of the institution and of the system. Institutional inefficiencies include organizational inertia and badly designed jobs and contracts; institutional ineffectiveness includes weak capacity for attaining the main missions and goals of the organization. A system's inefficiencies may be the result of poor coordination among institutions and the lack of some necessary units; a system's ineffectiveness may be the product of its inability to fulfil national missions.

However, these characteristics of NSIs have not yet been thoroughly studied by the main authors in this emerging tradition. Among the three founders of this concept, Lundvall (1988, 1992, 1996, 1998) has probably been more aware of the need to study efficiencies and effectiveness in NSIs empirically; however, his contribution has underlined the importance of the subject, rather than putting any substance in it. The many contributors to the collective volume edited by Nelson (1993) all pinpointed different types of inefficiency and ineffectiveness at the level either of the system or of particular institutions in specific NSIs. However, there was no systematic treatment of these subjects.

Few authors have tried systematically to explain what happens inside the institutions composing the NSI, how they are linked, and what routines make the system behave as such (except for the United States; Crow and Bozeman, 1998). This book is probably one of the first to examine the issues of efficiency and effectiveness within the R&D units that constitute the NSI, and this is certainly the first systematic study in Canada of the efficiency and effectiveness of the core components of its NSI.

I have suggested elsewhere (Niosi, 1999b) that systematic "benchmarking" (the construction of indicators of performance by different types of institutions based on empirical work) is the most useful way of assessing the efficiency and effectiveness of NSIs. This work goes in the direction of developing conceptual and methodological tools for studying the performance of such systems, particularly at the level of individual institutions – at the micro-level.

CONCLUSION

Countries differ in the way in which they conduct innovation, depending on resource endowments (both static and dynamic), market size, organizational idiosyncrasies and trajectories, historic public-policy choices about preferred public goods (defence, the environment, public health, and so on), and government roles in technological innovation. At the heart of those differences lie the national characteristics of the R&D units, in both the private and the public sectors, as well as of the regulatory and incentive frameworks that governments have built over the years.

Growing technological and organizational flows among countries tend somewhat to blur differences and to create convergence in productivity, but not in the underlying institutions of the NSI and in technological specialization of developed nations. *Thus the capacity to innovate remains located in a few industrial nations.* It is therefore probably premature to declare that NSIs are disappearing and that either global or supranational systems are emerging. To cope with this increasing porosity of national technological frontiers, I propose to differentiate between national, supranational, and domestic systems of innovation.

The concept of NSI is related to the new theories of international production and trade, based on the concept of increasing returns. In these theories, government intervention appears to be beneficial to the trading nation, by fostering creation of new knowledge-based industries through technology policy, by nurturing new productive organizations through industrial policy, by managing promotion of trade export, and/or by protecting these infant industries.

Drawing from the new competence theory of the firm and from the concepts of the learning organization and of the knowledge economy, one may postulate that a new approach is emerging – the competence theory of nations. The NSI perspective is a good candidate to become the structuring element in that new theory.

PART ONE

The NSI within Canada's Borders

2 Canada's R&D System

The entrenched image of Canada presents this country as both a late-comer and a laggard in the area of science and technology. This image is only partially right. Canada became involved in science and technology later than other present-day industrial nations. Also, it spends less than most other industrial countries on R&D. Today, with only 1.6 per cent of its gross domestic product (GDP) devoted to R&D, it ranks last among G7 countries, except for Italy, and behind several smaller industrial countries, such as the Netherlands, Sweden, and Switzerland. This chapter does not radically challenge these basic facts but rather proposes a historical perspective on the catching up of Canada, recalls the late emergence and main characteristics of Canada's national system of innovation (NSI), and, using the perspective developed in chapter 1, puts the emphasis on the building of institutions and policies that nurtured the postwar creation of the system. The first part of the chapter describes the origins and evolution of Canada's NSI; the second presents, on the basis of public figures, an overview of the main lines of the state of Canada's NSI in the 1990s.

ORIGINS AND EVOLUTION

Canada's NSI emerged in three separate phases. First, until the First World War, its development was embryonic. Second, that war provided a major stimulus for its development, and its growth was slow but constant up to 1939. At that time, Canada's NSI looked pretty similar to that of several developing countries of today. Third, after 1945, the system became consolidated. This part presents the development of Canada's NSI in terms of its three major groups of participants: industrial firms, government laboratories, and universities.

Few companies were conducting R&D in Canada in the early years of the twentieth century. In 1919, according to a report presented to the House of Commons, only thirty-seven private firms were undertaking R&D (Canada, House of Commons, 1919). Most of these laboratories were single-person operations. By 1930, a study conducted by the Canadian Manufacturers' Association found only fifty-one companies with in-house research, twelve conducting cooperative research and sixteen with in-house technological activities other than research. Fewer than fifty other corporations contracted out research to universities, government laboratories, and/or private consultants or received technology from their parent headquarters abroad (Canada, *Industry Canada*, 1930). It is difficult to know how accurate these figures are. Some authors (Hull and Enros, 1988) find that they underestimate the extent of Canadian industrial R&D.

In 1939, the Dominion Bureau of Statistics (DBS) produced the first precise, if brief portrait of all the research facilities in Canada. Business was the main performer of R&D: there were some one thousand industrial laboratories, employing 2,410 professional scientists, engineers, and technicians; their total annual expenditure was $10.7 million. These activities involved 54 per cent of all professional R&D personnel in Canada and 62 per cent of total R&D expenditures for that year. Unfortunately, the study did not distinguish in the industrial laboratories between those conducting R&D and those performing only routine tests or other technical services; the industrial distribution of the laboratories is also missing (see Table 2.1).

The second largest performer was the federal government. Its seventy laboratories represented 13 per cent of Canada's professional personnel and 15 per cent of R&D expenditures. They were the largest, with an average size of seven professional researchers and an average annual R&D expenditure of $32,423. By comparison, the industrial laboratories hosted on average only 2.4 researchers and spent only $10,700.

The university sector was the third major performer: it included 222 laboratories, with 22 per cent of all professional researchers in Canada, but only 13 per cent of the country's total R&D disbursements. The corresponding average measures for academic laboratories were 4.5 researchers and $9,800 per unit. There were also fifty-three provincial laboratories with 213 researchers and 4 per cent of Canada's total R&D expenditures, with averages of four researchers and $14,300 in spending (Table 2.1).

Table 2.1
Canada's R&D IN 1938

Type of laboratory	Laboratories Number (%)	Professionals Number (%)	R&D expenditures $million (%)
Industry	998 (69%)	2,410 (54%)	10.7 (62%)
Dominion	78 (5%)	573 (13%)	2.5 (15%)
University	222 (15%)	993 (22%)	2.2 (13%)
Hospital	89 (6%)	226 (5%)	0.9 (5%)
Provincial	53 (4%)	213 (5%)	0.8 (4%)
Municipal	26 (2%)	55 (1%)	0.2 (1%)
Total	1,466 (100%)	4,470 (100%)	17.3 (100%)

Source: Canada, Dominion Bureau of Statistics, 1941.

This picture shows an underperforming country (at that time Canada spent some 0.1 per cent of its GDP in R&D), which resembled the innovation systems in developing countries of present-day Latin America (Argentina, Brazil, and Mexico, in particular): many industrial companies conducting little or no research, a few large federal laboratories, and a very few diminutive provincial and university laboratories. Only a handful of universities were conducting graduate research. However, Canada was not doing so badly, when compared with the United States. Its 2,410 industrial scientists and engineers employed in R&D equalled 8.7 per cent of the American total for 1940 (Mowery and Rosenberg, 1993). In Canada, industry was responsible for 62 per cent of total R&D expenditures; in the United States, it paid for two-thirds. These figures mark some difference with the largest Latin American developing countries today, where industry spends less than 20 per cent of the gross expenditure on R&D (Dahlman and Frischtak, 1993; Katz and Bercovich, 1993).

Industrial Laboratories

No reliable data were collected on Canadian R&D between 1939 and 1955. Anecdotal evidence suggests that industrial R&D was growing (Eggleston, 1978: 378–94). New official figures came from the DBS in 1955, when 377 companies were registered as carrying out R&D worth $66 million, employing 2,914 scientists and engineers. These figures may represent a major underestimation, particularly of smaller companies. Among industrial firms in 1955, 318 had research establishments (in-house R&D), while most of the others contracted out research to universities, public laboratories, or other private companies. The split between domestic and overseas R&D expenditures indicates that $54 million was spent in Canada and $12 million (or 18 per cent) abroad, mostly in the United States and to affiliates. Three industries (transportation equipment, including aircraft, electrical apparatus and supplies, and chemical products) represented 25 per cent, 16 per cent, and 12 per cent of total R&D expenditures, respectively. The number of firms engaged in R&D programs in these industries was twenty-two, forty-four, and forty-six, respectively. These figures reflect the concentrated character of R&D activities: forty-four firms (or 14 per cent of all those with in-house research) were responsible for 65 per cent of the total expenditures. Table 2.2 gives some additional detail.

In 1955, several networks linking industrial companies, universities, and public laboratories were already in place. That year, the surveyed companies declared that almost 3 per cent of their total R&D expenditures (or nearly $2 million) went to pay for contractual research in Canada. By far the most R&D was conducted inside the companies: almost 79 per cent of R&D expenditures was destined for research conducted within the companies themselves. The balance (18 per cent) was composed of payments to others outside Canada. Large industrial R&D laboratories had been established in non-ferrous metals by Alcan Aluminum, Consolidated Mining and Smelting (later Cominco), and International Nickel (today's Inco); in chemicals, Ayerst, Canadian Industries Ltd, McKenna and Harrison, and Shawinigan Chemicals had large research laboratories; in food and beverages, Canada Packers, Canadian Breweries, and Maple Leaf Milling were important (Canada. *Canadian Yearbook*, 1954: 355).

By 1969, business enterprises represented 38 per cent of the Canadian gross expenditures in R&D (GERD), the federal government 31 per cent, universities 27 per cent, provincial governments 3 per cent, and private non-profit organizations 1 per cent (Canada. Statistics Canada, 1970). In 1969, the DBS had found 1,010 firms conducting R&D and reporting expenditures of $431 million. The most innovative industries, in terms of R&D expenditures, were electronic equipment and computers (22.2 per cent of the total), aircraft (12.4 per cent), primary metals (9.6 per cent), followed by chemicals, including pharmaceutical products (7.1 per cent each). These four industries accounted for over half of total industrial research in 1969. All forest industries combined, including pulp and paper, reported only 4.6 per cent of the total.

Table 2.2
Business R&D, by industry, 1955

Industry	R&D expenditure $million (%)	R&D professionals	Firms involved in R&D
Transportation equipment	16.6 (25%)	461	22
Electrical apparatus	10.8 (16%)	611	44
Chemical products	7.8 (12%)	515	46
Petroleum and coal products	4.7 (7%)	78	5
Non-ferrous metals	4.5 (7%)	225	15
Paper products	4.0 (6%)	202	35
Iron and steel products	3.0 (5%)	101	56
Rubber products	2.7 (4%)	55	9
All other manufacturing	4.7 (7%)	212	85
Mining, quarrying, and oil	3.0 (5%)	200	27
All other industries	4.1 (5%)	114	33
Total	65.9 (100%)	2914	377

Source: Canada, Dominion Bureau of Statistics (DBS), 1955.

By 1969, some 580 corporations had in-house R&D capabilities (Canada, Department of Industry, Trade and Commerce, 1969). The directory in which this information appears seems to be the first official public nominal listing of industrial corporations with R&D laboratories in Canada, even if it does not pretend to be exhaustive. Table 2.3 gives an account of the number of scientists and engineers in the research establishments of the major industrial performers. Some results deserve to be underlined. First, three-quarters of the largest corporations listed are foreign-owned and -controlled – the Canadian subsidiaries of either American or British firms – and they often operate in science-based industries, such as aircraft, chemicals, and electrical equipment. With two exceptions, Canadian firms were active in low-technology industries, such as metal refining and pulp and paper. Second, confirming the aggregate data of the DBS, R&D is concentrated around a few major activities just mentioned: transportation equipment (aircraft), non-ferrous metal refining, chemicals, and electronics. This 1969 portrait agrees with the 1955 picture presented by the DBS, of a high centralization of Canadian R&D in a few industries.

Table 2.3
Major Canadian corporations with R&D capabilities, 1969

Rank and corporation	Industry	Country of control	Scientists and engineers (no.)
1 Bell Canada/Northern	Telecommunication equipment	Canada	531
2 United Aircraft	Aircraft turbines	USA	271
3 Canadian Marconi	Telecommunication equipment	UK	222
4 Cdn. Westinghouse	Electrical equipment	USA	182
5 Canadair	Aircraft	USA	178
6 Alcan Aluminum	Aluminum refining	Canada	159
7 RCA Victor	Electronic equipment	USA	157
8 Imperial Oil	Petroleum	USA	150
9 Cdn. General Electric	Electrical equipment	USA	133
10 Ayerst Laboratories	Pharmaceutical products	USA	132
11 Uniroyal	Tires	USA	118
12 Computing Devices	Computers, microelectronics	USA	102
13 Du Pont of Canada	Chemicals	USA	101
14 De Havilland	Aircraft	UK	92
15 International Nickel	Nickel refining	Canada	92
16 Cdn Industries Ltd	Chemicals	UK	85
17 British American Oil	Petroleum	USA	81
18 International Cellulose	Cellulose, paper	USA	65
19 Orenda Ltd	Gas turbines	USA	61
20 Cominco	Lead and zinc refining	Canada	59
21 Domtar	Pulp and paper	Canada	54
22 IBM Canada	Computers	USA	54
23 Dow Chemical Canada	Chemicals	USA	52
24 Union Carbide Canada	Chemicals	USA	52
25 CAE Industries	Electronics, machinery	Canada	47
Total			3,230

Source: Canada, Department of Industry, Trade and Commerce (ITC), 1969.

Third, the two largest manufacturing industries in Canada – automobiles and pulp and paper – are notoriously missing. Canada was at that time one of the first motor-vehicle manufacturers in the world, and this industry was the country's largest (at two-digit level) in terms of both value of shipments and exports. In 1969, General Motors of Canada employed only two researchers; Ford and Chrysler did not report any. American corporations were importing motor-vehicle production technology from the United States, thus reducing Canada's total research effort and externalities. In pulp and paper, Canada was already one of the globe's largest producers and exporters, mostly under Canadian ownership and control; it was the second largest domestic industry. A majority of the Canadian producers maintained at the same time both small in-house R&D laboratories and a major cooperative program through the Pulp and Paper Research Institute of Canada (PAPRICAN). In 1969, PAPRICAN was the largest non-profit organization in the country, with fifty-three scientists and engineers. The Canadian producers imported, mostly from the United States, machinery and equipment embodying the latest innovations or bought them from the local subsidiaries of the same American firms.

The following twenty-five years would witness rapid expansion in both the number of industrial R&D performers and the number of industries with major involvement in research. Pharmaceuticals and biotechnology, electronic equipment and software, and transportation equipment became major activities of Canadian industrial research.

Since the 1960s, several debates have divided Canadian and foreign scholars about the determinants of R&D. Canadians have also discussed the specific causes of Canada's low technological performance. Ever since Schumpeter (1942), size has been considered a major determinant of R&D. Scherer (1970, 1992) confirmed its importance as a factor in R&D intensity but was reluctant to dismiss the smaller firm's contribution to innovation. Conversely, Soete (1979) found that the relationship between size and R&D effort was linear. Industry is also a well-known determinant of R&D expenditures: high-tech industries such as aerospace, electronics, and pharmaceuticals expend much more than traditional industries such as food, beverages, and textiles (Bound et al., 1984). Cohen and Kepler (1992), however, found large intra industry variations and postulated an unobservable, random process within industries. Nelson (1959) suggested that diversification was positively associated with R&D effort: firms with broader technology bases are more interested in supporting basic research programs than are specialized firms. Scherer (1970, 1984) found less evidence to support this relationship. Finally, foreign control is also supposed to be a key determinant of R&D

effort: foreign subsidiaries receive technology from their parent companies and are thus less obliged to conduct R&D in order to compete.

In Canadian debates, firm size has often been considered to affect R&D efforts strongly (Bones, 1979; Chand, 1981). Official data from Statistics Canada confirm the role of size of firm: over the years, twenty-five to thirty corporations have made more than 50 per cent of Canada's total R&D expenditures. One of Canada's problems, in this perspective, was the small average size of its industrial corporations.

Industry also appeared to be a major factor: a few industries, including in the 1930s and 1940s chemicals, electrical equipment, aircraft, and metals, have historically made the largest part of Canada's R&D expenditures. In the 1950s and 1960s, aircraft, energy, and then telecommunication equipment emerged as the main locus of Canadian innovation (Bones, 1979, Chand, 1981). It was convincingly argued that Canada had too many traditional and/or material-processing industries, which are do little R&D (such as pulp and paper, metal refining, and food products), and too few high-tech, R&D-intensive industries, such as electronics and pharmaceuticals. This factor would also help to explain Canada's technological underperformance.

However, foreign control of industry has been the preferred culprit (Britton and Gilmour, 1978, Bones, 1979, Chand, 1981). Observers have often argued that foreign firms tend to import technology from their parent corporations, thus reducing the overall national R&D effort. Other authors had found that Canadian and foreign-controlled firms exhibited the same (low) propensity to conduct R&D (see for example Safarian, 1966). An unpublished study for Statistics Canada by Niosi, Sabourin, and Wolfson (1994) arrived at a similar conclusion.

The preceding literature review shows that firm size and the composition of industry have traditionally been seen as the main causes of Canada's technological underperformance and backwardness in R&D. They certainly explain some part of Canadian underinvestment in industrial R&D. However, the NSI perspective suggests that industry also needs adequate policy incentives and institutions, and government leadership, in order to innovate.

Government Laboratories

As I noted above, Canada's national R&D system has always had a large number of major public laboratories. The federal and provincial governments not only financed R&D; they have also been major performers in this area.

In the nineteenth century, the country's first public laboratories appeared in geology in 1842, with the creation of the Geological Survey of Canada, devoted to the location and estimation of mines, forests, and water. Their goal was to provide basic information to investors on Canada's resources. Agricultural R&D followed, with the Dominion Experimental Farms, founded in 1886, designed to conduct research for the thousands of small and medium-sized Canadian farms. In 1913, the Department of Trade and Commerce created a Dominion Grain Research Laboratory, under the Board of Grain. In 1912, the Biological Board was founded, and it later became the Fisheries Research Board (Doern, 1972). These early public endeavours in science and technology aimed at exploiting Canada's natural resources and providing public-good, free knowledge to smaller firms and prospective investors.

The First World War provided the stimulus for Canada's first major entry into scientific and industrial research. In 1916, Ottawa created a national Advisory Council for Scientific and Industrial Research. This advisory board inquired into the situation of research in Canada and found that only a handful of companies, two or three universities, and a few government departments were performing some R&D. The dominion government then decided to create a National Research Council (NRC), inspired by the recently created U.S. body of the same name. The Canadian council would be the national institution for determining standards; it would carry out fundamental research in chemistry, physics, biology, and related fields, similar to that engaging university professors, and general and applied research in biochemistry and bacteriology (useful for industries such as fisheries and packaging); and it would promote research in order to facilitate the use of Canada's natural resources and its valuable waste materials (Canada, Advisory Council for Scientific and Industrial Research, 1921). The first laboratories of Canada's NRC were built in 1932, and its system of laboratories grew through the 1930s. In Doern's words, however, "For much of the 1920s and early 1930s, the NRC experienced considerable difficulty in securing its independence from successive ministers of Trade and Commerce, who viewed science, especially in this prolonged period of austerity and then depression, with a frugal eye" (Doern, 1972: 3).

In the 1930s, the NRC got some company in the form of newly created dominion laboratories: the Bureau of Mines created three large research facilities to coordinate and centralize its investigations: the Ore Dressing and Metallurgical Laboratory, the Fuel Research Laboratory, and the Ceramic and Industrial Minerals Laboratory. By the end of the 1930s, the national system of laboratories included, besides the NRC, research establishments under the aegis of the departments of Agriculture, Fisheries, Health and Welfare, Mines, National Defence, Public Works, and Transport.

In 1939, the NRC was still the largest Canadian laboratory, with three hundred researchers and a total budget close to $1 million. In the words of Robert Bothwell, it was "a council within a council, a laboratory, a granting agency, and a scientific panel, all rolled into one" (Bothwell, 1988: 18). It directed grants towards universities and put most of its own in-house research activities into industrial and applied research. Other public laboratories were advising government departments or creating public-good knowledge for agriculture, defence, industry, and mines.

The growth of the dominion research effort accelerated during the Second World War and afterwards. Federal R&D expenditures multiplied by six between 1939 and 1945, from $5.8 million to $34.5 million. The NRC grew from three hundred to five hundred researchers, to become the largest Canadian research establishment. In particular, it participated in the nation's nuclear program, which in time would produce a commercial electro-nuclear reactor, the CANDU. The NRC also hosted defence research during the war and participated in aircraft, radar, and many other crucial research projects. Technology transfer from the United Kingdom enormously accelerated during the war, as the British government tried to secure a safe place for advanced projects and supplies.

In the period after 1945, wartime projects proved useful in promoting industrialization. Some R&D projects move out from the NRC to other government laboratories. Thus, in the early 1950s, nuclear research split from the NRC to form Atomic Energy of Canada Ltd, a public corporation dedicated to nuclear research. Also, by 1947, the Department of National Defence (DND) took responsibility for all military R&D and the defence laboratories that carried out this research. In 1946, the NRC created a licensing agency called Canadian Patents and Development Ltd (CPDL), whose mission was to transfer to private industry the commercially useful results stemming from public research. The CPDL signed arrangements with other federal laboratories in order to become a central agency for the government's intellectual property.

Collaboration between industry and the federal laboratories went beyond the licensing of some public-research results to private business. A number of research projects were conceived in the public laboratories with an eye to their industrial applications. Anecdotal evidence illustrates – even before the war – several cases of private–public collaboration, over and above the routine tests that the NRC conducted for both industry and government. In the early 1930s, a major example occurred in separation of radium from Great Slave

Lake ores in cooperation with Eldorado Mines Corp. In the 1930s the NRC, in collaboration with Consolidated Mining and Smelting (today Cominco), DND, and Mines and Resources, developed a process to produce pure metallic magnesium that made Canadian mining companies highly successful in this industry and those using that metal (Eggleston, 1978: 109). Later, the wartime research that led to the CANDU reactor was also a major example of collaboration with private industry – in this case, with the largest electrical-equipment manufacturer and engineering firms. In the early 1950s, the NRC's wind tunnels served to help in the design of the wings for the De Havilland Otter aircraft, produced in Toronto. As well, in the 1940s, NRC research had assisted in the design of the first gas turbines for aircraft produced in Canada. The NRC also conducted contract research for private firms and assisted the federal government in technical and scientific areas.

Links between industry and government laboratories were not confined to the NRC. All other public laboratories also participated in the emerging system of innovation. One of the most relevant cases involves aerospace (see Inset 1).

Up to the mid-1960s, however, links between industry and government research were less pronounced in Canada than in the United States. In 1965, in the United States 53 per cent of the federal government's intramural R&D was allocated to development, as opposed to 16 per cent in Canada. Canadian insularity was attributable, according to several observers, to the smaller role of industrial – and specifically defence – R&D and to the lack of university research facilities (Lithwick, 1969: 92–3).

By 1961, federal laboratories in Canada hosted some eighteen hundred researchers. New labs had been created, including that of the Building Research Division, in 1947, to develop projects in such areas as acoustics, building insulation, and soil mechanics. The new division set up contacts with the industrial associations of building companies, the professional engineering and architects' associations, and other government laboratories to coordinate research, exchange ideas, and disseminate R&D results.

In 1958, the National Aeronautics Establishment had been created, within the NRC, to take over the flight, aerodynamic, and structural activities of the Division of Mechanical Engineering. Thanks notably to its development of the only wind tunnel available for industry in Canada, the NRC had been involved in aircraft design and testing since the Second World War and had participated in the design of every significant aircraft and engine type built in Canada up to 1969 (Green, 1970). See Inset 2.

Inset 1   Entering the Production of Satellites

Canada was the third country in the world – after the Soviet Union and the United States – to design and build a satellite. The first Canadian satellite, *Alouette 1*, was designed by Ottawa's Defence Research Telecommunications Establishment (DRTE) and launched by the U.S. National Aeronautic and Space Administration (NASA) in 1962. The NRC was responsible for its cosmic-ray instruments, while the satellite components were manufactured by private industry, under contract to DRTE. Canada did not choose to develop launch capabilities, in order to reduce the cost of its space program and because of the international arrangements that could be concluded with the United States.

Alouette 1 was a scientific satellite, but the telecommunication potential of satellites was immediately appreciated, and its advantages for such a large and sparsely populated country were evident. From the beginning, the work was organized with the aim of transferring the design capabilities from government laboratories to private industry. Over time, one major satellite manufacturer emerged – Spar Aerospace. In each satellite, the share of effort by government laboratories was smaller, and the role of private industry increased. In 1972, Canada built its first telecommunication satellite, *Anik A*, with the help of technology transferred by Hughes Aircraft, an American corporation. *Anik A* was launched by NASA. In the meantime, in 1969 a government corporation, Telesat Canada, was created to operate a commercial national communications system. Telesat was later privatized. In the early 1990s, remote sensing (collecting information about natural resources) was developed through a new series of satellites, RADARSAT. Over the years, the domestic design and construction capability was developed within Canadian private industry, with technical support from public laboratories. Also, the federal government has financed all the Canadian-designed and -built satellites, entirely at first, later only partially (Hartz and Paghis, 1982; Freedman and Crelinsten, 1993).

In the immediate postwar period, some of the new federal labs were set up outside the Ottawa region, helping to create a truly national system of innovation. In 1948, the Prairie Regional Laboratory was founded in Saskatchewan, to conduct research on the industrial use of agricultural waste and surplus. In 1952, a Maritime Regional Laboratory was created in Halifax to perform R&D on a variety of projects of particular interest for the Atlantic provinces,

Table 2.4
Federal government R&D organizations, 1969

Rank	Department/public corporation	Laboratories	Scientists and engineers
1	Department of Agriculture	2	847
2	Forest and Fisheries Canada	6	841
3	Energy, Mines and Resources	10	711
4	National Research Council	13	677
5	Atomic Energy of Canada Ltd	4	588
6	Deptartment of National Defence	17	362
7	Deptartment of National Health and Welfare	6	166
8	Department of Communications	2	102
9	Deptartment of Transportation	15	100
10	Indian Affairs	4	83
	Total	79	4535

Sources: Canada, ITC, 1969: Canada, DBS, 1970.

including marine research, industrialization of local agricultural produce, and steel-making processes. The trend towards geographical decentralization of the national laboratories was to accelerate and to contribute to the emergence of regional centres of innovation. By 1969, the growth of federal R&D had become phenomenal: ten departments and federal corporations carried out most of the public effort in research within some seventy-nine laboratories (Table 2.4). These units employed forty-five hundred scientists and engineers.

The provincial governments entered the R&D system of innovation at the same time as Ottawa, but with a smaller commitment; they concentrated their efforts mostly on the development of local natural resources and the support of small and medium-sized enterprises. Alberta (in 1921) and Ontario (in 1928) created the first major provincial organization for industrial research. After the Second World War, British Columbia, Saskatchewan, Manitoba, and Quebec followed them. By 1969, some forty-seven major provincial-government laboratories existed, employing 839 scientists and engineers (Table 2.5).

Table 2.5
Provincial research organizations, 1969

Province	Scientists and engineers (no.)	Laboratories (no.)
Alberta	119	5
British Columbia	52	2
Manitoba	68	6
New Brunswick	29	1
Nova Scotia	55	9
Ontario	332	16
Quebec	100	3
Saskatchewan	84	5
Total	839	47

Source: Canada, ITC, 1969.

Inset 2   Public Support for Aeronautical Innovation
Since the First World War, Ottawa has been actively involved in the development and promotion of aeronautical innovation. It created an Air Board in 1919 and requested the NRC to found in 1920 an associated scientific consultative committee. In the early 1930s, the NRC inaugurated the first aeronautical research laboratory in Canada. During the Second World War, the NRC worked on the development of a gas turbine for aircraft, starting in 1941. Wind tunnels were also built for private industry within the NRC. During a short period, the Canadian government created a crown corporation (Turbo Research Ltd, 1944–46), which designed and built the first gas turbine for aircraft in Canada, before being privatized. In 1954, the NRC created three committees, for cells and materials, for aerodynamics, and for propulsion. Still today, the NRC hosts three of the largest and most modern aeronautical research laboratories in Canada: the Aerodynamics, the Flight Research, and the Structures, Materials and Propulsion laboratories.

Canada did not simply support aeronautical research through its public laboratories. Like most other developed countries, it also funded much of the R&D effort by private companies – between 1968 and 1995, mostly through the Defence Industries Productivity Program (DIPP).

Between 1969 and 1985, DIPP provided the aerospace industry with over $940 million, of which over half went to Canadair, De Havilland, and P&W Canada. After 1995, the industry was funded through the Technology Partnership Canada program. The government also supported most university research in aerospace and the activities of other public laboratories working in related projects, such as those of DND (Green, 1970; Sullivan and Milberry, 1989, Ontario, 1990).

Universities

In the postwar period, the university system also grew rapidly. At the turn of the century only two universities in Canada were offering graduate degrees – Toronto and McGill. Still in 1950, doctoral research in Canada was confined to these two universities, and only one Nobel Prize had been awarded to Canadians, that to Drs Frederick Banting and J.J.R. Macleod, for the discovery of insulin at the University of Toronto. Nevertheless, Canadian university research was expanding rapidly in the late 1940s and the 1950s, financed mostly through NRC grants, which climbed every year to reach $3.75 million per year in the late 1950s, but always seemed insufficient.

The direct financing of research by the federal government, starting in 1959–60, gave a new momentum to university R&D and made it a key agent in the NSI. Higher education had been chronically starved by lack of funds: in 1963, the ratio of U.S. to Canadian expenditures on university research was 40 to 1 (Lithwick, 1969: 27). By 1969, it was 14 to 1, and there were some thirty research universities in Canada, including the five largest (McGill, McMaster, British Columbia, Waterloo, and Toronto). In practically all of them, medicine and engineering, together with natural sciences, dominated research (Table 2.6). These data, however, must be read with some scepticism, as the declarations were voluntary; the source may have suffered from underdeclaration. The largest performers, however, were represented.

From Confederation to the mid-1960s, university research was financed mostly by internal funds; other major sources were the federal government, which reimbursed provinces for at least 50 per cent of the operating costs of higher education, and later the NRC's research grants and scholarships. Though the provinces were responsible for education, including universities, Ottawa had to support these institutions or watch them suffer from lack of funds.

In 1968–69, university research in Canada cost some $125 million, of which 69 per cent came from the federal government, mostly

Table 2.6
Largest Canadian research universities, 1969

University	Researchers (no.)	Main fields
Waterloo	533	Engineering, chemistry
British Columbia	509	Engineering, medicine
McGill	395	Medicine, engineering
McMaster	336	Engineering, medicine
Toronto	256	Medicine, pharmacy
Total	2,029	

Source: Canada, ITC, 1969.

through the NRC and the Medical Research Council, 14 per cent from the provincial governments, 8 per cent from foundations, 3 per cent from business, and 6 per cent from other sources (Canada, *Canadian Yearbook*, 1972–73: 475). That year, universities awarded some 60,000 bachelor and first professional degrees, of which 1.2 per cent were in agriculture and forestry, 11.1 per cent in sciences, and 5.9 per cent in engineering and applied arts; they also conferred some 11,000 graduate degrees, of which 6.8 per cent were in agriculture and related sciences, 12.4 per cent in sciences, and 11.2 per cent in engineering and applied sciences. In other words, 18 per cent of all graduates with a first university degree and 30 per cent of all graduate degrees were in disciplines related to industry, natural science, and technology.

Coordination and Growth of the NSI

The Canadian government did not simply add new research institutions or new funds to the NSI. It also tried to coordinate it. The first such effort occurred during the First World War, when the NRC was created as a consulting body, to carry out research and to supervise and organize national scientific and technological activity. But, in spite of its increasing resources, the NRC never put much order in the system: universities were under provincial jurisdiction, and companies coordinated their technological activities through markets (licensing) and hierarchies (R&D support from parent companies abroad) and paid little attention to the new coordinating body. Also, the lack of public policy incentives made it difficult for the NRC to encourage industrial research. Between 1939 and 1945, the NRC increased its scientific personnel from three hundred to seven hundred. Its role as a government adviser, however, tended to diminish because of its increasing research function (Doern, 1972: 3). The years following the Second World War saw intense but uncoordinated growth of the system, with most government departments creating their own R&D institutions and the NRC founding new divisions and spinning off several institutions, such as Atomic Energy of Canada Ltd and the Defence Research Board.

The 1960s represented a watershed and may be called the era of the formation of an NSI. The Royal Commission on Government Organization (Glassco Commission) of 1963 recommended creation of a National Scientific Council and the reorientation of government research towards its original goal – supporting industry. In 1964, the Science Secretariat of the Privy Council was created, and in 1966, the Science Council of Canada. This new organism produced a massive number of studies, but as the Lamontagne Report (Canada, Special Committee, 1971–77) made clear in 1973, nobody truly coordinated national science and technology policies. The federal government led almost by default, as it financed and initiated most scientific and technical research, either in public laboratories and universities or in key industries, complemented by some self-organizing features of the system, including inter-institutional competition and cooperation.

During the 1960s, the links between different agents of the NSI grew very rapidly. The "linear" flow of innovation (Figures 2.1 and 2.2) among institutions seemed insufficient to explain the sequence of idea generation leading to innovation. Up to the 1960s, it was common to perceive university and public laboratories as carrying out basic research, government labs as conducting mostly applied research, and industry undertaking development based on university and government research. It was believed that, one way or another, knowledge would flow from one group of institutions to another, and economic development and welfare would naturally follow. In the 1960s, the credibility of this model received increasing challenges from empirical studies on spillovers and externalities in several industrial countries. Also, more mundane budgetary constraints pushed governments to increase the efficiency and the intensity of knowledge flows between economic agents. On the one hand, study after study showed that basic research did not guarantee industrial innovation and that the channels and the contractual arrangements for the transfer of technology between institutions were crucial to effective use of scientific and technical knowledge by industry. On the other hand, government funding for public laboratories could not increase at the rate it had since 1945. Important synergies and economies of scale in research had to be obtained through more systematic cooperation by the independent laboratories.

Figure 2.1
Canada's R&D institutions: four types, by activity

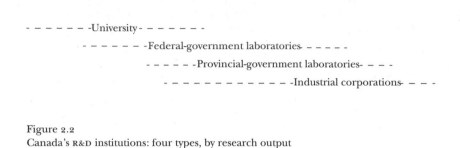

Fundamental research	Applied research	Development

- – – – – -University- – – – – – -
     - – – – – -Federal-government laboratories- – – – -
         - – – – -Provincial-government laboratories- – – -
           - – – – – – – – – – – -Industrial corporations- – – -

Figure 2.2
Canada's R&D institutions: four types, by research output

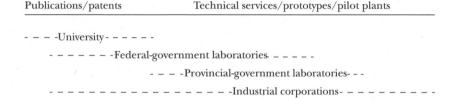

Publications/patents	Technical services/prototypes/pilot plants

- – – -University- – – – – -
   - – – – – -Federal-government laboratories- – – – -
      - – – -Provincial-government laboratories- – -
- – – – – – – – – – – – – – – -Industrial corporations- – – – – – – – -

More specifically, the Glassco Commission had concluded that government departments and agencies, including the NRC, had been only partially effective in promoting industrial research. Other types of incentives were necessary. The Science Council of Canada recommended that Ottawa contract out R&D to increase the technological capabilities of industrial firms. The council also suggested that it increase the national effort in university education and organize major R&D programs as multidisciplinary, multi-agent undertakings involving industrial, academic, and government R&D; further, federal scientific organizations "should actively seek to collaborate with industrial and university groups and to an increasing extent should be the initiators and co-ordinators rather than the performers of R&D" (Canada, Science Council, 1968: 26). Other observers insisted that the government had chosen first "to do much R&D itself and second that what it allocates to industry is almost all defense-oriented" (Lithwick, 1969: 101). On the basis of the Glassco Report, from the mid-1960s on, the federal government's role as a direct performer of R&D started to decrease, and the links among the agents of Canada's NSI increased while industrial R&D rose continuously.

Also, the number of industry, university, and government laboratories had grown exponentially. Canada had over one hundred government laboratories, mostly federal ones, and a similar number of other large university research centres, and over two thousand industrial and cooperative labs; the NSI was at work and was beginning to exhibit some valuable synergies and dynamism, even if it did not show major coordination, either by the market or by public hierarchies.

Between 1958–59 and 1970–71, federal expenditures on scientific activities tripled, from $225 million to $750 million. Five major programs were forging links among industry, academe, and government research organizations in the 1960s. The Defence Industrial Research Program (DIRP) began in 1961 to support military research with commercial applications, such as aircraft turbines. In 1962, the Industrial Research Assistance Program (IRAP) was launched "to create industrial research facilities within industrial companies and to expand existing facilities," as well as "to improve communications between research workers in government and industrial laboratories." Sponsored by the NRC, the program paid up to five years of salaries for scientists, engineers, and technicians engaged in approved R&D projects in industry. The Program for the Advancement of Industrial Technology (PAIT) was started in 1965 "to help industry help itself to improve its technological capacity and expand it innovation activity." The Industrial Research and Development Incentives Act (IRDIA), passed in 1967, provided "general incentives to industry for the expansion of scientific R&D in Canada"; it was sponsored by the federal Department of Industry, Trade and Commerce and was expected to foster cooperation between industry and universities on research related to industrial problems. The Defence Industry Productivity Program (DIPP) was set up in 1968 "to develop and sustain the technological capability of Canadian industry for the purpose of defence export sales or civil export sales arising from that capability" (Canada, DBS, 1970: 12–13). In 1969–70 the budgets of these five major programs totalled $63 million. The goal of all these major policy initiatives was to increase the competitiveness of Canadian firms both in domestic and in export markets. Competitiveness was supposed to result from increased technological capability, and the way to obtain this capability was to expand R&D and create synergy among the major institutions involved.

New federal tax deductions for industrial research appeared in the early 1960s (see Inset 3). They allowed private companies to deduct most R&D expenditures from taxable income. They represented new incentives for industrial research, whether in-house or contracted out. Later, new programs promoted cooperation between industry and universities, with emphasis on the academic side. In 1960, the Medical Research Council (MRC) was created under the NRC to promote basic and applied research, as well as clinical testing; in 1969, MRC became autonomous. It was followed, in 1978, by the Natural Sciences and Engineering Research

Inset 3   The Evolution of Tax Incentives for R&D, 1960–92

Before 1961 Current expenditures on R&D fully deductible in the year incurred; capital expenditures on R&D deductible at the rate of 33 per cent per annum

1961 Capital expenditures made fully deductible in the year incurred

1962–66 Incremental incentive introduced – tax deduction of 50 per cent of current and capital expenditures in excess of the base levels prevailing in 1961

1966–75 Incremental 50 per cent tax deduction replaced by (non-taxable) grants under IRDIA of 25 per cent of capital expenditures and 25 per cent of current expenditures in excess of the average level over previous five years

1977–78 Investment tax credit of 5 to 10 per cent, depending on region, introduced for both current and capital expenditures

1978 Incremental allowance (ITC) introduced – tax allowance of 50 per cent of current and capital expenditures in excess of the average level over the previous three years; general ITC rate increased to 10 per cent, 20 per cent in Atlantic Canada and Gaspé region, and 25 per cent for small business

1983 Incremental tax allowance eliminated. Tax credits rates for R&D increased by 10 percentage points to 20 per cent for general expenditures, 30 per cent for Atlantic Canada, and 35 per cent for small businesses. Partial refundability (20–40 per cent) of unused ITCs introduced for expenditures made before May 1986. Three-year carry-back of ITCs introduced, and carry forward extended to seven years. Limits on deductibility of ITCs eliminated. Scientific research tax credit (SRTC) flow-out mechanism introduced

1984 35 per cent credit limited to first $2 million of R&D expenditures per year; SRTC issues constrained by equity shares

1985 R&D recast as scientific research and experimental development (SR&ED).

1986 SR&ED incentives extended to payments made to federal granting councils

1987 Buildings excluded from SR&ED incentives. Carry forward extended from seven to ten years

1988 "Fast track" introduced for partial SR&ED ITC refunds before notice of assessment

Source: W.S. Clark et al. (1993), "Canada's R&D Tax Incentives: Recent Developments," in Canadian Tax Foundation, *Report of the Proceedings of the 44th Conference*, Ottawa.

Inset 4   Promoting Biotechnology

The rapid development of biotechnology in Canada in the 1980s and 1990s owes much to federal support. In 1987, under the aegis of the NRC, a large federal research centre was inaugurated in Montreal to host the largest biotechnology R&D facilities in Canada. The Biotechnology Research Institute of Montreal (BRI) contained four laboratories: for biochemical engineering and fermentation processes, genetic engineering, protein engineering and cell fusion, and molecular immunology. The Saskatoon National Laboratory was upgraded to become the Plant Biotechnology Institute. The Biology Laboratories in Ottawa were also revamped to become the Institute for Biological Sciences. Similarly, the Marine Laboratory in Halifax was modernized to become the Marine Biotechnology Institute. By 1998, the NRC hosted the five largest biotechnology R&D facilities in Canada, where companies of all sizes could conduct experimental research.

As in aeronautical research, federal assistance was not confined to providing research laboratories and results to private industry. Funding was also key, and it went both to industry (through the Strategic Technologies Program in the 1980s and early 1990s) and through the federal Centres of Excellence Program since 1988, funding cooperative research by industry, university, and public laboratories. The provincial governments, particularly Quebec and Ontario, developed their own centres of excellence programs with similar goals. By 1997, close to three hundred private firms – seventy-five with publicly traded shares as of September 1997 – were conducting biotechnology R&D in Canada, and the sector was thriving.

Source: Canadian Biotech News Service, Ontario, 1990; Walsh, Niosi, and Mustar, 1995.

Council (NSERC) and the Social Sciences and Humanities Research Council (SSHRC) to support research in the corresponding fields. In the 1980s, these councils created matching policies to promote collaboration between industry and universities. These include the Industrial Chairs Program and the Collaborative R&D Program at NSERC, the Health Partnerships Program at MRC, and the NSERC/SSHRC Chairs in the Management of Technology, as well as the Innovaction program. The result of these and similar policies was an upsurge in industry university collaboration (Doutriaux and Barker, 1995; Niosi, 1995).

Another major upgrading of the NSI occurred in the 1980s, when the federal government and most of the provinces adopted policies regarding venture capital. Venture capital tends to reduce the uncertainty and risk associated with the creation of new firms, particularly in high-tech areas, like biotechnology (Inset 4), where new companies have no collateral on the basis of which to borrow from commercial banks. In 1982, total funds available through venture capital financing represented only $350 million. Canada had no public policy related to venture capital. That year, the Federal Development Bank (now Business Development Bank) created a new venture capital division.

Later, in 1985, the federal government tried to correct this market failure through horizontal policies (tax incentives). The most successful of the resulting new institutions were the labour-sponsored venture capital corporations (LSVCCs), which have become the largest source of such capital in Canada. The total venture capital fund constantly increased, to $3.3 billion in 1992, $5 billion in 1994, and over $8 billion in 1998. By that year, close to 50 per cent of the funds invested in venture capital were in LSVCCs (Best and Mitra, 1997; Osborne and Sandler, 1998). A majority of the emerging firms funded by venture capital are technology-intensive and operate in biotechnology, computer software and hardware, medical and telecommunication equipment, and environment. The number of firms yearly funded by Canada's venture capital has grown from a few hundred in the 1980s to over one thousand in the mid-1990s. In 1998, over 1,300 firms obtained support from more than one hundred Canadian venture capital firms (Canadian Venture Capital Association, 1999). Venture capital was thus contributing to the rise of new firms in the knowledge economy, as well as increasing the incentive to conduct R&D in the private sector.

THE NSI IN THE 1990S

By 1995, Canada's national R&D system was composed of at least sixty-six hundred firms performing R&D, plus 150 federal and ten major provincial laboratories, each hosting more than twenty-five full-time researchers (Statistics Canada, 1997), and some thirty research universities with more than two hundred large research centres (each with over twenty-five scientists and engineers).

Reshuffling the R&D System

In the late 1980s and the 1990s, the federal government started a major reordering of the national R&D system in three directions – it modified the patent system, gave new missions to government laboratories, and redirected and curtailed funding programs.

First, Ottawa modified the patent system twice to give additional protection to new drugs. Canada had introduced its first patent law in

1869, two years after Confederation. This law was amended in 1923 in order to add compulsory licensing of new drugs: if a new drug was patented and the patentee did not manufacture that drug in Canada within two years of obtaining a patent, the commissioner of patents could grant a licence to an independent producer in order to ensure that the drug would be available in Canada. In 1969, the Liberal government introduced an amendment to the Patent Act that extended compulsory licensing to the import of both drugs and ingredients. A generic pharmaceutical industry immediately emerged in Canada, and the price of drugs fell. The large multinational pharmaceutical corporations responded by reducing their R&D in Canada; they even closed some laboratories.

In 1987, the Conservative government amended the Patent Act in order to extend patent protection for a drug to seventeen years after filing of the patent application (and thus effective protection of about ten years after market introduction of the drug); the large firms committed themselves to boosting their R&D expenditures in Canada to 8 per cent of sales by 1991 and to 10 per cent by 1996. In 1993, a new amendment to the Patent Act increased patent protection to twenty years after initial filing. The major pharmaceutical corporations, and a few generic producers, rapidly increased their R&D in Canada, contributing to the soaring private-industry R&D expenditures observed in the late 1980s and the 1990s: from 1987 to 1993, these expenditures increased by 240 per cent, from $107 million to $366 million. Also, this expansion augmented private funding of university laboratories in medical and pharmaceutical research.

Second, in the late 1980s and early 1990s, there was a major change in the missions of federal and provincial R&D funding in Canada. Networking, as well as scientific and technological collaboration between independent organizations, became more important. By 1993, some 30 per cent of all the 430 federal and provincial programs funding research by private firms, universities and government laboratories were supporting, exclusively or partially, collaborative research (Niosi and Landry, 1993). The systemic effects of these changes were considerable. Funding programs changed, as did the mandates, missions, evaluation procedures, and effectiveness criteria of government laboratories, where technological cooperation became key, to increase both revenues and visibility. The evaluation of public research institutions, traditionally conducted via publications and citations, is now increasingly based on their overspills on the economy, particularly on employment and production. Thus in the 1990s, the economic evaluation of their efforts has become a major exercise, as the public dollars spent need to be justified in terms of public welfare. Also, in 1990,

Ottawa liquidated the Canadian Patents and Development Corp. and shifted responsibility for transferring technology from the public laboratories to industry onto each laboratory and its supervising government department. In 1992, the Science Council of Canada was abolished as well, and the system was, more than ever, left to its own self-organizing mechanisms.

Third and finally, in March 1996, Ottawa announced a new science and technology policy. The new strategy aimed to improve performance in science and technology, but for the first time in decades there were no plans to increase government R&D. To improve the nation's performance, Canada would have need new priorities, information networks, more public–private partnerships, and intergovernmental cooperation. National laboratories were to increase technology transfer to the private sector. Federal agencies would promote national and international alliances and technology partnerships. But on the whole, the state was to be less a direct performer of R&D, less a direct financier, and increasingly a coordinator and a provider of direction (Canada, Department of Industry, 1996). A number of initiatives followed, including creation of Federal Partners in Technology Transfer, a new program that enrolled thirteen federal departments and agencies to promote commercialization of government-produced technology. DIPP gave way to the Technology Partnership Canada Program, under which firms could obtain R&D funds as repayable loans from Ottawa (Canada, Department of Industry, 1996).

Industrial Innovators

Between 1974 and 1995, intramural R&D expenditures in Canadian industry increased by almost 13 per cent per annum, and by 7.5 per cent if inflation is subtracted. In the early 1970s, industry had replaced the federal government as the largest funding support of R&D (Figure 2.3). The number of industrial corporations performing R&D increased by a factor of between five and seven. The share of GERD performed by business rose from 38 per cent in 1969 to 60 per cent in 1995. Meanwhile, government laboratories' participation decreased from 31 per cent to 16 per cent of R&D, and higher education's share from 27 per cent to 23 per cent (Canada. Statistics Canada, 1995). Compared to the American business sector, Canada's was still underinvesting. Business performed 72° per cent of U.S. national GERD, or U.S.$122 billion, against 54.4 per cent or $4,5 billion (current US$PPP) by Canada's business sector, for a ratio of 27 to 1.

Figure 2.3
GERD, by performing sector, 1963–97

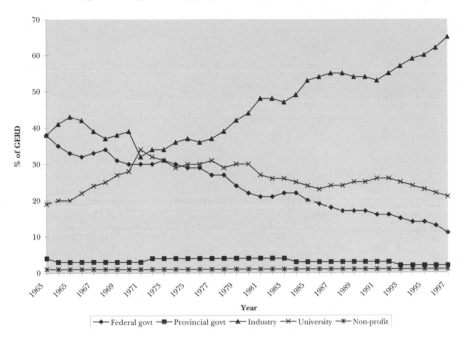

It is difficult to know exactly the scale of the private-sector effort in Canada. The figures above are based on Statistics Canada surveys conducted by the Service, Science and Technology Division. Several independent preliminary studies and fragmentary evidence suggest that these official figures may underestimate the private sector's effort, particularly in smaller firms, for three reasons. First, there are figures released by Revenue Canada under the Scientific Research and Experimental Development incentive program and analysed by Lipsett and Lipsey (1994); under this program, 5,644 companies of all sizes claimed in 1992 nearly $1 billion in R&D tax credits, a number far larger than the 3,566 performing firms estimated by Statistics Canada for that year (see Table 2.7). The differences still remain to be explained, but a major redesign of Canada's R&D statistics is in the making, with a better appraisal likely of the contribution of SMEs to innovation.

Second, the tracking of SMEs, particularly in new areas, is difficult; a comparative analysis of provincial and federal private and public nominal databases of R&D-active firms shows a similar pattern: the number of R&D-performing firms appears larger than the one estimated by Statistics Canada (see Quebec, Bureau de la Statistique du Québec,

Figure 2.4
GERD, by funding sector, 1963–97

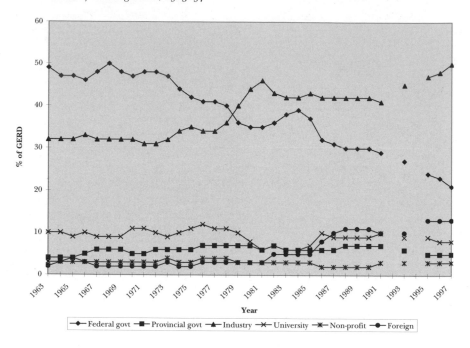

Table 2.7
R&D-active companies: figures from Revenue Canada and Statistics Canada, 1992

Province	Revenue Canada		Statistics Canada	
	Firms claiming tax credits (no.)	Amounts claimed ($million)	Laboratories conducting R&D (no.)	Total R&D effort of firms ($million)
Ontario	2,030	323	1,458	2,643
Quebec	1,762	460	933	1,280
British Columbia	851	82	509	279
Alberta	524	55	321	252
Maritimes and NWT	195	7	168	131
Manitoba	146	12	92	43
Saskatchewan	136	11	94	39
Total	5,644	949	3,566	5,512

Sources: Canada. Statistics Canada, 1993; Lipsett and Lipsey, 1994.

1993 and 1996). An ongoing study of the software industry in Canada found not fewer than two thousand firms conducting R&D, as against 864 cited by Statistics Canada for 1995 (Niosi and Chéron, 1998).

Third and finally, Canada's corporations have increased their R&D in foreign countries. In 1995, in the United States only, for instance, Canadian-owned and -controlled firms were spending nearly $2 billion (Serapio and Dalton, 1999), almost twice the figure that the American firms were spending in Canada. At least one hundred Canadian laboratories belonging to more than sixty Canadian-owned and -controlled corporations exist in the United States. There is no precise information available about Canadian laboratories in other countries, but patent figures and annual reports show that Canadian corporations are also active in R&D in western Europe, Japan, and a few large developing countries, such as Brazil, China, India, Turkey, and Mexico (see chapter 6).

There is a strong concentration of R&D activities in a few major Canadian firms. Even if corporate concentration of R&D has slightly diminished over time, the twenty-five largest performers of R&D still in 1995 represented 45 per cent of Canadian R&D expenditures in the business sector (Tables 2.8 and 2.9).

The industrial concentration of R&D is also evident. In declining order of shares, telecommunications equipment, aircraft and parts, engineering and scientific services, finance, insurance and real estate, other electronic equipment, pharmaceuticals and medicines, and business accounted for more than half of all business expenditure in Canadian R&D in 1995 (see Table 2.10). A comparison shows that this industrial concentration is not exclusive to Canada. In 1991, in the United States, the same industries – engineering and scientific services excluded – also represented over half of industrial R&D (National Science Foundation, 1993: 368).

Turnover among the top Canadian performers has been notable in the last quarter-century, resulting from both industry and company factors. When we compare the 1969 list of the twenty-five largest industrial performers of R&D with that of 1994, we see that nearly 60 per cent of the top 1969 performers do not show up in 1994; some companies disappeared (such as British American Oil, Orenda, and RCA Victor, and the pulp and paper firms), some occupy more modest positions in the ranking (such as chemical producers and electrical equipment manufacturers), and others were absorbed by competitors (such as Canadair and De Havilland, acquired by Bombardier in the 1980s). Some industries climbed to the top positions together with their leading companies; most notably, the pharmaceutical companies and the manufacturers of telecommunication equipment went up into the top

Table 2.8
Concentration of industrial R&D, 1973 and 1995

	Total intramural expenditures for R&D (%)	
Rank of corporations	1973	1995
Top 10	35	33
Top 25	51	45
Top 50	64	55
Top 75	72	61
Top 100	77	65

Source: Statistics Canada, 1995.

twenty-five, reflecting changes in both patent legislation and national technological advantages.

Another major change in Canadian R&D has been the declining role of foreign corporations. In 1969, 75 per cent of the top performers were foreign-owned and –controlled, compared to only 40 per cent in 1995. There were in all 447 foreign firms performing R&D in Canada; their total expenditures represented $2.5 billion of intramural R&D in 1995, or 32 per cent of the $7.7 billion of business expenditures in R&D (BERD). In 1995, foreign firms dominated R&D in several industries, including beverages and tobacco (90 per cent), pharmaceuticals (82 per cent), textiles (82 per cent), motor vehicles (80 per cent), other chemical products (77 per cent), business machines (62 per cent), and aircraft and parts (55 per cent).

University R&D and Industry

In the 1990s, university laboratories have become the second largest institutional actor in the national R&D system, relegating government labs to third place (Figure 2.4). The number of Canadian university campuses has grown (for example, the Université du Québec, founded in 1969, now has ten new major campuses); the number of advanced-studies programs, research centres in universities, and research programs and projects has increased at an even faster pace. And some of the French-speaking universities (notably Laval and Montréal) are now among the most research-intensive institutions in Canada.

By 1990, Canada had the world's highest percentage of twenty-two-year-olds with first college and university degrees: some 33 per cent of

Table 2.9
Top twenty-five industrial performers of R&D in Canada, 1995

Rank and corporation	R&D expend. ($million)	Country of control	R&D/sales (%)	Industry
1 Northern Telecom Ltd	2.332	Canada	15.9	Telecommunication equipment
2 Pratt & Whitney Canada	247	USA	14.5	Aircraft engines
3 IBM Canada Ltd	225	USA	2.2	Computers, software
4 Atomic Energy of Canada	159	Can. govt	48.3	Nuclear energy
5 Merck Frosst Canada	155	USA	34.8	Pharmaceuticals
6 Hydro-Québec	148	Que. govt	2.0	Electric utility
7 Ericsson Communications	127	Sweden	45.0	Telecom. equipment
8 Ontario Hydro	117	Ont. govt	1.3	Electric utility
9 Alcan Aluminum Ltd	104	Canada	0.8	Mines and metals
10 CAE Inc.	99	Canada	15.1	Electronic systems
11 Newbridge Networks	91	Canada	10.9	Telecom. equipment
12 Connaught Laboratories	86	France	21.8	Pharmaceuticals
13 Nova Corp.	84	Canada	1.9	Oil, gas, chemicals
14 Bombardier	82	Canada	1.4	Transp. equipment
15 Imperial Oil Ltd	74	USA	0.8	Oil and gas
16 Magna International	67	Canada	1.5	Automotive parts
17 Telus Corp.	62	Canada	3.7	Telecom. services
18 BC Telecom Inc.	59	Canada	2.5	Telecom. services
19 Bell Canada	58	Canada	0.7	Telecom. services

Table 2.9 *(Continued)*
Top twenty-five industrial performers of R&D in Canada, 1995

Rank and corporation	R&D expend. ($million)	Country of control	R&D/sales (%)	Industry
20 GM of Canada	56	USA	0.2	Cars and trucks
21 Apotex Inc.	56	Canada	14.9	Pharma-ceuticals
22 Rolls Royce Canada	54	UK	12.3	Aircraft turbines
23 Noranda	53	Canada	0.6	Metals, forest products
24 Allied Signal Canada	47	USA	11.1	Avionics
25 Hoechst Marion Roussel	44	Germany	13.0	Pharma-ceuticals

Source: Information from Evert Communications: *Research Money*, 17 July 1996, 4.

Table 2.10
BERD by industry, R&D expenditure intentions, 1995

Industry	% of BERD
Telecommunication equipment	15
Aircraft and parts	11
Engineering and scientific services*	9
Finance, insurance, and real estate	6
Other electronic equipment	6
Pharmaceuticals and medicine	6
Business machines	5
All other industries	42
Total, all industries (%)	100%
Total, all industries ($million)	$6,999

Source: Canada, Statistics Canada, 1995.
* Includes dedicated biotechnology firms.

Canadians at that age had a higher education diploma. However only 18 per cent of them had a degree in natural sciences or engineering; the proportion has not changed since 1969 (National Science Foundation, 1993). By comparison, 31 per cent of U.S. twenty-two-year-olds had a higher-education degree, and 13 per cent of them were in natural science or engineering. In Japan, 25 per cent of the twenty-two-year-olds had a higher degree, and 28 per cent of them had graduated in sciences or engineering.

Also, the links between industry and university in Canada have been developing very rapidly since the 1970s. A governmental study estimated that in 1980 business funded 4 per cent of university R&D, and in 1993, 11 per cent, against only 7 per cent in the United States (Doutriaux and Barker, 1995). In 1996, business contributed 10,3 per cent of university funds (*Research Money*, 10 Sept. 1997, 7).

The same authors estimate that the most common types of links between university and industry included research contracts awarded to university researchers by business firms, collaborative university–industry research projects, permanent industry–university research centres, provision of highly trained personnel to business by university, jointly organized industry–university training programs, and industrial spin-offs created by university researchers and others. A very tentative ranking of the major universities involved in industrial collaboration and some useful indicators appear in Table 2.11. The universities of Toronto, McGill, Montreal, British Columbia, and Laval, in descending order, dominate the rankings in almost every respect.

Also, by 1995, Canadian universities were spending some U.S.$2.3 billion, against U.S.$27.3 billion by American universities – a ratio of 1 to 12 (OECD, 1997). In financial terms, and relative to populations and gross domestic product (GDP), Canadian university research had caught up with the United States, a process that started in 1960.

Government Laboratories and Industry

In the 1990s, the government laboratory system had changed from what it was in 1969. The promotion of new technologies is now among its priorities. Government laboratories were in the 1990s, as in the 1930s, a few steps ahead of industry. NRC now included twenty divisions, including five biotechnology research centres, two Institutes for Information and Telecommunication Technologies, seven infrastructure technologies institutes (including aerospace, astrophysics, and surface transportation technology), and four institutes for manufacturing technologies (including the Industrial Materials Institute, the Institute for Sensor and Control

Table 2.11
Technology transfer activities, selected Canadian universities, 1992

Canadian university	Sponsored research ($million)				Selected outputs					
	A	B	C	D	E	F	G	H	I	J
Toronto	170	91	20	33	97	10	26	14	1115	20
McGill	154	71	31	48	57	10	10	12	110	19
Montreal	152	64	39	97	40	7	11	3	200	3
UBC	120	83	19	28	80	21	65	60	755	28
Laval	106	33	32	21	30	2	15	0	100	15
Alberta	79	43	8	18	40	12	60	20	410	28
McMaster	78	31	N/A	27	N/A	N/A	N/A	N/A	N/A	N/A
Queen's	62	39	8	17	33	6	23	33	761	12
Waterloo	60	30	6	11	N/A	7	60	22	2000	100
Calgary	60	28	N/A	16	N/A	N/A	N/A	N/A	N/A	N/A

Source: Doutriaux and Barker, 1995.
A: Total for university.
B: Federal-government support.
C: Industry-sponsored research.
D: Total private (includes industry).
E: Number of invention disclosures received.
F: Number of patents issued, 1992.
G: Number of active licences.
H: Number of biological agreements.
I: Royalties ($000), 1992.
J: Number of spin-offs, total.

Technology, and the Integrated Manufacturing Technology Institute). Some of these laboratories have been crucial in the development of new activities, such as biotechnology in Canada (Walsh, Niosi, and Mustar, 1995). Ottawa launched a few new technology institutes, independent from the NRC, such as the Canadian Space Agency, founded in 1989.

A second major shift was the gradual erosion of the role of federal laboratories in the system, partly because of the rise of business R&D, but also because of spending cuts by the federal government in the 1990s. The postwar period witnessed rapid growth of the number and expenditures of the federal laboratories. The proportion of Canadian domestic R&D performed by the government peaked in the mid-1980s, at nearly 22 per cent of GERD, and then declined slowly to 17 per cent in 1995.

Some public laboratories have been merged or have changed their departmental parents: Industry Canada took over several research laboratories from the Department of Communications, as did Natural Resources from the departments of Energy, Mines and Resources and of Forests, and a few units disappeared. Most federal and provincial laboratories lost some of their government budgets. Also, the Canadian Patents and Development Ltd (CPDL), established in 1946 to transfer government intellectual property to industry, was disbanded in 1990, and its intellectual property was sold. By the late 1980s, CPDL was one of the largest patent-holders in Canada.

Most of the federal departments and institutions active in research in 1969 were still there in 1994. Table 2.12 gives an idea of the largest departments/institutions in descending order of R&D budgets: Environment, NRC, Natural Resources Canada, and Agriculture. Complex funding patterns link government departments – including their laboratories – with other institutions, such as business enterprises and universities. Only two organizations (the Canadian Space Agency and Industry Canada) spend a major share of their R&D funds in industry, but all of them have some of their research allocations transferred to business. None of them makes the funding of university research a major mission.

These expenditures represent only one-third of Ottawa's outlays for scientific and technological activities. Another $1.3 billion in 1995 went to five funding agencies that have no direct involvement in research: the Medical Research Council, the Natural Science and Engineering Research Council, the Social Sciences and Humanities Research Council, the International Development Research Centre (IDRC), and the Canadian International Development Agency (CIDA). Most of these funds – except for the IDRC's and CIDA's – paid for research in Canadian universities.

In the early 1990s, provincial laboratories were playing a significant supporting role in the NSI, although their R&D expenditures represented only 1 per cent of Canada's total. In 1994, the Alberta Research Council was the largest, with a total budget of $43.8 million, followed by Quebec's Centre de recherche industrielle ($36.3 million) and Ontario's ORTECH ($28.8 million). These institutions were active mostly in industry, which provided 20 per cent of their funds that year.

The general trend, in Canada as in several other developed countries, including the United Kingdom and the United States, was a relative decline in the state's direct research activities and stagnation in direct public funding of innovation activities. In the 1990s, this trend brought reduced or frozen budgets for Canadian government laboratories and the privatization of a few of them. It also meant a retreat from direct subsidization of R&D. Among the casualties, the Defence

Table 2.12
Federal organizations performing R&D, 1995–96

Department or corporation	Total R&D expenditures ($million) (A)	Performed intra-murally (B)	Performed in university (C)	Performed in industry (D)
Environment	523	476	12	17
National Research Council	486	382	20	72
Natural Resources Canada	422	344	7	40
Agriculture	365	350	3	5
Canadian Space Agency	313	66	6	201
Industry Canada	300	144	6	141
Fisheries and Oceans	210	200	1	7
National Defence	197	111	9	76
Health Canada	189	152	16	5
Atomic Energy of Canada	164	147	1	12
Other	413	327	5	35
Total	3,582	2,699	86	611

Source: Canada, Statistics Canada, 1996.

Note: The difference between column A and the sum of the three remaining columns is made up of funds paid to other Canadian and foreign performers.

Industry Productivity Program was reduced from $167 million in 1993–94 to $90 million in 1995–96 and to $22 million in 1997–98. The NRC's budget fell from $502 million in 1990–91 to $486 million in 1995–96 and to $373 million in 1997–98. Also, all the science-funding agencies lost part of their budgets.

Provincial research organizations (PROs) were also falling behind. Between 1990 and 1994, they lost some 17 per cent of their aggregate budgets in current dollars. The British Columbia Research Council, the country's fourth largest PRO, was privatized in 1992. ORTECH was for sale in early 1999.

The Regional Dimension

The regions are the most visible subsets within Canada's NSI. Two regions account for over 80 per cent of industrial R&D: Ontario and Quebec. Ontario is by far the largest: in 1995, it was home to 55.5 per cent of Canada's business R&D, with $4.2 billion and 51 per cent of total Canadian R&D expenditures. Ontario dominated the industrial spectrum, particularly in telecommunication equipment, business machines, and financial R&D. Some twenty-two hundred industrial R&D units, according to Statistics Canada, existed in Ontario at the end of 1995 (Canada, Statistics Canada, 1997, Cat. 88–202). Ontario also received the most federal research money, because of the presence, mostly in the Ottawa region, of many large federal research establishments. Toronto and Montreal account for 50 per cent of all Canadian industrial R&D spending, with 25 per cent in each urban community.

Quebec is the second most important region, with 26 per cent of Canadian R&D and 28.3 per cent of the business total. Hosting some 2,575 private research units in 1995, Quebec industry led Ontario only in aircraft R&D and was second in most other fields. While second also in terms of government laboratories, Quebec was first as a performer of scientific research, with 40 per cent of the Canadian total. Quebec has nineteen universities and a large number of provincial hospitals conducting research. Ontario followed, with 28 per cent of total scientific expenditures. On a sector basis, Ontario conducted slightly more scientific research than Quebec in higher education but was outspent by Quebec in both hospital and business scientific research.

All other regions followed far behind Ontario and Quebec. British Columbia (with 943 industrial research laboratories) and Alberta (with 546) were third and fourth, respectively, by every possible measure, including industrial R&D expenditure, of which 7.2 per cent was conducted in British Columbia and 5.8 per cent in Alberta. The six other provinces combined hosted only 655 industrial research establishments in 1995 and received only 3.3 per cent of Canada's industrial R&D outlays (Canada, Statistics Canada, 1997, Cat. 88–202).

Despite of these regional differences, Canada's NSI is not simply a collage of regional systems. First, most large companies are coast-to-coast operations, and several own research establishments in more than one province. Second, Canadian technological alliances between industrial firms are most often national rather than regional. (Regions are defined as urban districts, or metropolitan agglomerations, sharing up to 1995 the same regional area telephone code). In Canada, regional alliances and cooperation are mostly either industry – university partnerships or informal (and thus less substantial in both strategic and budgetary terms) collaborations between firms. Canadian regions, even the largest, are probably too small to sustain many self-sufficient research programs; hence the importance of national (as opposed to purely regional) partnerships. Cooperation within industrial districts exists, but it comes second to national cooperation. Montreal, Toronto, Vancouver, and Ottawa are the largest of these R&D agglomerations (Amesse, Lamy, and Tahmi, 1989). International alliances are usually the largest in terms of the financial commitments of the partners, but they represented less than 20 per cent of all technological alliances of Canadian enterprises (Niosi, 1995).

Third, federal policies and funding are national and apply to all companies, whatever the region. They are much more far-reaching and substantial, in financial terms, than those of any provincial government. True, Quebec has developed dozens of policies and programs to support technological development within industrial firms and universities. These policies helped Quebec industry catch up relative to Ontario (Niosi and Landry, 1993). Still, most companies operating in the province require supplementary competencies and knowledge that they must obtain outside Quebec. Whatever the intensity of the public effort, the size of the region (seven million people, fewer than fifteen hundred companies with industrial laboratories) does not allow any degree of technological autarchy. Also, as we saw above, PROs perform only 1 per cent of Canada's total R&D effort. In the meantime, the federal government funded 41 per cent of Canada's $11 billion GERD in 1995 and performed directly, via its own labs, 17 per cent of this amount.

The role of the federal government is particularly significant in university research. The provincial governments, which have jurisdiction in education, starved the universities for about a century, while Ottawa provided some of the small amounts of research funds available to them. In the 1990s, provincial austerity is also putting the university system in jeopardy, particularly in Quebec. Regional systems of innovation are suffering from underinvestment in higher education by the provincial governments.

Also, federal laboratories collaborate with, and transfer technology to, companies of all regions, even those (such as agricultural farms, construction companies, and fisheries) that conduct no R&D. In addition, the largest labs operating in all provinces, including Quebec, are owned and controlled by Ottawa.

Finally, the evolution of the R&D personnel shows a continuous decrease of the provincial component of the research workforce. Between 1983 and 1993, the total number of R&D personnel in Canada increased by 33 per cent. The most sizeable growth took place in industry – a jump of 64 per cent to 60,530, or almost half of the 127,000 national total. The next highest increase was in higher education, to a total of 44,620. In the federal government, there was a modest increase of 100 researchers, to a total of 16,400; in the same period, the

R&D personnel working for provincial governments dropped by 16 per cent, to 3,500 (*Research Money*, 21 Aug. 1996, 8). It is difficult to argue that provincial influence is growing when the total provincial effort is declining.

However, the gographical deconcentration of the new federal laboratories is helping to create regional poles of advanced technology in several provinces. In biotechnology, for instance, the NRC's Plant Biotechnology Institute in Saskatoon is now at the centre of a cluster of both new firms and foreign subsidiaries in agro-biotech. In Montreal, the Biotechnology Research Institute is at the core of cluster of human biotechnology firms.

Outputs of the R&D System

Canada's R&D effort produces every year between two thousand and three thousand new patent applications by Canadian residents. In 1992, for instance, Canadian residents made 2,873 applications in Canada (OECD, 1995) and received more than two thousand in the United States (National Science Foundation, 1993). What sectors were the most advanced in Canadian technology? I applied the concept of revealed technological advantage (RTA) to find out the areas in which Canadian firms showed major inventiveness. The RTA concept uses the U.S. patent database and relates the strength of every industry in a given country (in terms of number of patents granted in the United States) to the total strength of the same industry of all countries other than the United States, as shown by the patents granted to those foreign inventors in the United States; this ratio (the numerator of the fraction) is then normalized (divided) by the relative size of the inventive effort of the country. The algorithm thus reads as follows:

RTA =

$$\frac{\dfrac{\text{Number of patents granted to industry X of country Y in the United States}}{\text{Number of patents granted to industry X of all foreign countries in the United States}}}{\dfrac{\text{Number of patents granted to country Y in the United States}}{\text{Number of patents granted to all foreign countries in the United States}}}$$

If the value of this index exceeds 1, then country X shows an RTA in that particular industry; if the index is inferior to 1, then country X is at a technological disadvantage in that industry (Pavitt, 1982; Pavitt and Patel, 1990). Table 2.13 shows the distribution of the RTA index in Canadian industries. By 1988–91, Canadian industry seemed technologically strong in some areas in which it also shows major commercial advantages, such as mining products; pulp, paper, and cellulose; metallurgy, rail-transportation equipment; aircraft; and telecommunication equipment. New areas of technological strength are biotechnology and metal products. Conversely, Canada is weak, as one could expect, in such fields as textiles, semiconductors, photographic equipment and films, pharmaceuticals, organic chemicals, computers, robots, and laser equipment; but Canadian technology appears also to be weak in areas where its industry was supposed to be a leader, such as heavy electrical equipment and nuclear energy.

Commercial results from R&D-intensive industries are quite a different matter. A recent study of advanced technology products suggests that Canada shows a commercial deficit in some areas in which it has some technological advantages, such as biotechnology. Conversely, areas of technological weakness, including advanced materials, show commercial strength (see Table 2.14). On the whole, however, the negative trade balance is consistent with the weak domestic R&D effort that is often presented in the literature.

However, since 1991 and for the first time in its history, the Canadian balance of technological services has become positive; in 1993, Canada's receipts for foreign-purchased R&D and other technological services exceeded payments by $214 million. Two sectors accounted for the Canadian surplus: telecommunications equipment and business machines. All other sectors reveal a deficit (Canada, Statistics Canada, 1995).

The Canadian R&D system still exhibits a bias towards fundamental and pre-competitive research, because of its heavy investment in higher education and public research (as shown in Table 1.1) and the private sector's comparatively weak – but increasing – interest in performing commercial R&D. By 1991, Canada was responsible for 4.2 per cent of the world's articles in scientific and technical journals, but only 0.23 per cent of its patents and 2.1 per cent of all patents granted in the United States (National Science Foundation, 1993).

At least three explanations have been put forward to explain the apparent underinvestment of the Canadian private sector in R&D: the overwhelming importance of resource-based industries such as mining and metallurgy, pulp and paper, and hydrocarbons, which are not R&D-intensive; foreign control of much Canadian manufacturing, where subsidiaries and affiliates of multinational corporations would spend less than their Canadian competitors but import technology from their parent companies abroad; and the small size of many Canadian-owned and -controlled firms. It seems difficult at this moment to assign a specific weight to each of these competing explanations. A more precise response would probably need better data;

Table 2.13
Revealed technological advantages (RTAs) of Canadian industry, 1988–91

	1980–83	1984–88	1988–91
Industries with technological advantage			
Food and beverage	1.77	1.40	1.27
Mines	1.10	1.15	1.31
Paper and cellulose	2.96	2.43	2.09
Inorganic chemicals	1.77	1.89	1.51
Bleaching, dyes, fluid treatment	1.09	1.06	1.11
Biotechnology	0.00	1.01	1.44
Water treatment	2.17	2.13	1.61
Metallurgy	1.17	1.24	1.18
Metal products	0.75	1.47	1.35
Construction	2.56	2.65	3.15
Aircraft	2.08	1.37	1.02
Rail transportation	1.55	1.56	2.14
Shipyards	1.77	2.31	2.66
Other transportation	1.37	1.21	1.30
Telecommunication equipment	0.89	0.82	1.03
Telephone and telegraph equipment	1.51	1.68	1.03
Measurement and controlling equipment	0.97	1.01	1.11
Ammunition and explosives	1.19	0.84	1.65
Other industries	1.33	1.32	1.28
Industries with technological disadvantage			
Textiles	0.38	0.32	0.35
Organic chemicals	0.46	0.42	0.43
Pharmaceutical products	0.66	0.58	0.77
Alloys and metal composites	0.31	0.27	0.71
Computers	0.62	0.43	0.41
Semiconductors	0.29	0.38	0.26
Robots	0.00	0.39	0.69
Electrical equipment	0.98	0.99	0.77
Nuclear reactors and systems	0.65	0.83	0.52

Source: Kelly, 1993.

Table 2.14
Canadian trade balance in advanced technology products, 1994

Product	Balance ($million)
Aerospace	2554.4
Advanced materials	41.9
Opto-electronics	(81.0)
Nuclear technology	(163.8)
Weapons	(195.8)
Biotechnology	(213.0)
Flexible manufacturing	(680.2)
Life sciences	(700.7)
Information and communication	(2,556.3)
Electronics	(3,853.8)
Total	(5847.9)

Source: Research Money, Oct. 1995, 2.
Note: Figures between parenthesis denote deficits.

some of the apparent riddle may be simply a case of underestimation of total private R&D, particularly in the new areas of computer software and advanced materials, in which SMEs predominate and where traditional definitions and samples still need improvement. Also, Canadian-owned and -controlled corporations have extensive R&D operations abroad, closer to their major markets and to centres of highly innovative scientific and industrial research (see chapter 6). When the foreign R&D activities of Canadian firms are taken into account, their technological underinvestment seems less substantial.

THE FINANCING OF INNOVATION IN CANADA: VENTURE CAPITAL

In the postwar period, and up to the early 1970s, as we have seen, the overall trend was one of increasing involvement by the state in the financing and direct execution of R&D, as it sought to create incentives for industrial innovation. As we saw in chapter 2, the federal state was funding, still in the 1960s, close to 50 per cent of total GERD, and the provinces, almost 5 per cent (Figure 2.4). Since then, the public sector has held a decreasing role, as new, private-sector or mixed private–

public institutions appeared, mainly in the 1980s and 1990s, to finance and execute R&D. Thus by 1997 the combined share of federal and provincial financing was closer to 25 per cent, having shrunk by half, while business itself was funding over 60 per cent (including 50 per cent by Canadian industry and another 13 per cent by foreign business).

The sources of these private funds are three-fold. First, many large and medium-sized firms are now able to finance in-house R&D and innovation projects with retained earnings. Second, equity markets as well as non-equity (debt) markets are also available to them. Third, in the 1980s and 1990s, Canada has witnessed the rise of a set of private and mixed-capital venture capital institutions funding emerging innovative firms, particularly in the new areas of computer software, electronic hardware, biotechnology, automation, and materials. There are no available figures on the first two types of sources, but some good estimates exist on the size and the role of venture capital firms in the growth of new, high-tech firms.

The rise of venture capital in Canada paralleled that of the United States. In Canada, the first venture capital firm (Charterhouse Canada, an Anglo–French foreign subsidiary) was created in 1952. In 1958 a second appeared, and the third was founded in 1963. A few other companies emerged between the early 1960s and the late 1970s (Macdonald, 1987). However, the rise of the venture capital industry occurred in the 1980s, with marked reductions in taxes on capital gains and the growth of pension capital funds looking for profitable investments. At that time, there were both supply and demand for venture capital. Initial sources included large banks and insurance companies, government organizations, rich individuals, and foreign investors looking for good investments in new areas. In the last ten years, we have witnessed the rise of pension funds and hybrid private–public institutions, including labour unions, among the most dynamic lenders of venture capital. New demand came from the emerging high-tech industries of biotechnology, computer software, telecommunication equipment, environment, industrial automation, and other electronic activities. Since the mid-1970s, hundreds of new high-tech companies arrived every year in these burgeoning science-based industries, and more and more were supported by the growing venture capital firms.

A few figures may help to explain the process of growth of both supply of and demand for venture capital. The Canadian Venture Capital Association (CVCA) consisted of some twelve firms in 1974, seventy in 1985–86 and over one hundred in 1998. The total capital pool in Canada, estimated to be $1.3 billion in 1985, was over $8 billion in

Table 2.15
Venture capital in Canada, 1996

Industry	Investments (no.)	Companies financed (no.)	Amounts invested ($million)
Biotechnology	133	54	159
Communication	65	42	95
Computer-related	195	22	222
Electronics	81	46	87
Energy/environmental	31	17	30
Industrial automation	22	15	45
Medical/health	85	37	111
Total technology	612	328	749
Total traditional	269	197	344
Total	881	525	1,094

Source: CVCA, 1997.

1998 (CVCA, 1999). In 1987, 265 enterprises were financed, for a total of $346 million. Ten years later, the amounts had tripled. In 1996, 881 investments had been approved for 525 companies, for a total of $1.1 billion.

Technology has always been the main area of investment of venture capital, but its share grew from 32 per cent of amounts invested in 1987 to 69 per cent in 1996. This year, some 62 per cent of the investees were technology-based firms (Table 2.15).

Venture capital seemed to play a pivotal role in the development of at least some of the new knowledge-intensive industries in Canada, particularly in biotechnology, where in the late 1990s it financed close to 15 per cent of the 300 existing firms. The role of venture capital may be less important in other areas, such as the production of computer software, where it financed close to 4 per cent of firms in 1996. (Two hundred software-producing firms out of some five thousand in Canadian industry were supported by venture capital.)

An in-depth study based on the CVCA's data showed that, between 1991 and 1994, some 21 per cent of the exits of venture capital investment consisted of write-offs. Company buy-backs, initial public offerings, acquisitions, and mergers formed almost all of the other (successful) types of exit (Mackintosh, 1997).

A learning process seems to have occurred in the Canadian venture capital industry, where dozens of firms have been entering in the last twenty years with a fair rate of success. The NSI thus boasts not only technological learning, but also an investment learning process.

CONCLUSION

During the last thirty years Canada has partially caught up with other OECD countries (see Table 2.16). In 1961–62, it devoted only 0.9 per cent of its GDP to R&D, compared to an average of 1.64 per cent for the OECD countries, including 2.8 per cent by the United States. The Canadian effort represented only 55 per cent of the average of these countries. In 1995, Canada's GERD represented 1.6 per cent of its GDP, or 75 per cent of the average OECD effort. That year in the United States GERD made up 2.58 per cent of GDP. Canada has participated in the generalized catching up of late industrializers, as well as in the general retreat of the state from direct performance and the increase in business-financed and -performed R&D. The catching up, however, is most noticeable for 1985–95, when several countries such as Canada, Denmark, France, and Japan increased their expenditure, while others, such as (West) Germany, the United Kingdom, and the United States decreased spending. Convergence results thus from both catching up and falling behind (Abramovits and David, 1996).

Canada's national R&D system has historically been oriented towards the "upstream" areas of the innovation process. Its effort appears strong in fundamental research – as shown by the disproportionate share of higher education within total R&D expenditure and the high proportion of Canada's publications in the world's scientific and technical literature. Conversely, Canada's private industry is performing less R&D than its American counterpart and also compared to several smaller countries, such as the Netherlands, Sweden, and Switzerland. Canada's industry shows several areas of strength in terms of patents, such as paper and cellulose, metallurgy and metal products, telecommunication equipment, aircraft, rail transportation, construction, and food products. It appears weak in areas such as textiles, semi-conductors, computers, and organic chemicals. However, Canadian firms have gained technological strength in most new science-based industries, such as biotechnology, telecommunication equipment, and even robotics and advanced metal-based materials; these two are, however, areas in which Canada is still lagging behind other industrial countries.

During the twentieth century, Canada's NSI was built through at least three stages. The first was one of laissez-faire and slow growth under market forces, up to 1914. The second period started with the First

Table 2.16
Convergence of GERD/GDP in industrial countries, selected years, 1961–95

Year	Can.	USA	UK	Italy	Fra.	(W.) Ger.	Japan	Neth.	Den- mark	Aver- age*	S.D.†
1961	0.9	2.8	2.4	N.D.	1.5	1.2	1.3	1.4	N.D.	1.64	0.65
1975	1.1	2.3	2.2	0.8	1.8	2.2	2.0	2.0	1.0	1.71	0.55
1985	1.44	2.93	2.31	1.13	2.25	2.72	2.77	2.09	1.25	2.10	0.64
1995	1.60	2.58	2.19	1.14	2.34	2.27	2.84	2.05	1.83	2.14	0.49

Source: Information from OECD.
* Average for these selected countries.
† Standard deviation of the nine countries vis-à-vis the OECD average. These countries were selected on the basis of the stability and reliability of series as well as their importance within the OECD.

World War and continued till 1939, with the federal government increasingly active as both financier and performer. The third stage, from the Second World War to the present, is characterized by federal, and lately provincial, efforts to involve business in R&D, a growing public role within the NSI, together with an intense systemic integration. By the 1990s, Ottawa's direct role as a performer had diminished, and the system worked increasingly by itself, under federal regulations and stimuli.

All efforts to coordinate and promote R&D exclusively from the top down were resisted by many company managers, provincial leaders, and university researchers. But underinvestment by private firms led governments to create first, between 1940 and 1965, a large in-house research establishment, and then, beginning in the mid-1960s, hundreds of programs, in order to stimulate scientific research in universities and technological research in industry. These programs gave some leverage to (mainly the federal) governments and some unity and coherence to the NSI. It would be erroneous to pretend that top–down coordination prevailed; some order came by way of self-organization of markets. Whatever its level of unity and coherence, Canada's NSI – like probably most NSIs in industrial countries – was the product of both market forces and public policies. In Canada, as a late industrializer, the latter were probably more powerful than the former.

Compared to other industrial countries, the Canadian NSI exhibits again some similarities with Italy in terms of its late, postwar development (Malerba, 1993), but not in terms of the industries and types of institutions that it developed. In spite of government efforts to promote high technology, Italy specialized in light, design-intensive industries (textiles, garments, leather, shoes, electrical appliances) that are declining activities in Canada; conversely, like Canada, Italy also promoted a few heavy industries with some success (car manufacturing, petro-chemicals, aircraft) but was far less successful than Canada in high technology.

Like Sweden, Canada started industrialization in the nineteenth century on the basis of a similar endowment of natural resources: forests and mining-related activities started manufacturing (Edquist and Lundvall, 1993). Sweden, however, developed earlier than Canada a group of large domestically owned and-controlled corporations that conducted in-house R&D within the country's borders – Alfa-Laval, Asea, Ericsson, Saab, and Volvo, to name a few. The equivalents appeared much later in Canada, after 1945 (Apotex, Bombardier, Magna, Mitel, Newbridge Networks, NorTel, and Nova). In some cases, they were foreign subsidiaries bought by Canadian firms in the interwar years (Alcan, Inco) or the postwar period (i.e., Northern Telecom in 1956; Canadair and De Havilland in the 1980s). As we see in chapters 7 and 8, the internationalization of Canada's industrial R&D also started much later than Sweden's.

It seems now crucial to study Canada's national R&D system at a micro-level, where laboratories are the key institutions and most decisions are taken. Too many dimensions of the behaviour and performance of Canadian research laboratories are now understudied and need to be clarified. They include management methods, performance evaluation, technology transfer, patterns of cooperation, revenue sources, and the whole national network of interactions between private, university, and public laboratories. The following chapters (3–5) examine these areas.

3 Canada's Domestic R&D System

The core of Canada's domestic R&D system consists of one hundred large and medium-sized private and public enterprises concentrating some 77 per cent of Canada's industrial R&D expenditures, together with one hundred government and nearly two hundred large university R&D laboratories. This study targeted all R&D laboratories employing twenty-five or more scientists and engineers. Our unit of analysis was the R&D laboratory, not the firm, because R&D management practices, including networking of all sorts, are best understood and monitored at the level of the laboratory, not at the level of the corporation or other, more distant parent institutions (such as government departments, which are responsible for public institutions; universities, responsible for academic research laboratories; and parent corporations). Using many different public sources, we estimated that there were, in 1993 and within Canadian borders, some three hundred private, one hundred and ten government, one hundred and fifty university, and twelve non-profit R&D laboratories in that size range.

We mailed out questionnaires to the heads of all those laboratories, except for a few cases of personal interviewing. Several labs responded that they employed at that moment fewer than twenty-five R&D persons; some organizations informed us that their units had been closed. The "actual" population takes these adjustments into account. The population, number of valid responses, and response rates appear in Table 3.1. Table 3.2 shows the regional distribution of the actual population.[1] Inasmuch as we can judge (a few questionnaires did not identify the respondent), the responses constitute representative samples of the population, in terms of region, industry (in the case of private laboratories), and the federal–provincial distribution (in the case of public laboratories).

We made slight differences among the questionnaires addressed to the four types of R&D laboratories, in order to reflect organizational and goal variance. The questionnaires, with nearly forty questions, were modified versions of those used in the U.S. study, as some of the issues and/or pre-coded responses did not apply to Canada. Also, we added a few questions in order to have a better grasp of networking activities between R&D labs.

The questions concerned the activities of the laboratories, missions, the origin of budgets and allocation made of them, inputs and outputs, links with external units through technology transfer and cooperative activities, obstacles and difficulties encountered in accomplishment of goals, and other related issues, such as effectiveness criteria and internal organization. These data were useful because they give some flesh to the concept of NSI. New concepts and theories must be developed through their exposure to real world problems and data, not merely through more theorizing. In other words, the hypothetico-deductive method (developing a hypothesis from theory, testing it with data, and modifying the theory acordingly) is the best method in empirical science (Bunge, 1967; Ghiselin, 1969).

---

1 Bureau de la Statistique du Québec, 1993; Evert Communications, *Canadian Corporate R&D* (Ottawa, 1993); Contact International, *Canadian Biotechnology 1993 Company Directory* (Ottawa, 1993); Gale Research Corp., *Research Centers Directories* (New York, 1994); Industry, Science and Technology Canada, *Répertoire des laboratoires et installations de recherche au Canada* (Ottawa, 1990); Ministry of Superior Education and Science, Quebec, *Répertoire des regroupements de recherche des établissement universitaires du Québec, 1992/3* (Quebec, 1993); Canada, Statistics Canada, *Répertoire des établissements scientifiques et technologiques de l'administration fédérale* (Ottawa, 1988).

Some of these sources existed only for Quebec, but this fact did not introduce overrepresentation of that region. Indeed, only five of 313 Quebec industrial laboratories, and only two of 135 government laboratories, did not appear in national directories. The only national listing available for university laboratories is the Gale Research Corp.'s directory, which originates in the United States and addresses more directly American organizations, with Canadian organizations not uniformly and completely covered.

Table 3.1
Target population, number of valid responses, and response rate, 1993

| | Target population | | Valid | Response rates |
Type of laboratory	Estimated	Actual	responses (no.)	% resp*100/ Actual
Industrial	313	252	59	23
Government	135	104	44	42
University	220	191	40	21
Non-profit	12	12	5	42
Total	680	559	148	26

Table 3.2
Regional distribution of Canadian laboratories with twenty-five or more R&D employees, 1993

Region	Industrial (%)	Government (%)	University (%)
Ontario	47	39	18
Quebec	37	15	63
Prairies and BC	14	33	15
Maritimes	2	13	4
Total	100	100	100

Table 3.3 enumerates some of the characteristics of the sample; I decided not to compute separately the non-profit organizations in order to ensure confidentiality. There are major differences among the three samples. On average, government laboratories were larger by any possible measure, followed by industrial and university research units. However, industrial and university labs were more homogeneous than government establishments.

Each sample represents a different proportion of Canada's R&D effort. The sample covers a much larger proportion of the government sector, where most intramural R&D takes place in large labs; it also reflects a larger response rate. Thus our sample of government labs represents 91 per cent of Canada's research professionals and 56 per cent

Table 3.3
Some characteristics of laboratories sampled, 1992

	Industry	Government	University
Average total personnel 1992	127	245	95
Standard deviation	214	367	95
Average R&D professionals 1992	96	151	80
Standard deviation	167	191	86
Average R&D budget 1992	$13.6 m.	$25 m.	$4 m.
Standard deviation	$29.4 m.	$43.8 m.	$6.4 m.
Median total personnel 1992	60	133	51
Median R&D professionals 1992	48	100	47
Median total budget 1992	$50 m.	$12 m.	$3 m.
Total personnel 1992	7,262	10,797	3,790
Total R&D professionals 1992	5,593	6,622	3,041
as % of Canada's	18%	91%	8%
Total budgets 1992	$750 m.	$1,070 m.	$159 m.
as % of Canada's	14%	56%	6%

Source: for Canada's totals, OECD, *Main Science and Technology Indicators 1993* (Paris, 1994).
Note: Averages, medians, and standard deviations take into account a few cases of missing responses.

of public laboratories' R&D budget. As for the university sample, if all professors were considered researchers, large university laboratories would constitute only a small fraction of academic research, in terms of research personnel (8 per cent) and budgets (6 per cent). This estimation would reflect the more scattered character of academic research, where laboratories undertake only a small portion of total R&D activity, particularly in the social sciences. Finally, the responding industrial labs represented some 18 per cent of Canada's industrial researchers and 14 per cent of its total business expenditure on R&D.

ASSESSMENT OF THE DATA

The three types of research laboratories differed in major characteristics: goals, organization, source and allocation of R&D budget, effectiveness criteria, and links (transfers, cooperative research, and other) with external institutions. This section outlines nine of the basic differences.

Missions

As we expected, missions and objectives differed widely among samples. Within industry, commercial applied research was the major mission: 90 per cent of the laboratories conducted this type of R&D; development followed, with 83 per cent of the cases; pre-commercial applied research, with 43 per cent, and assistance to parent company, with 42 per cent (Table 3.3). A few other were never picked as the most important – assistance and transfer to governments and transfer to private organizations. This range of responses reflects the commercial goals of the industrial lab, where the uncertainty and risk associated with basic and pre-commercial research tends to concentrate R&D activities at the more profitable end of the research spectrum: for 73 per cent of the labs, the single most important goals was either commercial applied research or development.

Conversely, government and university units were, as expected, more oriented to the upstream, more fundamental side of research. Government centres displayed a more variegated set of goals. Pre-commercial applied research and transfer to private organizations were the single most important objectives of a majority of organizations (68 per cent of labs put them as the most important or a very important mission). They were followed by assistance to private organizations (61 per cent), assistance to government (57 per cent), commercial applied research (53 per cent) and development (44 per cent), transfer to government (39 per cent), and assistance to parent organization (41 per cent). Basic research was important for only a few laboratories. Clearly, in the public laboratories, service to industry has often displaced service to government as a major goal.

University labs were the least differentiated set. Three-quarters of them responded that basic research was their single most important goal, and 97 per cent considered it either the most important or very important. All other missions came far behind. Pre-commercial applied research (58 per cent called it very important or most important), and transfer to private organizations (55 per cent) also appeared as important objectives.

Sources of Funds

The three types of laboratories also differed on the main sources of funds. The most common sources of funds for industrial laboratories were their own firm (Table 3.5), followed by government contracts, funds transferred from parent organization, and industrial grants. Those companies using government contracts and grants

Table 3.4
Major laboratories' missions

Mission	% of each category considering the mission the most important or very important		
	Industry	Government	University
Basic research	7	32	97
Pre-commercial research	43	68	58
Commercial applied research	90	53	8
Development	83	44	13
Assistance to government	5	57	25
Assistance to parent organizations	42	41	10
Assistance to private organizations	15	61	22
Transfer to government	5	39	20
Transfer to private organization	17	68	55
Support marketing	47	4	2

Table 3.5
Sources of funds for laboratories, 1992

Source of funds	Average % of funds from each source (weighted)		
	Industry	Government	University
Government contracts	12	13	45
Direct appropriations from government	0	72	4
Lab. organization	52	0	1
Parent organization	19	0	3
Industrial grants	9	13	16
Other	8	2	31

were usually financed by several government departments. However, Industry Canada emerged as by far the largest funding agency for industrial research, being used by 40 per cent of all industrial labs in our sample. Government units were the biggest users of direct appropriations from governments, by far their most common source of funds. Government contracts and industrial grants followed, being used by two-thirds of the public labs. Finally, university labs depended most on government contracts and grants, followed by government grants, industrial grants, parent-organization funds, and other sources.

Allocation of Funds

The distribution of research funds is closely linked to both missions and sources. Industrial laboratories used their funds most frequently in development and commercial and pre-commercial research and seldom for other purposes (Table 3.6). Government labs showed diversified expenditures, as their missions were diverse too. They spent more frequently on pre-commercial and basic research, together with assistance to outside organizations, technology transfer and development. University labs, as we saw above, were involved more in basic research than in any other area. This was also their main area of expenditure: all academic laboratories put funds in this area. The only other activity that came close was pre-commercial research, where 75 per cent of the labs spent some resources.

Budgets: Recent Evolution

R&D budgets had remained usually constant over the short period (three years before the study took place). Our data also show great stability of research budgets for 1990–92. Within industrial laboratories the median R&D budget remained fixed around $6 million, probably reflecting the recession and its impact on company profits. Government units saw their median budgets increase slightly from $11 million in 1990 to $12 million in 1991 to $12.2 million in 1992. In university labs, the median R&D budget grew somewhat more, from $2 million in 1990 to $2.5 million in 1991 to $3 million in 1992. This latter increase probably reflects the effect of provincial and federal centres of excellence programs, which tended to concentrate research funds in the most productive university labs. Also, under the new patent laws, pharmaceutical companies increased dramatically their R&D expenditures, including external contracts to university labs.

Outputs

Resources and missions yielded differing results. As one could expect, industrial laboratories concentrated more on production of technical knowledge for internal use (internal reports), prototypes and devices,

Table 3.6
Distribution of industrial R&D funds in laboratories, 1992

	Average % (weighted)		
Task	Industry	Government	University
Basic research	6	17	68
Pre-commercial research	28	24	17
Commercial research	23	21	6
Development	30	8	3
Assistance to parent organizations	7	8	0
Assistance to outside organization	3	11	1
Technology transfer	2	6	4
Other	1	5	3

Table 3.7
Research outputs in laboratories, 1992

	% devoting 20% or more of annual person-hours to specific outputs		
Type of output	Industry	Government	University
Published articles	2	45	67
Patents, licences	2	7	5
Algorithms, software	37	9	20
Internal reports	36	27	20
Prototypes, devices	39	14	7
Papers for seminars	0	11	15
Demonstration of devices	14	14	2
Other	19	18	7

and algorithms and software. Another major output was the demonstration of devices (Table 3.7). Both government and university labs produced published articles, papers for conferences, and internal reports, but public labs were slightly more involved in marketing of research through demonstration of devices and the building of prototypes, because of the more pre-commercial emphasis of their activities.

Commercial Activities

Commercial activities were increasingly important in all types of laboratories. They include technology transfer and cooperative networks. More than half of respondents were active in technology transfer, but the proportions vary among our three types of R&D units. Some 39 per cent of the industrial labs conducted technology transfer, and 55 per cent of the university units and 89 per cent of government labs. The motives for technology transfer also varied (Table 3.8). Only one motive cuts across the whole sample: the growth of cooperative R&D seemed to push all types of laboratories to transfer their technology or to look for other labs' technologies. Among industrial units, the hope of increasing profits was the major motive, followed by an aggressive competitive strategy. Among government labs, cooperative research, economic development, and legislative mandates were key in explaining technology transfer. University research centres were also carried along by the wave of cooperative R&D, but participation in industry–university research centres and exchange of technical information and personnel also motivated technology transfer.

Among the forty-three industrial laboratories, profits for the unit were by far the most important benefit obtained through technology transfer (it was also the "single most important" benefit chosen by fourteen respondents). New users and clients were the second most popular choice, followed by an unexpected benefit – a more realistic approach among scientific and technical personnel. Technical knowledge was also obtained from outside organizations selling or buying technology from the firm (Table 3.9).

Most of the thirty-nine government laboratories involved in technology transfer gained clients and users from this activity, but also a more "real world" approach (the most important benefit for ten research organizations) and greater public visibility (an intangible asset that may be necessary in periods of tight government budgets). Also, technology transfer permitted labs to draw in scientific and technical personnel from elsewhere to collaborate and increase their competence via the knowledge of their transferees.

Increased public visibility, contact with the "real world," drawing together of research personnel, and increased technical knowledge were the benefits that academic labs had obtained from technology transfer. As publicly funded entities, both university and government laboratories shared some of the motives and benefits of technology transfer. Conversely, industrial units did not need to rely on special

Table 3.8
Motives for technology transfer

Motive	% that find the motive "very important"		
	Industrial	Government	University
Legislative requirement	0	41	22
Economic development emphasis	0	46	18
Growth of cooperative R&D	35	49	50
Participation in industry university or government university centre	9	23	45
Exchange of technical information or personnel	9	26	41
Company's or parent's profits	65	0	27
Hope to increase lab's budget	0	18	0
Scientists' and engineers' personal satisfaction	17	31	32
Scientists' and engineers' interests in entrepreneurship and wealth	17	3	14
Offensive competitive strategy	43	0	0
Defensive competitive strategy	26	0	0
Other	9	10	5
Total units active in technology transfer	23/59	39/44	22/40

projects to "draw together" their personnel; they sought not public visibility, but profits. Transfers also brought problems. Industry, however, conducted technology transfer in the normal course of its affairs, and so technology transfer did not create major problems (Table 3.10). Compared to benefits, difficulties look minor and less widespread.

Conversely, university and government laboratories have had to integrate technology transfer in their more quiet style of fundamental research. This new activity has sometimes led to disputes over intellectual property and other matters and reduced time for research and, in the case of university, for teaching. Nevertheless, in the balance of technology transfer, benefits seemed to have outnumbered problems in all types of laboratories.

Table 3.9
Major or single most important benefits to laboratories of technology transfer

	Number of units declaring benefit		
Benefit	Industry	Government	University
Profits for laboratory	21 (91%)	12 (31%)	4 (18%)
Profit for individual scientists	2 (9%)	4 (10%)	4 (18%)
Increased public visibility	13(56%)	29 (74%)	17 (77%)
Approval of government officials	1 (4%)	23 (59%)	12 (54%)
More "real world" approach by lab personnel	17 (74%)	30 (77%)	17 (77%)
Drawing together scientific and technical personnel	11 (48%)	29 (74%)	16 (73%)
Gained technical knowledge from outside organizations	16 (70%)	24 (61%)	14 (64%)
Gained clients, users	18 (78%)	31 (79%)	10 (45%)
Other	1 (4%)	1 (2%)	3 (14%)
Total involved in technology transfer	23 (100%)	39 (100%)	22 (100%)

Table 3.10
Major and most important problems engendered in laboratories by technology transfer

	Number of units indicating each type of problem		
Problem	Industry	Government	University
Diminished time for research	4 (17%)	10 (26%)	6 (27%)
Changes in lab's agenda	1 (4%)	6 (15%)	3 (14%)
Disharmony and disputes in lab	2 (9%)	10 (26%)	3 (14%)
Conflicts over intellectual property	3 (13%)	4 (10%)	7 (32%)
Interruptions from outsiders	1 (4%)	2 (5%)	1 (4%)
Other	1 (4%)	1 (2%)	5 (23%)
Total units involved	23 (100%)	39 (100%)	22 (100%)

Part of the technology transfer took place through licences and sale of patents (Table 3.11). It is often argued that in times of intense and rapid technological change, patents are less often used to protect intellectual property and to transfer technology. Our research seems to confirm this view. A minority of industrial laboratories that were active in technology transfer held patents (48 per cent) or licensed technology (35 per cent). Conversely, among the thirty-nine government units conducting technology transfer, 51 per cent held patents, but 69 per cent licensed their technology. Only 55 per cent of university labs active in the field held patents and licensed their technology. Patenting and licensing seemed more important in government and university labs (where they are often used as criteria for the lab's evaluation) than in industry, where secrecy is increasingly used as a means of appropriating intellectual property and where licensing technology is often seen as a second-best option, after internal use within the company.

Cooperative R&D agreements are becoming more common in the organization of innovation. They allow all partners to increase the speed of innovation, get complementary technologies and know-how, reach economies of scale and scope, and reduce costs of R&D. Most units were active in cooperative agreements, either with foreign units or with other industrial, government, university, and non-profit labs. More than 50 per cent of the laboratories in each category conducted cooperative R&D (Table 3.12). But industrial labs were least involved, and most of them were collaborating with other industrial research units in Canada. Conversely, a vast majority (three-quarters) of the public labs were active in this area, most often with domestic industrial firms, but also with foreign partners or with other government R&D institutions and university research centres. University labs were also very active in cooperation, but their main partners were government labs, followed by foreign research units.

Why do laboratories cooperate with external organizations? Motives varied (Table 3.13). One motive cuts across the three groups – the prospect of increased revenues, either for the lab or for the parent organization. Other motives are more specific: desire for new technology was common to a majority of both industrial and public labs; the search for fundamental scientific knowledge was important to most university research units, but was much less relevant elsewhere.

Difficulties

During the normal course of their activities, laboratories encounter problems of all sorts, which vary according to the type of unit. Nearly one-third of industrial research organizations found that they had not

Table 3.11
Number of laboratories patenting and licensing, 1990–92

Activity and year	Industry	Government	University
Patenting			
1990	11 (19%)	16 (36%)	6 (15%)
1991	11 (19%)	19 (43%)	8 (20%)
1992	11 (19%)	20 (45%)	12 (30%)
Licensing			
1990	9 (15%)	19 (43%)	7 (18%)
1991	7 (12%)	25 (57%)	9 (23%)
1992	8 (14%)	27 (61%)	12 (30%)
Total	57 (100%)	44 (100%)	40 (100%)

Table 3.12
Cooperative agreements, 1992

| Type of agreement | No. of laboratories involved | | |
	Industry	Government	University
Cooperative R&D agreement	30 (51%)	33 (75%)	21 (53%)
Foreign agreement	14 (24%)	25 (57%)	16 (40%)
With government lab(s)	13 (22%)	24 (55%)	17 (43%)
With industry	21 (36%)	29 (66%)	14 (35%)
With university research centre(s)	15 (25%)	20 (45%)	15 (38%)
With non-profit research lab(s)	7 (12%)	13 (30%)	5 (13%)
With other lab(s)	0	3 (7%)	1 (3%)
Units in sample	59	44	40

enough trained scientific and technical personnel. And one-quarter complained about the focus on short-run commercial benefits to the exclusion of longer-run development of technological and scientific knowledge. On the whole, however, industrial laboratories had less to complain about than government and university labs (Table 3.14).

Government laboratories experienced other difficulties. Insufficient government R&D funding was the most important; more than 50 per cent found this a very important or the most important problem. The

Table 3.13
Main motives for cooperation by laboratories

Motive	No. of laboratories		
	Industry	Government	University
Desire for fundamental knowledge	1	5	11
Desire for new technology	17	17	6
Desire to contribute to other parties	3	12	7
Incentives from other parties	7	7	2
Incentives from public regulation	2	2	0
Opportunities for personnel exchange	1	1	3
Increased profits	15	12	10
Other	0	1	4
Total units involved in cooperation	30 (100%)	33 (100%)	21 (100%)

Note: Multiple-choice question.

relative lack of well-trained scientific and technical personnel affected more than a quarter of them. Government accounting and paper-work requirements, and the excessive amount of red tape affecting management and/or performance, also received mention. In short, public labs, heavily dependent on government funds and supervision, pointed to their parent governmental organization as being responsible for nearly all their major difficulties.

Academic laboratories seemed to experience more difficulties than the other two types of units. Insufficient government funds affected 75 per cent of them. Nearly half complained about a heavy load of teaching and advising. Insufficient personnel, lack of physical space, and outmoded equipment (all certainly linked to the alleged scarcity of public funds) were also obstacles for one-quarter of them. Government accounting requirements were also a problem.

These findings contradict somewhat the recent evolution of R&D budgets that we saw above. The median R&D budgets increased by approximately 50 per cent in university laboratories, and by nearly 10 per cent in government research units, but they were stagnant in industrial laboratories, where the only perceived problem somewhat related to funding is the lack of scientific and trained personnel. It is difficult to say whether public and university labs suffer from a real lack of funds – which may be the case given the state of the public purse – or if this is another case of the French say: "L'appétit vient en mangeant" (Hunger comes when you eat).

ORGANIZATION AND STRUCTURE OF R&D LABORATORIES

Large industrial, governmental, and academic organizations usually owned or controlled several laboratories. This is the case for a majority of big Canadian corporations, whether locally or foreign-controlled. It is also the case for government departments, such as Agriculture Canada, the Department of National Defence, and Industry Canada, and for central research laboratories, such as the NRC. Also, in the last ten years, the proliferation of networks of centres of excellence, either federal or provincial, among university labs has created multi-unit academic organizations, stretching from Halifax to Vancouver. It is thus not surprising that, within larger organizations, it is common to find several labs under the same organizational umbrella (Table 3.15).

We asked laboratories whether they constituted the central research unit or a divisional lab of their parent organization. Usually, before the research was conducted, our preliminary sources would let us know whether the labs occupied a pivotal or a more peripheral position. Overall, we gathered information on nearly as many central as divisional laboratories, but the latter were slightly more numerous in the industrial and the government samples. Our data yielded the results that appear in Table 3.16. The two types of laboratories – central and divisional – differed in a number of dimensions within each of the three samples. Industrial central labs seem more involved in commercial applied research and get more government contracts, while divisional units appear to play a more modest role in both aspects (Table 3.17). Government central labs, as one could expect, were the largest by any standard: they had the biggest R&D budgets and more personnel than central industrial and academic labs (Table 3.18). Organizations with an internal departmental structure were the most frequent within central laboratories, while divisional labs were equally divided among those with departmental or other internal structures (typically ad hoc or structured around principal investigators) (Table 3.19).

Several other statistical relations were also highly significant for public laboratories. Divisional units conducted more basic research and published more articles (more than 20 per cent of their output consisted of this type of result) than central labs. Nevertheless, they also owned more patents (Table 3.20) and were more active in tech-

Table 3.14
Laboratories declaring important difficulties (%)

Difficulty	Industry	Government	University
Not enough trained scientific and technical personnel	32	27	25
Insufficient government R&D funds	17	55	75
Outmoded equipment	9	5	20
Lack of space	14	5	35
Government accounting requirements	3	20	25
Heavy teaching and advising load	N/A	N/A	45
Focus on short-term benefits	25	16	5
Too much red tape	10	23	10
Inability to keep pace with scientific and technical development	15	11	13
High administrative costs	5	9	5
Insufficient computing power	9	5	3
Government health and safety regulations	3	0	0
Disputes with other units	14	9	0
Other	5	7	8

Note: Multiple-choice question.

Table 3.15
Position of laboratories within the parent organization

Position	No. and % of laboratories		
	Industry	Government	University
Sole R&D unit	18 (30%)	3 (7%)	3 (8%)
One of several laboratories	34 (58%)	39 (91%)	28 (72%)
Independent functioning unit	7 (12%)	1 (2%)	8 (20%)
Total	59 (100%)	43 (100%)	39 (100%)

Note: Missing responses: one in each government and university samples.

Table 3.16
Central versus divisional laboratories

Type	No. and % of laboratories		
	Industry	Government	University
Central	28 (48%)	15 (41%)	20 (56%)
Divisional	30 (52%)	22 (59%)	14 (44%)
Total	58 (100%)	37 (100%)	34 (100%)

Table 3.17
Industrial laboratories with/without government contracts

Type	Government contracts	No government contracts	Total
Central	18	9	27
Divisional	11	18	29
Total	29	27	56

Pearson correlation coefficient = 0.03.
Missing observations: 3.

Table 3.18
Total R&D budgets in central and divisional government laboratories, 1992

Type	< $10 million	≥ $10 million	Total
Central	3	12	15
Divisional	11	10	21
Total	14	22	36

Pearson correlation coefficient: $p < 0.05$.
Missing observations: 8.

nology transfer. Among university labs, as among government R&D establishments, central units were usually larger than divisional ones (Table 3.21). In this type of laboratory, internal organization was conducted exclusively in groups led by principal investigators – an arrangement that was also predominant in divisional laboratories (Table 3.22).

Table 3.19
Organization within government laboratories, 1992

Type	Departmental organization	Other than departments	Total
Central	14	1	15
Divisional	12	10	22
Total	26	11	37

Pearson correlation coefficient = 0.01; Fisher's exact test (two-tail): p = 0.01.
Missing observations: 7.

Table 3.20
Patents in central and divisional government laboratories, 1992

Type	One or more patents	No patents	Total
Central	3	7	10
Divisional	13	5	18
Total	16	12	28

Pearson correlation coefficient: $p < 0.05$; Fisher's exact test (two-tail): $p < 0.05$.
Missing observations: 16.

Table 3.21
Total R&D budgets in university laboratories, 1992

Type	< $2.5 million	≥ $2.5 million	Total
Central	6	13	19
Divisional	9	5	14
Total	15	18	33

Pearson correlation coefficient: p = 0.06.
Missing observations: 7.

EFFECTIVENESS CRITERIA

Industrial, university, and government laboratories differed in their effectiveness criteria. Only one criterion was important for them all – namely, "producing knowledge useful in developing commercial prod-

Table 3.22
Internal organization of university laboratories, 1993

Type	Principal investigator-led groups	Other	Total
Central	20	0	20
Divisional	11	3	14
Total	31	3	34

Pearson correlation coefficient: $p < 0.05$; Fisher's exact test (two-tail): $p = 0.06$.
Missing observations: 6.

Table 3.23
Effectiveness criteria, 1993

Criterion	% of laboratories considering the criterion very important or the most important factor		
	Industry	Government	University
Contributing to basic scientific knowledge	15	46	98
Producing commercially useful knowledge	88	77	53
Meeting needs of constituent group	36	91	28
Increasing resources of laboratory	20	27	53
Training graduate students	–	–	100
Training undergraduates	–	–	33
Other	15	2	5

ucts and processes." Industrial R&D units used almost exclusively this criterion, which represented the single most important criterion of effectiveness for two-thirds of the industrial sample and a very important one for another 24 per cent (see Table 3.23). Once again, there was less variation within the industrial sample than in the other two. Government units concentrated more on meeting the needs of a specific constituent group (industry, trade association, or governmental organization); this was the most important criterion for nineteen of them (43 per cent of the sample). Another thirteen (30 per cent) picked the most popular industrial response – that is, producing knowledge

Inset 5   Basic and Applied Public Research: NRC's Plant Biotechnology Institute

In 1948, the NRC opened the Prairie Research Laboratory with a mission to conduct research on alternative uses of western Canada's crops. Later the unit expanded its goals to include studies on oilseed crops, uses of agricultural residues, and industrial fermentation processes. In the early 1980s, Ottawa designated the NRC as the main federal agency for the development of biotechnology, and, in 1983 the Prairie Lab was renamed the Plant Biotechnology Institute (PBI) and given an enlarged mandate, to include research on molecular biology and genetic engineering. PBI works on crops that are important for Canada, such as barley, canola, grain legumes, and wheat. In 1980, the provincial government and the University of Saskatchewan created a 120-acre research park, called Innovation Place, to capitalize on the NRC lab. In 1989, PBI and the province organized a joint venture to build the L.F. Kristjanson Biotechnology Complex at Innovation Place, where PBI located its transgenic plant centre, which in 1991–92 produced the first transgenic wheat and later transgenic fieldpeas and modified canola. By 1997, Innovation Place had attracted some thirty-five agriculture-related companies, both Canadian and foreign-owned. These included AgrEvo and BASF from Germany; Groupe Limagrain from France; Dow Agro-Sciences, Monsanto, and Mycogen from the United States; and Philom Bios and Prairie Plant Systems from Canada. PBI has a staff of 110 researchers and hosts over one hundred guests.

Over its fifty-year history, the Saskatoon facility has conducted collaborative and contract research with dozens of partners, including Agriculture Canada, the Canadian Wheat Board, Monsanto Canada, Mycogen, the Saskatchewan Wheat Pool, and the University of Saskatchewan.

Sources: PBI Bulletin (May 1998 and Jan. 1999); Research Money, 5 Feb. 1997, 7.

useful in developing commercial products and processes. Academic laboratories used the most numerous and differing effectiveness criteria. The single most important was contributing to the advance of fundamental scientific knowledge, with thirty-one (or 78 per cent) of the first choices. Training graduate students was second, and very important to all of them. Increasing the lab's resources and producing commercially useful knowledge were important for more than half.

A minority (15 per cent) of industrial laboratories still considered it very important to produce basic scientific knowledge. This distinctive subgroup makes up what we can call the "science-based industrial lab," following the classification developed by Keith Pavitt (1984).

CONCLUSION

By 1993, the core of Canada's NSI was composed of some 560 laboratories employing at least twenty-five researchers. The approximately
one hundred government labs were the largest by any measure, followed by industrial and university research units. The outputs of these
three types of establishments differed by sector: university units were
producing mostly published articles; industrial ones, prototypes and
devices, algorithms and software, and internal reports; and government labs, both articles and internal reports.

However, the reality of Canada's R&D system is a far cry from the stylized scheme of three watertight compartments, with academic laboratories conducting basic research, government establishments doing
pre-commercial applied research, and industrial units developing
products and processes (see Inset 5). Under the new liberalized and
open-market environment, and the new policy environment promoting cooperation and competitiveness, many university labs – mainly,
but not exclusively, in the health sciences and engineering – have been
given a variety of missions and have adopted more for-profit effectiveness criteria. The same kinds of changes seem to be taking place in
government labs, where publishing goals and evaluation criteria are
now being challenged by other types of assessments of relevance to the
NSI approach: within public labs, assistance to private industry is now
more important than assistance to government. We found that some
industrial R&D units are also under the influence of the new technological paradigms (biotechnology, electronics, advanced materials, optics) and conduct basic research. Sources of funds and research
outputs thus are much more variegated than in the stylized concept.
Most important, the number of government and university labs that
are patenting and licensing has increased enormously in only three
years, and more than half of the units in each category are now conducting cooperative research, even if motives vary.

These rapid changes do not happen without difficulties emerging.
Government and university laboratories find that they receive insufficient public R&D funds, and university research units complain about
the heavy teaching and advising load (which takes time from the increasing research commitments). All types of units find that they cannot recruit enough trained scientific and technical personnel.

On the whole, however, under the new governmental incentives,
Canada's NSI shows a fairly high degree of synergy and seems to be
heading towards more dense interaction, coordination, and collaboration among its laboratories and adopting a more for-profit orientation
across the board. Links among research institutions of all sorts, in

Inset 6   Newbridge Networks' R&D
Founded in 1986 by Dr Terrence Matthews, Newbridge's mission was from the start to produce telecommunication equipment, originally time-division multiplexers. Later, in 1991, the company embraced ATM equipment to deliver networks, and it became a world leader in this fast-growing technology. Hedquartered in Kanata, near Ottawa, the company experienced explosive growth, and its R&D activities followed suit. Its sales jumped from $553 million in 1994 to $1,620 million in 1998; during the same period, its R&D expenditures grew from $39 million to $259 million, representing 16 per cent of sales. By that time, Newbridge was the second largest Canadian manufacturer of telecommunication equipment and one of its top five industrial R&D performers. Its main R&D facility is still located in Kanata, but it opened R&D facilities in 1995 in Vancouver, in 1996 in Halifax, Nova Scotia, and in 1997, in Hull, Quebec, to complete its national network of labs. The firm cited government support and the presence of research universities as one of the most important factors in its locating new R&D units in these provinces. However, by late 1995, the bulk of its 850-strong R&D workforce was located in its central laboratory in Kanata. Smaller R&D facilities operated also in Wales and in the United States. Among its many research collaborations, Newbridge is a member of Communications and Information Technology Ontario (CITO), a provincial centre of excellence, whose "mission is to strengthen the global performance of Ontario information and communication technologies through university/industry research partnerships involving the exchange of people, ideas and technologies." It also boasts a major alliance with Siemens of Germany.
Sources: Research Money, 15 Nov. 1995, 2; 26 Aug. 1998, 5; Newbridge and CITO websites

other words, are increasing (see Inset 6), and government labs are at the forefront of this movement. An NSI is now well entrenched, and government incentives to cooperate were, if not the only factor, a major one promoting links among institutions; public laboratories and research universities seemed particularly sensitive to government incentives to cooperate with industry, as much of their budgets come from government appropriations and subsidies.

4 Linking the Units: Technology Transfer

INTRODUCTION: CHANGING R&D MANAGEMENT

In the 1980s and 1990s, there was a radical change in the way in which R&D in Canada was managed by industry, government laboratories, and universities. Before 1980, these innovating units were often working in isolation from each other. There was some technological cooperation and transfer, but most R&D managers believed that this activity was too volatile to be conducted with the help of external units, let alone competitors. Besides, it was considered evident that universities should concentrate on fundamental research, public laboratories on applied research, and corporations on development. One way or another, knowledge would flow from universities to public laboratories, and then to companies, where it would be translated into new and improved processes and products. National prosperity would follow.

These certainties were challenged from the late 1970s on by at least five developments. First, western Europe and Japan, and then South Korea and Taiwan, were catching up with Canada (and the United States); although their investment in basic or applied research was minimal, they were able to reduce the technological gap with industrial countries by acquiring North American technology, becoming acquainted with its science, or simply copying its products and processes. The emphasis of their policy was on inward technology transfer and technical diffusion, not science, and they could often reap the benefits of public and university R&D in Canada, the United States, or western Europe faster than American or European firms would.

Also, in Southeast Asia, corporations, government laboratories, and universities also seemed to behave differently from their Western – particularly North American – counterparts. Cooperation between companies was common, and technology transfer from public and university laboratories to industrial firms was also frequent. In fact, public labs were usually conducting development activities in close connection with private corporations. The result seemed to be less duplication, the achievement of critical masses, and faster technology transfer. A new, radically different system of innovation was challenging the West (Freeman, 1987).

Second, the Canadian (and u.s.) trade balance in high-technology products with Southeast Asia was becoming increasingly negative. The ability of those nations to incorporate foreign science and technology allowed them rapidly to increase their competitiveness and penetrate u.s., Canadian, or European markets.

Third, the three decades of postwar prosperity ended abruptly with the first oil crisis in 1973. Long-term growth in GDP and productivity were now declining. Public finances started showing signs of strain. Government financing of research universities, government laboratories, and private companies' R&D could not continue growing at the same rate. If these labs were to maintain and increase their revenues, they would have to do so through greater efficiency and more private revenues via profitable activities, not from public moneys.

Fourth, global competition became more intense with the opening of the national markets, entry of the Southeast Asia newly industrialized countries (NICs), and internationalization of companies of all sizes. In order to survive, North American companies had to accelerate innovation and adopt new technologies and new management methods. The only route to these ends was through technology transfer and technological cooperation among national R&D establishments.

Finally, the end of the Vietnam War in 1975 and the collapse of the Soviet Union in 1989 reduced the priority of military R&D in several countries with heavy commitments in defence, including France, Sweden, the United Kingdom, and the United States. Commercial and civilian research was now at the top of the agenda, including in Canada, and it required more interaction of public and universities laboratories with private companies in pursuit of commercial applications for government and academic research. Civilian R&D required new management schemes: heavy, cost-plus R&D government contracts were out; lean and flexible R&D was in.

All these factors pushed universities and public laboratories to look for private money through technology transfer, cooperative R&D, and contract research, and at the same time they encouraged business to look for advanced research to obtain new knowledge. The result was a

massive increase of technological collaboration and technology transfer, among these three components of NSI. This chapter examines
technology transfer, and the next one analyses technology transfer and
cooperation among Canadian R&D laboratories. The two activities are
different. Technology transfer is the sale of an existing technology
from one laboratory or corporation to another; in other words, it is a
commercial activity, and as such it is materialized through licensing,
training, and/or assigning of product or process design from one firm,
government, or university laboratory to another. Technology transfer
thus is one major mechanism of technology diffusion, together with
imitation (Rosenberg and Frischtak, 1985). Technological cooperation, in contrast, is an agreement between independent parties (corporations, public laboratories, and/or universities) jointly to develop
future new or improved processes and/or products, through commonly executed R&D (Chesnais, 1988). In other words, technology
transfer is the sale of a certain technology already developed by the
selling party, while technological cooperation is the association of two
or more innovating units to create new technology through joint R&D.

TECHNOLOGY TRANSFER: BASIC FIGURES

In 1992, a majority of Canadian laboratories in our sample were conducting technology transfer, and licensing activities, measured
through licences sold per year, were increasing (Table 4.1). Activities
were more or less intense according to the type of laboratory. Transfer
occurred more often in government laboratories, where in 1992 thirty-
nine labs out of forty-four conducted technology transfer, and nearly
two-thirds were licensing their technology. Also, between 1990 and
1992 the licensing trend was upward in all the public units. The new
environment of declining government appropriations and new rules
of intellectual property in government laboratories were forcing them
to gain fresh revenues and industrial visibility through technology
transfer and licensing.

Conversely, less than half (only twenty-three) of the industrial laboratories were involved in outward technology transfer, and only a
handful were licensing any technology at all to external parties. This
finding confirms the view that most industrial laboratories produce
technology for their parent organization, not for transfer outside.

In technology transfer, university research centres found themselves
somewhere between government and industry. By 1992, more than
half of them (twenty-two) were conducting technology transfer, but
only a third were licensing any technology; the licensing trend from
university labs, however, was definitely upward. In 1990–92, the environment of university research was far less constrained than the one in

Table 4.1
Technology transfer in Canadian laboratories, 1990–92

	% active			
Year	Industry	Government	University	Total
Licensing 1990	15.2	43.1	17.5	24.4
Licensing 1991	11.9	56.8	22.5	28.7
Licensing 1992	13.6	61.3	30.0	32.9
Technology tranfer in 1992	39.0	88.6	55.0	58.7

government labs: government grants for academe were still increasing, and regulations on intellectual property had not been changed so radically and swiftly as those in public laboratories.

In the United States, Coursey and Bozeman (1992), using basically the same methods, had found that in 1990 42.4 per cent of government laboratories were conducting technology transfer, compared to 69.9 per cent of university research centres. The differences, while significant, may be explained partly by the three-year gap between the two studies: the transformation of Canadian public labs, during which government regulations pushed them to collaborate, started in the early 1990s. Three years earlier the Canadian figures might well have been similar to the American ones. Perhaps in 1990–92, American universities were still more involved in technology transfer than their Canadian counterparts, but the situation has changed radically in the last few years because of the increasing outward orientation of at least the more research-oriented universities (see chapter 2).

Motives

The analysis of the motivations behind technology casts new light on the process (Table 4.2). The growth of alliances and cooperation was the major motivation for technology transfer in the whole sample for both public and university laboratories, but less so for industrial units. In private-industry research, profits for either the laboratory or the parent organization were by far the most important reason for technology transfer. The other major determinant in industry was implementation of an aggressive competitive strategy, such as capturing of a market through licensing to an associate or independent company. Government labs transferred technology because of regional-development and other legislative requirements. In university labs, participation in industry–university consortia and exchange of personnel or technical information were also major motives.

Table 4.2
Motives for technology transfer

Motive	No. of laboratories considering the motive very important			
	Industry	Government	University	Total
Growth of cooperation	8	19	11	38
Regional development	–	18	4	22
Personnel satisfaction	4	12	7	23
Participation in industry–university consortia	2	9	10	21
Exchange of personnel or technical information	2	10	9	21
Lab or parent profit	15	–	6	21
Legislative requirement	–	16	5	21
Offensive competitive strategy	10	–	–	10
Personnel interest	2	1	3	6
Defensive competitive strategy	6	–	–	6
Other	2	4	1	7

Strategies

Personal contacts were by far the most common way of relating to external users in all three types of laboratories (Table 4.3). Contractual and cooperative R&D followed in importance for the entire sample, but its weight differed by type of lab. Cooperative R&D was key for government R&D units, but less so for industry. Conversely, contractual R&D was the second most favoured strategy for both industry and university labs.

Person-to-person strategies were most frequent: cooperative and contractual R&D (and other strategies such as presentations, participation in consortia, informal visits to potential clients, and external visitors to the lab) involve direct relationships between people. Conversely, fliers, newsletter, and other written material sent by mail did not seem very popular in promoting technology transfer.

Advantages and Disadvantages

Technology transfer brought both benefits and problems to R&D laboratories, according to their managers. Benefits were sector-specific

Table 4.3
Strategies used by laboratories for promoting technology transfer

	Most successful strategy			
Strategy	*Industry*	*Government*	*University*	*Total*
Personal contacts	21	34	19	74
Contract R&D	10	18	14	42
Cooperative R&D	5	26	10	41
Seminars, conferences	6	13	8	27
Consortia	4	16	7	27
Informal visits	10	14	2	26
External visitors	5	14	5	24
Presentations at professional meetings	6	10	8	24
Sales/gift of patents, etc.	6	13	3	22
Personnel exchanges	5	11	3	19
Presentations at government meetings	1	11	5	17
Central office	4	5	8	17
Fliers, newsletters, etc.	2	5	1	8
Other	–	1	–	1

Note: Multiple-choice question.

(Table 4.4). In industry, all twenty-three labs involved in technology transfer reported some major benefit. Profits for the unit were the most important of them. Most government labs also declared some major benefit; the most common was a more "real world" approach among scientific and technical personnel, followed by the desire to encourage personnel to collaborate on technology transfer and technological development and greater visibility for the lab. All twenty-two university research centres reported some major benefit from technology transfer: visibility was the most frequent, and the only one that really mattered. These results are similar to those that Coursey and Bozeman (1992) had obtained from the American survey. In their study, increased public visibility was by far the most important benefit for both university and government labs: 24 per cent and 27 per cent of labs, respectively, had pointed to that particular advantage. In Canada, public visibility was the main advantage for 30 per cent of university research centres, but for only 16 per cent of public labs; for the latter, a more "real world" approach was far more important. Between the 1990 U.S. survey and the 1993 Canadian survey, pressures for more technology transfer in government labs – at least in Canada – relegated visibility to a second place.

Technology transfer did not take place without problems (see Table 4.5). Even if these looked less serious and frequent than benefits, a majority of laboratories involved in this activity experienced some difficulties. The most frequent concern, across the board, was time taken from other research-related activities. In government labs, technology transfer had also often led to disharmony, while in university research centres it had produced intellectual-property disputes as well. In the American survey, the list of problems was again different. Government labs found that technology transfer had taken time from other research activities (the single greatest problem) and moved research from fundamental research (a major problem), while in Canada technology transfer had led to disharmony within the lab. As for universities, in the United States, the principal problems were the same as for public labs. In Canada, disputes over intellectual property were now more important than the other two factors. Again, because of similar regulatory and economic environments of American and Canadian laboratories, I tend to interpret the differences as stemming from the rapid changes in Canadian universities and public labs in the 1990s, pushing them to more technology transfer and technological cooperation.

Success and Impact

How successful were the laboratories in transferring technology? In the questionnaire, two separate questions measured success. One asked lab managers to rate themselves at getting others interested in using the lab technology. A majority of all types of laboratories that transferred technology considered themselves very successful in this activity, but the self-rating varied by sector (Table 4.6). Less than half of industrial laboratories have transferred technology, and three-quarters of them thought that they did it successfully. Just over half of university units had participated in technology transfer, and most of them considered the operation successful. Labs were more sober when they assessed the commercial effects of technology transfer (Table 4.7). Some 60 per cent of those involved considered the impact very good or excellent. However, this figure applies to only one-third of the whole sample. Again, industrial units seemed more able to deliver commercial benefits to their clients in technology transfer, with government labs rating second and university labs a distant third.

Table 4.4
Benefits obtained by laboratories from technology transfer

	Single most important benefit			
Benefit	Industry	Government	University	Total
Profits for the lab	14	1	1	16
Increased visibility	1	6	7	14
Drawing personnel to collaborate	3	7	3	13
"Real world" approach	–	10	2	12
Gained clients, users	4	4	–	8
Government approval	–	1	3	4
Gained knowledge from users	1	2	–	3
Other	–	1	2	3
Profit for personnel	–	–	–	–

Note: Multiple-choice question.

Table 4.5
Problems with technology transfer

	Single greatest problem, major problems			
Problems	Industry	Government	University	Total
Time taken from other activities	4	10	6	20
Disharmony	2	10	3	15
Intellectual property disputes	3	4	7	14
Reduced time for fundamental R&D	1	6	3	10
Interruptions from outsiders	1	2	1	4
Teaching undermined	–	–	3	3
Other	1	1	2	4

Note. Multiple-choice question.

EXPLAINING TECHNOLOGY TRANSFER

As we saw above, not all laboratories conduct technology transfer: 39 per cent of industrial, 88 per cent of public, and 55 per cent of university laboratories were active in this field. Units that transfer

Table 4.6
Levels of success in technology transfer

Success level	Industry	Government	University	Total
Very good/excellent (7–10)	18 (75%)	24 (62%)	13 (56%)	55 (64%)
Average (4–6)	5 (21%)	14 (36%)	5 (22%)	24 (28%)
Ineffective (0–3)	1 (4%)	1 (2%)	5 (22%)	7 (8%)
Total	24 (100%)	39 (100%)	23 (100%)	86 (100%)
Does not apply/no response	35	5	17	57

Table 4.7
Commercial impact of technology transfert

Impact level	Industry	Government	University	Total
Very good/excellent (7–10)	18 (78%)	21 (55%)	9 (47%)	48 (60%)
Average (4–6)	4 (17%)	14 (37%)	4 (21%)	22 (28%)
Ineffective (0–3)	1 (5%)	3 (8%)	6 (32%)	10 (22%)
Total	23 (100%)	38 (100%)	19 (100%)	80 (100%)
Does not apply/no response	36	6	21	63

technology differ from those that do not; also, some of the characteristics of labs conducting transfers are similar among industry, government, and university.

Industrial laboratories that conduct technology transfer are larger than those that do not, suggesting that some critical mass is required for this activity to take place (Table 4.8 and Inset 7). Also, these labs are more financially independent: compared to labs that are not involved in transfers, parent companies are the source of a smaller percentage of their funding. Not surprisingly, these R&D units allocate to technology transfer some part of their budget, while the laboratories that do not transfer their results do not devote any money to technology transfer. The laboratories that transfer technology also sign more cooperative agreements in general and with industry in particular, and the search for profits is their main motive for cooperative agreements.

Table 4.8
Characteristics of industrial laboratories involved in technology transfer

Characteristic	No.	Pearson probability
They are more often larger than those who do not.	57	0.003
Parent company is the source of a smaller share of the budget.	56	0.03
They allocate some share of their budget to TT.	57	0.000
They also do more cooperative R&D,	59	0.07
particularly with industrial partners.	31	0.006
R&D cooperation is motivated by profit.	32	0.001
Technology transfer is an explicit mission.	58	0.008
Contributing to basic science is not an important mission.	58	0.008

Note: Results of 2x2 correlations.

Inset 7   Technology Transfer from Industry: IBM Canada

IBM Canada is the wholly owned subsidiary of the IBM Corp. It has been present in Canada since the end of the nineteenth century, producing tabulating equipment. It opened its first computer-related plant (for memory cards and power systems) in Don Mills, Ontario, in 1951 and its second one (for semiconductors) in Bromont, Quebec, in 1972; it exports production of both establishments. It set up the IBM Canada Laboratory in Toronto in 1967 to conduct R&D on software for the global enterprise. IBM Canada is IBM's largest software facility in the world. By 1990, it employed some 1,500 people, developing applications and enabling and communications software for the world market, as well as Computer Aided Software Engineering (CASE) products. By 1996, it was spending some $229 million on R&D. It was the third-largest R&D facility in Canada; it spent every year over $50 million on university research and cooperated with Canadian universities for advanced research and training.

Early in 1998, IBM Canada announced a new licensing agreement (financial terms undisclosed) with Electronic Data System Corp. (EDS) that gave EDS's system integration branch total access to a full range of software produced by IBM; it put an umbrella on other licences allowed by IBM.

Sources: IBM Canada, The IBM Canada Story (Toronto, 1990); Computing Canada, 5 Jan. 1998, 2.

Inset 8   Technology Transfer from Universities and Government Labs:
Performance Plants Inc.
Technology transfer from university to industry, as well as from government laboratories, has increased enormously in the 1990s. A new biotechnology company has benefited from several such transfers to enter into new promising fields. Performance Plants Inc. (PPI) was founded in 1996 by members of the Plant Biotechnology Group at Queen's University, Kingston, Ontario. PPI is located on the university campus, in the new Biosciences Complex, and had in early 1999 some twenty-six employees and managers, including sixteen researchers. It is a classic biotechnology spin-off from university research. Its research projects span five areas. Two of them use technology transferred from government laboratories. The Cold Tolerant Plant uses a technology that PPI developed collaboratively with Agriculture Canada and was licensed exclusively to the company. The Fibre Reduction project has generated transgenic canola and tobacco leaves using a tobacco seed-coat promoter isolated and patented by Agriculture Canada and also licensed exclusively to PPI, which has proprietary technology in related areas.

Early in 1997, PPI received an infusion of $1,5 million in venture capital from a private firm located in Dorval, Quebec. The decision to create PPI emanated from PARTEQ – Queen's University's technology transfer office – and the search for the initial venture capital investment took approximately one year. The funds were planned for developing and demonstrating proprietary technologies, seeking additional investments, and organizing market and technology alliances.
Sources: Queen's University; *Research Money*, 22 Jan. 1997, 6.

Government laboratories undertaking technology transfer (see Inset 8) share some of the characteristics of transfer-active industrial R&D establishments (Table 4.9). Contrary to their industrial counterparts, they are smaller than the average, but only in terms of R&D personnel; they allocate funds to technology transfer – their most important mission. They also spend more funds on pre-commercial R&D and to assist outside organizations. In other words, they transfer technology because they produce industrially useful knowledge and reserve some funds to transfer it. However, some characteristics of transfer-oriented public labs are exclusive to them: over 75 per cent of their budgets come from direct government appropriations. Clearly, the message from public authorities pushing government labs to transfer technology to the private sector has been heard. However, revenues from this activity are still not very sizeable.

Table 4.9
Characteristics of government laboratories involved in technology transfer

Characteristic	No.	Pearson probability
They are smaller in terms of R&D personnel.	44	0.03
Technology transfer is their most important mission, and thus	44	0.01
they spend over 25% of their budget on pre-commercial R&D	43	0.015
and over 5% on assistance to outside organizations.	43	0.035
Producing commercially useful knowledge is used as a criterion of effectiveness.	44	0.035
More than 75% of their budget comes from direct government appropriations	39	0.036
They are more often divisional than central laboratories,	37	0.010
and research is not organized through ad hoc groups,	44	0.031

Note: Results of 2x2 correlations.

Besides, producing knowledge useful in developing commercial products and processes is very important to public laboratories, or their most important criterion of effectiveness. Also, these labs undertaking technology transfer are more often divisional than central laboratories and thus oriented more to applied than to fundamental research (Table 4.9). Finally, they are not organized like university research, through more or less ad hoc groups, but more like industrial research, through departments, divisions, and branches.

Again, transfer-oriented university laboratories share some characteristics with their industrial and government counterparts. They are also larger (typically over $2.5 million in annual budgets and over sixty full-time personnel), allocate funds to technology transfer, and select R&D projects after an assessment of their commercial benefits; they also consider pre-commercial R&D and technology transfer one of their most important – or the single most important – missions. These units are more usually funded by the Natural Sciences and Engineering Research Council, which gives them usually over 35 per cent of their total grants and government contracts (Table 4.10). Also they consider creation and demonstration of devices an important output of their laboratories.

In all the three sectors, transfer-oriented research laboratories do not transfer technology as a sporadic or casual activity. The role is embedded into their missions and into their effectiveness criteria, and they allocate funds to it. Usually, these labs are also larger and have a view to profits when selecting R&D projects. Their research can be sold because it is conceived from the start for commercial purposes.

CONCLUSION

Under constraints similar to those of their American and European counterparts, Canadian university and public laboratories are increasingly transferring their technology to the private sector. Cooperation, concern for economic development, and new legislative requirements, combined with decreasing public funds, are pushing both types of labs to devise strategies for technology transfer, including increased personal contacts with external clients and more contractual and more cooperative R&D. All the units involved in technology transfer (39 per cent of industrial, 88 per cent of government, and 55 per cent of university labs) drew one benefit or another in this activity: profit for the organization was the most important advantage for industrial research centres; public labs gained attained visibility, a more "real world" approach to R&D, and collaboration; and universities were mostly content with their increased visibility. A majority of the labs conducting technology transfer in each of the three categories considered themselves successful in this activity.

Technology transfer brought not only benefits, but also some problems. Industrial laboratories found that it has taken time away from other research-related activities. Government units also discovered that it has brought some kind of disharmony, as rewards and evaluation of performance varied among employees. Academic labs complained about intellectual-property disputes and time lost from research and teaching. None the less, two-thirds of all the R&D labs involved in technology transfer rated themselves as very successful in this field; however, only in industry was the commercial impact of the transfers very noticeable. In government and university units the economic results were more mixed, in line with the somewhat more complex motivations for technology transfer.

All R&D units active in technology transfer were larger than those not involved, suggesting that minimum thresholds are necessary for this activity. All of them considered technology transfer an important activity, not a sporadic source of revenues. Thus they have made it an explicit mission and allocate to it some portion of their budget. Industrial units were also more active in technological cooperation with ex-

Table 4.10
Characteristics of university laboratories involved in technology transfer

Characteristic	No.	Pearson probability
They have larger budgets.	39	0.001
They are larger in total personnel and in	40	0.004
terms of R&D staff.	38	0.070
Pre-commercial R&D is a most important		
mission,	40	0.002
as is technology transfer.	40	0.000
They select projects with an eye to commercial		
benefits,	40	0.002
and allocate funds to technology transfer,	40	0.067
even if over 35% of their total grants and		
public contracts come from NSERC.	40	0.014

Note: Results of 2x2 correlations.

ternal organizations and less dependent on their parent company for funds. By contrast, in public labs, government appropriations represented a larger share of the revenues, suggesting that they transfer technology under departmental pressure. Nevertheless, these units were spent more on pre-commercial R&D (as opposed to fundamental research) and on assistance to outside organizations. Even university labs transferring technology behave in some ways like industrial labs: they select projects with an eye to their commercial profitability; pre-commercial R&D and technology are their most important missions.

My main conclusion is that technology transfer requires the painful adoption of appropriate internal routines: new missions, adequate project selection, incentives, evaluation methods, effectiveness criteria, and budget allocations. Existing contracts and skills and established patterns of work organization are difficult to dislodge and slow to change, because of organizational inertia.

5 The Rise of Cooperative R&D

Technological cooperation between government laboratories and private enterprises, or between university research and industry, has existed in Canada for more than a century (Hull and Enros, 1988; Niosi, 1994, 1995). What is new since the early 1980s is the intensity of the technological collaboration between firms and among industries, government, and university R&D units. This collaboration takes many forms: company-to-company alliances for the development of new and improved products and processes; large research pre-competitive consortia involving private firms and public laboratories; and industry–university cooperative research centres.

The growth of technological cooperation in industry has resulted from several converging forces: the triple technological revolution of information technologies, advanced materials, and biotechnology, which has made R&D increasingly complex and science-intensive; the internationalization of firms of all sizes and the opening of markets in most countries, which have increased economic uncertainty; new management methods originating in Japan, which emphasized vertical cooperation between assemblers and suppliers, instead of competition between suppliers for access to assemblers; and the growing electronic hardware industries, which required some degree of vertical and horizontal cooperation between producers to assure standards.

Governments have motives of their own for promoting technological cooperation. Collaboration increases diffusion of new technologies among industrial partners; it also increases the chance of getting R&D

results and accelerates the production of the innovation. Consortia are more likely to create the "critical masses" necessary to conduct large or risky research projects for national purposes, in the areas of defence, environment, health, or telecommunication. Finally, collaboration reduces duplication: instead of supporting several competing projects, governments will probably obtain less expensive, faster, and/or better results by disbursing only one industrial grant. Hence the new legislative requirements for government laboratories, in which cooperation has become the new password, and also the emergence of many programs, in Canada and abroad, supporting cooperative industrial innovation (Niosi and Landry, 1993).

Universities increasingly seek industrial cooperation in order to gain access to new sources of revenue. Companies cooperate with university research centres so as to obtain new knowledge in the advanced technologies of materials, information, and biotechnology. Government laboratories collaborate with external parties in order to gain resources, complementary knowledge, and visibility.

All these convergences do not occur without problems. University and government laboratories are used to being evaluated on the basis of publications and the number of graduate students they attract and graduate. Public labs are usually evaluated through patents and publications, not on the basis of industrial relevance. Also, in the pre-collaborative era, all intellectual property stemming from research conducted in both university and government labs belonged either to the university or to the crown. Industrial cooperation on a massive scale is changing missions, methods of budget allocation, reward systems, rules on intellectual property, evaluation routines, research tempos, and effectiveness criteria in both university and public labs.

Industrial R&D units are also affected, though perhaps less dramatically. Secrecy seems now less important for them than speed to market. The shortened life cycle of products and processes has played havoc with the traditional closed industrial laboratories; it is now better to share a novelty than to keep it under exclusive ownership but be late to market. We may expect fewer problems in the industrial labs than in public and university research centers. But problems will surface in all of them.

TECHNOLOGICAL COOPERATION

By 1992, a majority of large Canadian laboratories of all three types were cooperating with external units (Table 5.1). Today, more than half of all labs in each category conduct cooperative R&D. Three-quarters of all government labs, and just over 50 per cent of university and industrial research units, were involved in partnerships.

Table 5.1
Technological cooperation by Canadian R&D laboratories

Type of partner	No. and %			
	Industry	Government	University	Total
All types	30 (51%)	33 (75%)	21 (53%)	84 (59%)
Domestic government labs	13 (22%)	24 (55%)	17 (43%)	54 (38%)
Domestic industrial labs	21 (36%)	29 (66%)	14 (35%)	64 (45%)
Domestic university labs	15 (25%)	20 (45%)	15 (38%)	50 (35%)
Domestic non-profit labs	7 (12%)	13 (30%)	5 (13%)	25 (17%)
Foreign partners	14 (24%)	25 (57%)	16 (40%)	55 (38%)
Other	–	3 (7%)	1 (3%)	4 (3%)
Units in sample	59	44	40	143

Government laboratories dominated all categories of cooperative agreements. More than half of them were active and cooperated with other government labs, and with industrial firms and participated in foreign alliances. Industrial R&D establishments were less involved in cooperation, and most often they worked with other Canadian firms. Universities were more often involved with government labs and with foreign companies.

MOTIVES

Motives for cooperation varied (Table 5.2). Within industrial R&D establishments, desire for new technology and increased profits were the main motives. Public laboratories were looking for new technology and profits too, but they also wanted to contribute to other parties, typically to assist their departmental parents within government. University research centres were pushed to collaborate both by a drive towards acquisition of fundamental knowledge and by the search for profits. New knowledge, either technical or fundamental, and revenues were the main across-the-board explanations for the cooperative drive.

Advantages and Disadvantages

Evaluations of the contribution of alliances to laboratories, in terms of research effectiveness, show that the three sectors differed markedly in

Table 5.2
Main motives for cooperation

Motive	Industry	Government	University	Total
Desire for new technology	17	17	6	40
Increased profits	15	12	10	37
Desire to contribute to other parties	3	12	7	22
Desire for fundamental knowledge	1	5	11	17
Incentives from other parties	7	7	2	16
Personnel exchange opportunities	1	1	3	5
Incentives from public regulation	2	2	0	4
Other	0	1	4	5
Total number of units cooperating	30	33	21	84

Note: Multiple-choice question.

terms of advantages obtained (Table 5.3). Not surprisingly, cooperation improved the research effectiveness of industrial laboratories
mainly in commercial and pre-commercial applied research. Government labs benefited mostly in pre-commercial applied research but
also, somewhat unexpectedly, in commercial applied R&D and technology transfer. University research centres gained in basic and pre-
commercial applied research.

Technological cooperation brought, as we anticipated, problems for
a majority of laboratories (Table 5.4). Sixty per cent of industrial labs
involved in cooperation experienced some difficulties. Among government research centres involved in cooperation, difficulties appeared in
78 per cent of the cases. Finally, 86 per cent of university labs doing so
showed some problems.

Problems differed, but limited funding, difficulties in dividing the
intellectual property produced by the collaboration, and complex
contracts were found across the board. Industrial laboratories complained about the difficulties in dealing with non–private-sector
partners, which had different goals and priorities, different organizations and cultures, and a marked lack of urgency in relation to
market opportunities. They also found contracts too complex,
clearly pointing to transaction costs in the tradition of Coase and
Williamson (Coase, 1937; Williamson, 1985). This problem also af-

Table 5.3
Main area in which technological cooperation assisted research, 1990–92

| Area | No. of laboratories | | | |
	Industry	Government	University	Total
Basic research	7	7	12	26
Pre-commercial applied research	10	17	10	37
Commercial applied R&D	11	14	2	27
Technology transfer	7	13	5	25
Total	35	51	29	115

Note: Missing frequencies: 28.

Table 5.4
Problems experienced in cooperation by laboratories, 1990–92

Problem	Industry	Government	University	Total
Limited funds available	3	8	7	18
Complexity of contracts	6	5	2	13
Disputes over intellectual property	3	3	2	8
Different cultures, goals	7	–	–	7
Small number of partners	–	6	–	6
Government red tape	–	–	4	4
Difficult access to companies	–	–	3	3
National security issues	–	2	–	2
University overheads	–	–	2	2
University bureaucracy	–	–	1	1

fected public labs. These, however, experienced major difficulties in finding suitable partners: too many of the latter did not carry out any R&D, or were too small, or did not want to commit funds to collaborative research. University research centres found that government-funding agencies were slow and bureaucratic, and that their own university bureaucracies were also slow or requested too large overheads.

These figures are somewhat higher than those found in a previous study on technological alliances in Canadian industry (Niosi, 1995).

That research found that nearly one-third of the firms were experiencing problems with cooperation. The alliance study, conducted in 1990–91, addressed only firms; it was mostly done before the 1990–92 crisis that affected Canadian firms and put financial issues at the top of R&D concerns. In the alliance study, the sharing of intellectual property rights was the key difficulty hindering cooperation, followed by the complexity of contracts, particularly in assessment of partners' contributions to the alliances. By 1993, after a long recession and the beginning of government cuts to R&D grants, funding had become the main obstacle to technological cooperation.

The Propensity to Cooperate

We saw above that not all large Canadian R&D laboratories cooperated with external units. Only 59 per cent conducted collaborative R&D. How can we characterize the collaborative labs? Using the methods developed in the previous chapter for technology transfer, we compared the units with and those that lacked cooperative R&D activities. The results appear in Tables 5.5 to 5.9.

Industrial laboratories conducting alliances resemble those that are also active in technology transfer. In fact, 65 per cent of the labs that transfer technology are also conducting cooperative R&D (Table 5.5). Among industrial units active in alliances, large and small units do not behave in the same way (Table 5.6). Larger industrial R&D establishments have signed relatively more foreign agreements, while smaller units conduct more cooperative research with domestic non-profit organizations and government labs. Also, smaller private labs enter into technological cooperation to obtain new technology.

Government laboratories conducting cooperative R&D also look very much like those that are transferring technology (Table 5.7). Among these, basic research is rarely an important mission; they allocate funds to development, and their internal organization is more like that of an industrial unit than an academic one: they are organized through vertically linked departments and divisions, instead of freely formed, ad hoc research groups.

Within government laboratories involved in collaborative research, at least two types of units seem to emerge (Table 5.8). One is oriented more towards industry. This group is composed of smaller labs that own more patents, get more external revenues from the licensing of those patents, have fewer contacts with university research centres, and think that assistance to the parent organization or any other government organization is not an important mission. Also, they allocate more of their budget to pre-commercial applied R&D.

Table 5.5
Characteristics of industrial laboratories involved in cooperative R&D

Characteristic	No.	Pearson probability
They have technology transfer to private firms as an important mission.	59	0.012
Increasing the resources of the lab is a major effectiveness criterion.	58	0.0095
They consider the commercial benefits of R&D projects that they select.	55	0.025
Government policies also have an impact on the projects that they select.	59	0.048
They receive industrial grants from government.	56	0.094
They allocate fund to technology transfer.	57	0.004
Prototypes and devices constitute more than 10 per cent of output.	55	0.022
Demonstration of devices is one outpout.	55	0.078
They are not organized in ad hoc groups	59	0.091
They believe growth of cooperation is a major factor in technology transfer.	23	0.003
They tend to conduct technology transfer.	59	0.077

Table 5.6
Size of industrial laboratories and cooperative agreements

Characteristic	No.	Pearson probability
Larger laboratories have more foreign agreements.	29	0.047
Smaller ones have more alliances with non-profit laboratories	30	0.025
and with public laboratories	26	0.068
and are more motivated to look for new technology in alliances.	30	0.055

Table 5.7
Government laboratories with cooperative R&D

Characteristic	No.	Pearson probability
They are one among several labs under the same parent organization.	43	0.010
Basic research is seldom an important mission.	44	0.061
Direct government appropriations represent over 75 per cent of revenues.	43	0.002
They spend over 5 per cent of budget in development.	43	0.093
They are not organized in ad hoc groups.	44	0.029
They look for public visibility through technology transfer.	44	0.076

Conversely, those public laboratories oriented more to other public organizations are larger than the former; they consider assistance to government a major mission, they do not enter alliances with a profit motive, and they allocate fewer funds to pre-commercial applied R&D (PAR&D). In fact, they are similar to those public labs that conduct more collaborative work with university labs. Among government labs, larger, central units tend to cooperate with other public organizations, while smaller, specialized R&D units are more likely to ally themselves with industry and to allocate funds to do so.

Finally, when we compare university research centres that enter into cooperative agreements with those that do not, several characteristics appear (Table 5.9). First, those involved in cooperation are larger than the average, with budgets typically over $2.5 million. Also, they are more prone to selecting R&D projects with a view to profitability and receive a higher percentage of industrial grants than the average – typically over 3 per cent of their total budget. Conversely, government R&D contracts constitute a smaller proportion of their budget. Also, their parent organization (typically a university or a consortium of universities) does not contribute to their revenues. When allocating funds, these collaborative research centres allocate some funds to development and to technology transfer, but not to (free) assistance to outside organizations. They transfer technology for profit, be it for the laboratory or for its scientists and engineers. Finally, patents and licences are important outputs of the university laboratory involved in cooperation.

Table 5.8
Types of government laboratories according to main partners

Characteristic	No.	Pearson probability
Public labs with more industrial cooperation		
They are smaller than the average.	32	0.093
They own more patents.	27	0.024
They conduct university alliances less often.	32	0.016
Assistance to parent government organizations is less important.	32	0.003
They allocate more funds to pre-competitive applied R&D.	31	0.004
Public labs with more cooperation with government		
They are larger.	31	0.036
Assistance to government is their major mission.	32	0.004
They do not enter into alliances with a profit motive.	32	0.062
They allocate fewer funds to pre-competitive applied R&D.	31	0.045
Public labs with more university alliances		
They own fewer patents.	27	0.058
They get fewer revenues through licensing.	25	0.053
They are motivated not by the contribution of other parties to alliances	32	0.035
but by assistance to government,	32	0.016
and they allocate fewer funds to pre-competitive applied R&D.	31	0.007

REVENUES, TECHNOLOGY TRANSFER, AND COOPERATIVE R&D

Cooperation and technology transfer have been on the rise for the last decade or more. How have they affected revenues and the overall management of the laboratories? Government and university laboratories have dramatically increased such activities since the early 1990s; conversely, industrial units have been less active in both patenting and licensing. In 1992, a majority of each of the three types was involved in technological cooperation (Table 5.10).

Table 5.9
University laboratories involved in cooperation

Characteristic	No.	Pearson probability
They are larger.	39	0.076
They are more prone to select for-profit R&D projects.	40	0.092
They have more industrial grants in their budgets.	39	0.076
They have fewer public contracts.	37	0.069
They receive fewer funds from their parent organization.	37	0.068
They often spend funds in development activities	40	0.078
and in technology transfer	40	0.092
but not in assistance to outside organizations.	40	0.044
They usually transfer technology either for the lab's profit or	23	0.014
for the profit of their scientists and engineers.	23	0.036
Patents and licences are important outputs.	40	0.050

Patenting and licensing were undertaken in order to obtain new technology through barter, but also with a view to increasing revenue – a motive that we found in all types of laboratories. How did these new or increased activities affect budgets and revenues? Table 5.10 shows that the number of university and government labs with patenting and licensing increased markedly but that the number of units drawing revenues from these activities grew less substantially. The prospect – or the actual pinch – of falling government appropriations, subsidies, and grants, plus the development of science and technology policies promoting cooperation and industrial support, has probably stimulated both public and university labs to look for patents and to license some of their research results. Industrial units were also pushed to cooperate by federal and provincial technology policies (Niosi and Landry, 1993) but were less keen to transfer technology to outside parties or to get revenues from them. The main mission of industrial laboratories still is to produce technology for the parent company. Hence the diverging patterns of public and quasi-public labs as opposed to private ones in technology transfer and licensing.

Table 5.10
Results of licences and cooperation, 1990–92

Type of lab/result	No. of laboratories		
	1990	1991	1992
University			
Patents	6	8	12
Licences	7	9	12
Revenue from licences	3	4	5
Cooperation agreements	N/A	N/A	21
Total units in sample	40	40	40
Industrial			
Patents	11	11	11
Licences	9	7	8
Revenue from licences	4	4	4
Cooperation agreements	N/A	N/A	30
Total units in sample	59	59	59
Government			
Patents	16	19	20
Licences	19	25	27
Revenue from licences	10	13	15
Cooperative agreements	N/A	N/A	33
Total units in sample	44	44	44

Nevertheless, budgets have been stagnant for industrial and government units, while increasing rapidly for university laboratories (Table 5.11). In fact, between 1990 and 1992, years of recession for Canada, the increase in the budgets of industrial labs was marginal (3 per cent on average, 6 per cent in terms of median). In government labs, similarly, the average budget decreased while the median budget grew (minus 2 per cent and plus 6 per cent, respectively). Conversely, against all odds, university labs saw their budgets grow rapidly: by 17 per cent (mean) and 45 per cent (median).

We also saw above in chapter 3 that the three types of laboratories differ in the relative significance of their sources of funds. Industrial

Table 5.11
Laboratories' total budgets, 1990–92

| | $million (current dollars) | | | | | |
| | Industry | | Government | | University | |
Year	Mean	Median	Mean	Median	Mean	Median
1990	13.2	5.0	25.4	11.5	3.5	2.0
1991	13.2	5.0	26.0	11.6	3.8	2.5
1992	13.6	5.3	24.9	12.2	4.1	2.9

Table 5.12
The rise of government licensing revenues

Variable	Correlation	No.	Prob.	Beta	Sigma T
CHANGE2	0.6076	31	.000	.412491	.0007
CHANGE3	0.6100	32	.000	.456238	.0002
PNOBASIC	0.3675	32	.039	.289830	.0095
TOTPRFG2	0.3900	30	.033	.270027	.0158
Constant				.022	.0000

Notes: CHANGE2 shows recent (1990–92) changes in the allocation of budgets.
CHANGE3 shows recent (1990–92) changes in the productivity of the laboratory.
PNOBASIC shows problems resulting from the fact that technology transfer has moved R&D away from basic research.
TOTPRFG2 shows the increase in the R&D personnel.

labs depend on their own funds and/or the company's funds, government units rely mostly on government appropriations, and university research centres get their revenues primarily from government subsidies and contracts and secondarily from industrial grants.

Explaining Government Units' Revenue Patterns

Between 1990 and 1992, licensing did not represent an increasing source of revenue for industrial or university laboratories, although it did for government units. Here, the regression line tells a complex and interesting story (see Table 5.12). Government laboratories whose licensing revenues are rising are those that changed the allocation of their budgets and increased productivity, with some increase in R&D personnel. This change brought some problems, however, as technology transfer has led the units out of their more traditional research agendas.

Government Laboratories

Public laboratories have seen direct government statutory funds decreasing as a share of their budgets, while government contracts and industrial grants have increased. The sale of patents, royalties from licensing, and other types of private-sector revenues have not, however, become a major source of revenues (Table 5.13). *In other words, while the number of public laboratories owning patents and conducting technology transfer and technological cooperation with industry grew rapidly in the early 1990s, on the whole, sources of revenue have remained fairly steady.* In the early 1990s, direct appropriations from government declined as a source of revenues for government labs (from 95 per cent to 88 per cent), but they were partially replaced by government contracts and by more industrial grants. The new types of industrial revenues, however, did not yet constitute a sizeable item in budgets. Also, the number of public labs receiving either industrial grants or other industrial revenues did not change in the three-year period: each year, 66 per cent of them received industrial grants, and 11 per cent "other" revenues. However, in 1992, 61 per cent of government units were licensing some technology to outside parties; one is tempted to conclude that these agreements were bringing in negligible revenues.

As for government contracts and grants for public laboratories, they came mainly from federal departments. Industry, Science and Technology Canada (ISTC) gave contracts to fifteen government laboratories, the Department of National Defense (DND) to eight, Supply and Services Canada to six, and Energy Mines and Resources Canada to five. The NRC provided funds for seven laboratories, and NSERC for three.

Industrial Laboratories

We saw above that industrial R&D units were using a more variegated set of funding sources than either university or government laboratories (chapter 3). What Table 5.14 shows is essentially a bi-modal distribution: some 60 per cent of the industrial labs generate between 77 per cent and 80 per cent of their funds through sales of services to the company that owns them or to other companies. Some 40 per cent of the labs generate between 60 per cent and 80 per cent of their revenues from the company to which they belong through internal budgets. Both groups generate some complementary revenue from government contracts and industrial grants; other private-sector revenues are not important in terms of the number of labs involved (just three or four of them) but represent a major source of revenues for these few units in terms of the proportion of budget that they bring in.

Table 5.13
Sources of income in government laboratories, 1990–92

Source of funds	Median of % of total budgets		
	1990	1991	1992
Direct appropriations from government	95 (n = 35)	91 (n = 35)	88 (n = 41)
Government contracts	5 (n = 22)	6.5 (n = 24)	8 (n = 29)
Industrial grants	5 (n = 29)	9 (n = 29)	8 (n = 29)
Other	5 (n = 5)	5 (n = 5)	5 (n = 5)

Table 5.14
Sources of income in industrial laboratories, 1990–92

Source of funds	Median of % of total budgets		
	1990	1991	1992
Lab organization	77 (n = 36)	80 (n = 39)	78 (n = 40)
Parent organization	80 (n = 23)	60 (n = 24)	65 (n = 23)
Government contracts	15 (n = 28)	20 (n = 27)	20 (n = 29)
Industrial grants	24 (n = 17)	30 (n = 20)	25 (n = 22)
Other	16 (n = 3)	29 (n = 3)	22 (n = 4)
Direct appropriations from government	0 (n = 0)	0 (n = 0)	0 (n = 0)

Public organizations were major sources of contracts and grants for academe (Inset 9). NSERC was by far the most prominent funding agency: twenty-seven out of the forty university research centres in our sample obtained grants from it. It was followed by the Medical Research Council (supporting fourteen laboratories), Health and Welfare Canada (nine), and the Social Science and Humanities Research Council (seven). Provincial departments and granting agencies supported university labs, which constituted the majority of the "other" category (some twelve units received grants or contracts from them).

CONCLUSION

A majority of large laboratories (with twenty-five researchers or more) in Canada are now conducting cooperative research, with government

Inset 9   PAPRICAN: Pulp and Paper Research
The Pulp and Paper Research Institute of Canada (PAPRICAN) is the old-
est and still the largest non-profit cooperative research centre in Canada.
It was created in 1925 at McGill University, with the financial support of
industry and the federal government. Later, the Quebec government also
provided economic support. In 1956, the centre built a separate research
laboratory, in Pointe Claire, Quebec, within McGill's campus; in 1978, it
set up a similar agreement with the University of British Columbia, and it
opened a second R&D unit at UBC in 1986. Later, it extended its partnership to the École polytechnique of the Université de Montréal. With a total of 380 researchers, it studies process innovation for pulping,
papermaking, and recycling, product quality and uniformity, environmental protection, energy and water conservation, and a sustainable and economic fibre supply. By 1995, PAPRICAN had spent $33,4 million of R&D
on behalf of its thirty-two members. Most research was contracted out to
Canadian universities.
Sources: PAPRICAN web site; *Research Money.*

research centres being the most active. They were motivated by the desire for new technology but also for profits and new sources of revenue. In government labs, their missions pushed them to cooperate
with other public organizations. University labs were also looking for
new fundamental knowledge.

Practically all laboratories that conducted cooperative research obtained some major benefits from it, but problems abounded – limited funding, disputes on intellectual property, and the complexity of
contracts. These difficulties produced significant transaction costs.
In addition, several companies (one-third of those conducting technological collaboration) found that government and academic partners had different cultures, goals, and tempos and that these factors
inhibited success. Public labs experienced difficulties in finding companies sufficiently large and committed to R&D to risk their funds.
University research centres often found government bureaucracies
too slow in supporting alliances.

When characterizing the laboratories that cooperate and those than
do not, one is struck by the similarities between those that cooperate
and those that transfer technology. In fact, two-thirds of industrial R&D
units that transfer technology also conduct cooperative agreements.
All of them allocate funds to pre-commercial applied R&D and to technology transfer and/or development, consider potential profits when
selecting R&D projects, and produce prototypes and demonstration devices.

Inset 10   PRECARN and IRIS: Intelligent Systems
The PRECARN consortium was created in the late 1980s as a non-profit organization, combining industry, government, and university organizations for pre-competitive research. Soon it specialized in intelligent systems, and in 1989, it promoted formation of the Institute for Robotics and Intelligent Systems (IRIS). By early 1999, PRECARN and IRIS had spent over $75 million on research in this area with the support of Industry Canada. Participants include some twenty-three university groups (including the Laval University's Artificial Vision Laboratory and McGill Centre for Intelligent Machines), ten government organizations (including Alberta and Saskatchewan's research councils, Atomic Energy of Canada Ltd, the Canadian Space Agency, the Department of National Defence, Hydro-Québec, and Ontario Hydro), and at least fifteen Canadian corporations, including CAE Electronics, Inco Ltd, MacDonald Dettwiler Associates (Vancouver), MPB Technologies (Montreal), Spar Aerospace, and Syncrude Canada (Alberta).

PRECARN has three types of members. Regular ones pay $25,000 per year and have free access to research results and full voting rights, as well as participation in the board. Associate members are universities and government organizations; they pay the same amount as regular ones but have no voting rights. Small business members pay half the amount of larger firms.

In addition, in public laboratories with cooperative projects direct government appropriations typically represent over 75 per cent of revenues; thus technology transfer and cooperation are new activities that do not yet generate substantial revenues. Government labs behave differently regarding cooperation. Smaller, divisional R&D units are more active in industrial, for-profit cooperation. Larger, central ones cooperate more with government and quasi-public organizations – including universities – regardless of profitability; in doing so, they consider only their mandates and missions.

University laboratories that are active in cooperation are larger than average and often select R&D projects not solely for their potential in terms of publication but also for the profit that they can bring to the lab and/or to its researchers. They usually have industrial grants but fewer government contracts. They allocate funds to technology transfer and to development and look for patents and licences as important outputs.

The main conclusion is that technology transfer and technological cooperation are no longer sporadic, spontaneous, and occasional activities for the laboratories. Labs have embedded them in their strategic routines, in their missions, fund-raising, and fund allocation; in their effectiveness criteria and evaluation methods; and in their reward systems and output decisions. Increasing numbers of government policies and incentives also support them. In the new technological, economic, and fiscal environment of the 1990s, a lab's coherent strategy for the adoption of these internal routines may well make the difference between survival and disappearance.

The intense relationships between R&D organizations (see Inset 10) support again the concept of the NSI. The innovating agents are not isolated establishments, but networking organizations, searching for ideas and funds within other, external units. The trends point clearly towards increasing systemic coordination and interaction within national borders. As the following chapters show, however, national borders are somewhat porous and open to foreign influences and exchanges.

PART TWO

The Internationalization of Canada's NSI

6 Towards a North American System of Innovation?

In the last few years, the concept of national systems of innovation (NSIs) has nurtured an abundant literature (for example, Lundvall, 1992; Nelson, 1993; Niosi, Saviotti, Bellon, and Crow, 1993; Niosi, and Bellon, 1994; Patel and Pavitt, 1994; Archibugi and Michie, 1995; Freeman, 1995; Edquist, 1997). Empirical studies and theoretical discussions are now abundant about "national" and also subnational ("regional"), "sectoral," and even "supranational" systems of innovation. NSIs have been defined as sets of interrelated economic agents (firms with innovative capabilities, government laboratories, and research universities) aiming at the production of science and technology within national borders. Interaction among these units may be technical, financial, legal, or social (Niosi, Saviotti, Bellon, and Crow, 1993: 212).

The state plays a key role in an NSI. In OECD countries, governments contribute, on average, close to half of the resources of the system. They also provide priorities (for example, defence, health, environment, or national unity), incentives to innovate (for example, R&D funds in the form of subsidies and tax credits) resources (financial and human), and rules (for example, legislation on intellectual property determining which technological assets are to be protected by law and which are not and financial legislation concerning venture capital).

The internationalization of systems of innovation has been analysed in terms of two perspectives. One approach has been to consider that all NSIs are open systems receiving scientific and technological inputs from abroad through various channels, such as foreign-funded and-performed R&D, international alliances, and scientific cooperation (Niosi and Bellon, 1994). The other perspective has been to refer to "supranational" systems of innovation – actual, potential or future (Edquist, 1997). Both emerging views are probably more complementary than competing. Also, Archibugi and Michie (1995) have insisted that technology becomes globalized through several mechanisms and stages: first, through foreign trade; next, through foreign direct investment (FDI); and finally, through the international production of technology by means of expatriate R&D and international alliances.

The concept of a supranational system of innovation (SSI) has not been explored yet. No author has enumerated the specificity and characteristics of such a system. What degree of coherence and interrelationship among units based in different countries is necessary for an SSI? What kind of supranational regulation – if any – is needed to provide goals and incentives to such a system? Are the international flows among members of an SSI different from other international flows or from the domestic national or regional flows of its components?

The possibility of such an SSI's existing has, however, been suggested. The European Union is the most likely candidate. In the 1980s and 1990s in western Europe, programs such as BRITE, ESPRIT, EURAM, EUREKA, JESSI, JOULE, and SPRINT have provided goals and priority areas, promoted intra-European cooperation, harmonized policy instruments, and levelled fields in science and technology among companies of different countries. Before them, the Airbus consortium, the European nuclear research centre (CERN), the European space agency (ESRO), and other collective research and manufacturing initiatives provided resources and specific goals to collaborative ventures in several areas.

According to the empirical literature on the emerging European SSI, these are the three main traits of such a system (see, among others, Caracostas and Soete, 1997): First, there are at least some supranational policies in science and technology providing priorities, incentives, and rules of functioning to the system on top of national and subnational regulations and institutions. Second, international technological flows among the countries of such a system are abundant, including international technological alliances, direct investment flows for production, and R&D among organizations based in member countries. Third, countries within the system are the most important technological partners for each other.

On the basis of these characteristics, I propose the following definition for a supranational system of innovation: *A supranational system of innovation (ssi) is a set of national systems of innovation (NSIs) showing some degree of coherence and interdependence, on the basis of a common body of science and technology policies, a significant degree of interaction among units belonging to different NSIs, and the preferred technological outsourcing of each partner country among the other nations of the system.*

This chapter is about one of the most likely candidates to become an ssi – the North American Free Trade Agreement (NAFTA), framing the trade area linking the United States, Canada, and Mexico. In order for North America to become an ssi, it must meet of all the above-mentioned conditions. First, the three North American countries should have put in place (or at least should be negotiating) a harmonization of their science and technology policies. Second, international technological flows among the three partners must be nourished. Third, the main partner for each member country, in terms of international technological flows, should be one of the others.

THE NORTH AMERICAN SYSTEM

The size and functioning of the three NSIs in North America are strikingly different. The United States hosts the largest and most diversified NSI in the world, with a total R&D annual expenditure over U.S.$180 billion by 1996, scattered in almost every industry. Canada, the seventh largest NSI in the world, spends approximately 1/18th of that amount (some U.S.$10 billion), with a clear concentration on a few major industries, such as telecommunication equipment, aircraft, engineering, biotechnology, and software and related services (Canada, Statistics Canada, 1997). Mexico spends 1/120th of the U.S. total in R&D (some U.S.$1.5 billion) (OECD). In 1993, per capita R&D expenditures amounted to $641 in the United States, $314 in Canada, and $17 in Mexico (all figures in current U.S. dollars, at purchasing parity power, or PPP) (OECD).

Both the American and the Canadian NSIs are strongly rooted in national science and technology policies, but most of their innovative efforts take place within the private sector. Also, the United States and Canada are the only developed countries, together with Norway, where over 30 per cent of the population between eighteen and twenty-five years old attends university; both nations boast some of the largest agglomerations of university research in the world, which are host to important local and foreign R&D laboratories. By 1995, some 17 per cent of Canada's business expenditure on R&D (BERD) was financed by foreign enterprises, as was 18 per cent of that of the United States. In 1993, there were close to 1.5 million scientists and engineers in the U.S. R&D system, and some 127,000 in Canada, of whom over half in each nation were employed in industry (Table 6.1). Finally, both U.S. and Canadian corporations have made significant foreign direct investment (FDI) abroad, including expatriate R&D, both in each other's territory and in other developed countries. The level of internationalization of the U.S. and Canadian R&D systems is fairly high.

Conversely, R&D in Mexico – as in most developing countries – takes place in the public sector (government laboratories, public universities, and state enterprises), and very little in the private sector. In 1993, for instance, only 33,440 researchers were conducting R&D in Mexico, including over 90 per cent who were employed by the public sector and less than 10 per cent (some two thousand people) by the private sector (CONACYT/SEP, 1995: 58; information from OECD). Only 1 per cent of Mexico's BERD is financed by foreign sources. Thus Mexico attracts little foreign R&D in the private sector, and Mexican firms conduct little FDI or R&D abroad. Mexican firms and private citizens receive less than one hundred patents per year in the United States (or less than 1 patent per million population, against 277 patents per million in the United States and over one hundred per million in Canada). Under these conditions, one can even wonder whether Mexico has an NSI at all.

Trade and Investment within NAFTA

Canada and the United States have for most of the twentieth century been each other's largest trading partners. Also, FDI flows between them have been large and growing since the beginning of the century. Similarly, the United States has been Mexico's largest trade partner and its largest foreign direct investor for decades. Conversely, Mexico and Canada have only recently discovered each other, in terms of trade, investment, and technology, and their mutual share of commerce or FDI is still low in absolute and relative terms.

A few policy initiatives have brought some coherence to the Canadian–U.S. system in several industries, in terms of both FDI and R&D. The two most important, before the Canadian–U.S. Free Trade Agreement (FTA) of 1987, are worth mentioning. First, in 1959, Canada and the United States entered into an agreement to share defence production; the resulting program was called DIPP (Defense Industry Productivity Program). It made assistance available to Canadian producers for R&D so that they could compete with their American counterparts in a few designated areas. Later, Canada signed similar agreements with several European nations, but none of them reached the scale of the North American DIPP. Second, the Canada–U.S. Auto Pact of 1965

Table 6.1
The North American NSIs compared, 1993

Indicator	Size (U.S.$million)		
	United States	Canada	Mexico
GERD (U.S.$million)	165,480	9,104	1,563
GERD per capital (U.S.$)	641	315	17
BERD (U.S.$million)	117,400	5,184	162
Business firms' researchers (no.)	764,500	35,480	867
BERD financed from abroad (%)	7%	17%	0.6%
Total R&D personnel (no.)	1,500,000	127,000	27,000

Sources: OECD, Main Science and Technology Indicators (Paris, 1996); National Science Foundation (NSF), 1996.

triggered massive direct investment from the American (and lately Japanese) car manufacturers into Canada. Canada became a large vehicle producer through the importation of automotive manufacturing technology, without the equivalent growth of an associated R&D capability. Neither of these agreements represented a major abandonment of the traditional laissez-faire policy of both countries in favour of coordination of science and technology policies.

The North American Free Trade Agreement (NAFTA) among Canada, Mexico, and the United States, effective 1 January 1994, has increased these trends. Both it and the FTA were aimed at increasing both trade and investment within North America through elimination of tariff and non-tariff barriers and creation of a set of common regulations on intellectual property, services, competition, and other areas (Canada, Foreign Affairs and International Trade, 1997). It is clear that the goal has largely been attained.

In the last ten years, as a consequence of both the FTA and NAFTA, trade among the three countries has increased dramatically. Since 1989, Canadian merchandise exports to the United States have increased by over 120 per cent, from $101 billion in 1989 to over $223 billion in 1996 (Figure 6.1). U.S. exports to Canada rose by over 78 per cent, from $88 billion in 1989 to $157 billion in 1996 (Figure 6.2); Canadian exports to Mexico grew by over 20 per cent in only two years from $1 billion in 1994 to $1.3 billion in 1996 (Figure 6.3); and imports from Mexico grew from $5.6 billion to $7.2 billion (Figure 6.4).

Figure 6.1
Canadian merchandise exports to the United States, 1988–96

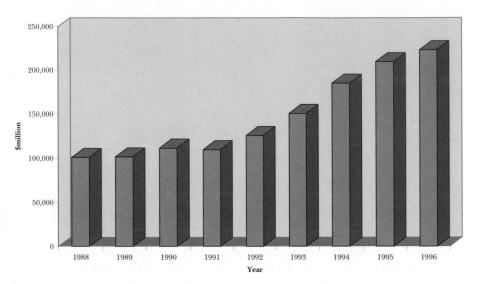

Figure 6.2
Canadian merchandise imports from the United States, 1988–96

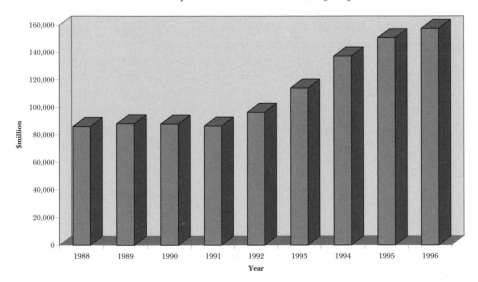

Figure 6.3
Canadian merchandise exports to Mexico, 1988–96

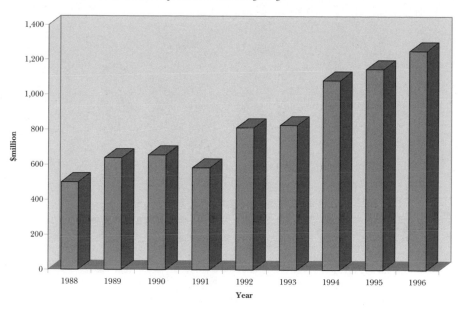

Figure 6.4
Canadian merchandise imports from Mexico, 1988–96

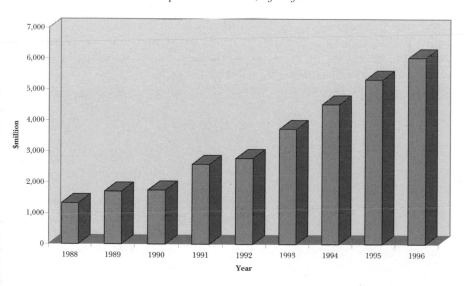

Figure 6.5
U.S. direct investment in Canada, 1988–96

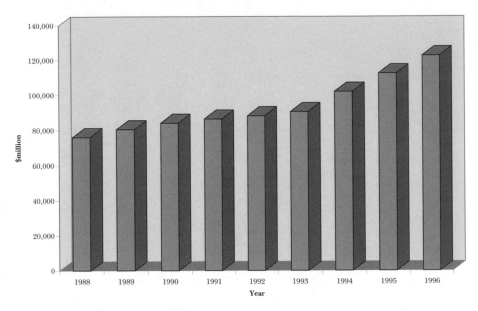

FDI has also soared. U.S. FDI in Canada increased by over 50 per cent between 1989 and 1996, from $80 billion to $123 billion (Figure 6.5). Canadian investment in the United States rose even faster, from $56 billion in 1989 to $93 billion in 1996. Mexican FDI in Canada, almost non-existent in the early 1990s, reached $239 million in 1996 (Figure 6.6), while Canadian FDI in Mexico, very low six years ago, was worth $1.3 billion in 1996.

Inter-country R&D

While trade and investment show impressive increases and the constitution of a North American trading bloc, the internationalization of technological production has not followed. First, Canadian R&D in the United States has in fact decreased during the period, while total foreign R&D in the United States grew dramatically. Also, in the long term, Canadian industrial R&D has not risen as a proportion of foreign-funded R&D in the United States: in 1977, as in 1993, Canadian affiliates in that country represented 8 per cent of all foreign R&D expenditures, and Canada was in 1977, as in 1993, only the sixth largest foreign investor in American industrial R&D (see Table 6.2).

Figure 6.6
Mexican direct investment in Canada, 1988–96

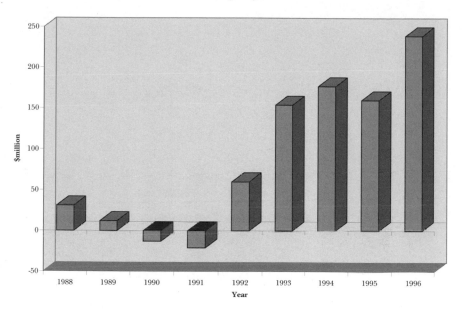

Table 6.2
Foreign R&D expenditures in the United States, 1977–96

	Expenditures (U.S. $million)				
Country	1977	1987	1989	1995	(% change) 1989–95
Canada	74	1,666	1,758	1,396	−20
France	62	366	572	1,644	187
Japan	23	307	800	1,867	133
Netherlands	190	542	703	838	19
Sweden	10	128	214	807	277
Switzerland	241	765	1,195	3,088	158
UK	155	833	1,645	2,497	52
(West) Germany	101	1,139	1,503	3,976	165
Total (all countries)	933	6,521	9,455	17,666	87

Sources: NSF, 1993, 1996.

Figure 6.7
Canadian direct investment in Mexico, 1988–96

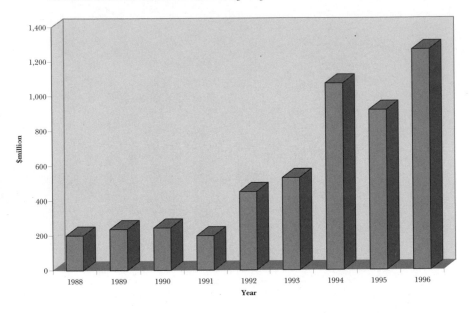

Table 6.3
R&D expenditures by majority-owned foreign affiliates of U.S. parent companies, by country, 1982–95

	Expenditures (U.S. $millions)			
Country	1982	1989	1993	(% change) 1989–93
Germany	893	1,496	2,568	72
UK	805	1,673	1,639	−2
Canada	545	914	1,030	13
France	263	545	942	73
Japan	104	488	862	77
Belgium	181	317	460	45
Netherlands	101	360	392	9
Italy	136	294	304	3
Mexico	38	37	N.D.	N.D.
Ireland	31	134	669	399
Total, all countries	3,647	7,048	10,954	55

Sources: NSF, 1993, 1996.

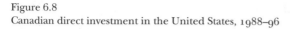

Figure 6.8
Canadian direct investment in the United States, 1988–96

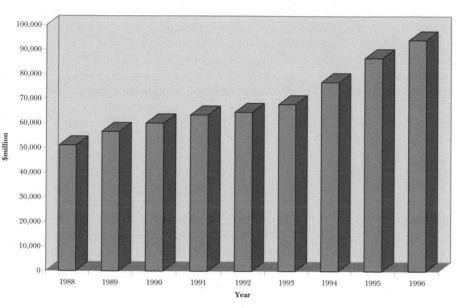

In the meantime, U.S. R&D expenditure in Canada increased only modestly in absolute terms, from U.S.$545 million in 1982 to U.S.$1030 million in 1993 (Table 6.3). In relative terms, however, Canada received a declining proportion of R&D performed by majority-owned foreign affiliates of U.S. parent companies: its share slipped from 15 per cent of the U.S. total in 1982 to 9 per cent in 1993. Canada is still, however, the third-largest destination of U.S. R&D expenditures abroad, but not the preferred one. In Canada, foreign firms undertook in 1995 some 20 per cent of total Canadian industrial R&D expenditures. American firms represented 72 per cent of the foreign total (Canada, Statistics Canada, 1997: 70). The United States is also the largest recipient of Canadian expatriate R&D. Some two-thirds of the patents obtained through Canadian overseas R&D are granted to Canadian subsidiaries operating in the United States, and nearly one-third to those operating in western Europe (Niosi, 1997).

It is safe to conclude that the U.S. NSI represents the largest partner for the Canadian NSI but that the converse is not true: Canada is an important partner, but not the foremost one, of the US NSI. Within NAFTA, Mexico is not a technological partner, but more a user of American and Canadian technologies.

International Alliances

Hundreds of technology alliances exist between American firms and their counterparts in western Europe and Japan. By the end of the 1980s, one of the most complete databases available found close to six hundred alliances between American and European corporations and over three hundred between American firms and Japanese counterparts. Thus in terms of international technology alliances, the United States is, within the Triad (European Union–Japan–North America) the largest partner for both western Europe and Japan. Unfortunately, the MERIT-CATA Database does not provide figures for Canada. But we can gain some similar information from our previous study of Canadian alliances (Niosi, 1995).

While figures are not perfectly comparable (we obtained the MERIT-CATA Database mostly from public announcements in the newspapers, and Canadian data, through interviews), it is clear that in 1992 western Europe was the preferred destination of strategic technological alliances of Canadian firms, totalling some 47 per cent of them, followed by the United States (32 per cent), Japan (12 per cent), and the rest of the world (Table 6.5). This preference of Canadian firms may be explained by two factors. The first is the massive increase in European alliances within that continent since 1984, following implementation of BRITE, ESPRIT, EURAM, JESSI, and the other intra-European programs, including at least one accepting foreign partners (EUREKA). The second is the technological complementarity between Canada and western Europe. Compared to the European Union (EU), Canada's industry is strong in new biotechnology, but weak in traditional pharmaceuticals, where many EU corporations are major players. Also, Canadian firms are stronger than most of their European counterparts in some areas of information technologies (such as telecommunication equipment and software) and weaker in others (such as robotics and consumer electronics). Conversely, Canadian high-tech industry closely resembles its American counterpart. Thus between Canadian and U.S. firms there is more competition than cooperation. Technological complementarities are the main condition for the development of alliances, and they are more evident between North America and western Europe than between the United States and Canada.

CONCLUSION

In North America, there are at least two NSIs, and the existence of the third is still open to debate – or a matter of definition. Within NAFTA, the internationalization of technology production has been much slower

Table 6.4
Distribution of strategic alliances among economic blocs, 1985–89

Industry	USA/EU	USA/Japan	EU/Japan
Automotive	24	39	16
Aviation/defence	31	3	0
Biotechnology	124	54	20
Chemicals	54	28	21
Electrical equipment	22	4	4
Food and beverage	4	2	2
Information	256	132	57
Medical instruments	19	5	6
New materials	52	40	23
Total	586	307	149

Source: NSF, 1993.

Table 6.5
Canadian international alliances in various economic blocs, 1992

Industry or technology	USA	EU	Japan	Others	Total number
Advanced materials	9	11	2	2	24
Biotechnology	16	27	3	2	48
Information	16	30	9	11	66
Transportation equipment	9	8	4	1	22
Total	50	76	18	16	160
Total (%)	32%	47%	12%	9%	100%

Source: Niosi, 1995.

than that of production and trade. This confirms the arguments of Archibugi and Michie and of Patel and Pavitt about globalization as starting with trade and investment for the exploitation of existing technology and moving only later to international production of new technology.

While a regional trading bloc is now emerging in the framework of NAFTA, it would be difficult to argue that an SSI is now being put in place. I suggest two major reasons for this specific (trade-before-technology) pattern. First, the internationalization of technology production proceeds much faster between North America's largest economies and non-NAFTA partners than within NAFTA, because of the different capabilities of the countries involved and the relative sizes of their markets. Thus firms based in the larger European countries and Japan, not Canadian or Mexican ones, are becoming the largest technological partners of American corporations. Second, for an SSI to emerge, supranational science and technology policies should develop. These policies are evident in EU –, for example in ESPRIT, EUREKA, and JESSI, which forge alliances and technology transfer among companies based in different European countries. Nothing of the sort takes place in NAFTA, and there are only sectoral agreements and ad hoc arrangements on specific issues, but no substantial, international technology policies. Each of the three members has its own set of domestic goals and policies on science and technology, and no major tentative coordination is on the political agenda. The absence of supranational policies in these fields is probably the major factor explaining the absence of a North American SSI. This situation is much more evident when one compares NAFTA with the EU.

Also, the scientific and technological gap among the three partners in NAFTA makes the largest of them their most important supplier of technology and a magnet attracting most of the foreign R&D activities of the second one in a search for wider markets and larger pools of ideas. Nothing of the sort happens in the EU, where the four major economies of comparable size (France, Germany, Italy, and the United Kingdom) are more harmoniously coupled to several other smaller industrial countries with similar, though more specialized technological capabilities.

NAFTA fails to meet at least two of the three conditions of an SSI: it has no supranational science and technology policy, and its member countries are not each other's main technology partner. The whole North American picture is rather one of two (or three) different, but open NSIs, displaying mutual interaction and influences, but still fairly autonomous and evolving on the basis of their own technological and organizational trajectories within a context of increasing globalization of trade and investment. In the next two chapters, I analyse some of the "borders" of Canada's NSI, on the basis of Canada's industrial R&D abroad, under the hypothesis of an open system exchanging information with external environments.

7 Canadian R&D Abroad: The Patent Record

In the last two decades, Canadian industrial research abroad has been growing rapidly. Some large and a few small and medium-sized Canadian-owned and -controlled corporations conduct R&D abroad. This chapter gives an overview of their foreign research activities on the basis of their overseas original patents.

FOREIGN R&D BY MULTINATIONAL CORPORATIONS

In the 1990s, the literature on foreign R&D has expanded dramatically, following the rapid increase in overseas R&D by multinational corporations (MNCs). The traditional explanation for expatriate R&D by MNCs had been provided by Ronstadt (1984); overseas R&D was an auxiliary activity needed to assist technology transfer from the parent company to the foreign subsidiary, through adaptations required by specific raw materials or different manufacturing processes in the host country. This explanation was in line with the product life-cycle theory of international business.

In the late 1980s and early 1990s new explanations emerged, as it became evident that the life-cycle explanation did not hold any more. Most expatriate R&D was concentrated in a few areas (pharmaceuticals and biotechnology, computers and computer software, consumer electronics, chemicals, automotive, and other high- and medium-technology industries). More extended studies showed that the goal of these R&D investments was more often to acquire technology, to create new products and processes for local and world markets, and to keep abreast with technological developments than to assist parent companies with technology transfer (Cantwell and Hodson, 1991; Cheng and Bolon, 1993; Kenney and Florida, 1994; Dalton and Serapio, 1995).

THEORIES ON THE INTERNATIONALIZATION OF R&D

Theories of the MNC help us to understand the internationalization of R&D, as well as the international expansion of NSIs. Here I examine eight.

The Product Life-Cycle Model

The product life-cycle (PLC) model argued that firms become multinationals as they transfer abroad the innovations produced in their home country for their national markets. Economies of scale in R&D and frequent interaction with affluent customers will have the effect of keeping R&D at home. Vernon and Wells (Vernon, 1979; Vernon, and Wells Jr, 1991) have recognized that the PLC model has lost some of its original appeal, because some large corporations are now able to develop at home new products to serve several different international markets at the same time and even to develop abroad new products for the world market. In the original model, the internationalization of R&D activity involved the transferring abroad of the capabilities necessary to modify or adapt to a different (usually less prosperous) market the basic technology produced in the domestic market. In this perspective, foreign R&D laboratories are essentially technology transfer and support operations. On the basis of case studies, Ronstadt (1984) concluded that technology transfer units are the most frequent type of expatriate R&D laboratories within U.S. MNCs.

The Specific-Asset Approach

This perspective posits that corporations become multinationals in order to benefit from past investments in R&D and in organization. These investments provide them special assets that are difficult to transfer because they consist mostly of knowledge. As knowledge markets are imperfect, companies prefer knowledge transactions in the form of transfer of these assets to foreign subsidiaries. In doing so, they become MNCs (Kindleberger, 1969; Caves, 1971; Hymer, 1976). Hymer emphasized the ownership advantages of proprietary technology; Caves stressed the presence of intangible assets resulting from investments in R&D, advertising, or organization as a predictor of multinational activity (Caves, 1982). Like the PLC model, they assumed that domestic R&D produced these special intangible assets in the home country of the corporation. They also found that R&D was mostly concentrated in large firms and that it promoted foreign investment. But the R&D functions tended to remain close to corporate headquarters (Caves, 1982).

Transfer Costs and the Internalization of Markets

David Teece (1977) emphasized the large technology transfer costs involved in arm's length sales of technology. He concluded that the main explanation for the existence of MNCs was the internalization of markets. Peter J. Buckley and Mark Casson (1976) draw the same conclusion. Casson (1987) later argued that ownership advantages in the Hymer–Caves–Kindleberger tradition were not a necessary condition for the internationalization of firms. Combining neoclassical trade theory and transaction costs, he insisted that location and transfer costs were sufficient conditions to explain multinational operations. More recently, he suggested that the internationalization of R&D could proceed on the same basis (Casson, 1991). There could be location specialization in R&D, on the basis of comparative advantage, as different types of R&D required various immobile inputs. Corporations could locate some types of R&D in different countries on the basis of comparative advantage. From this perspective, it makes no difference whether R&D is located at home or abroad.

The Comparative-Advantage Approach

National endowment of factors also affects the type of technologies that MNCs transfer abroad. Japanese MNCs were found to manufacture abroad products similar to those developed in Japan (Kojima, 1978). These products were making intensive use of factors that were abundant in Japan (capital and skilled labour).

The Eclectic Model

The eclectic model (Dunning, 1989) reconciled most of the hypotheses of the previous authors: firm-specific advantages, national home-country advantages, and host-country location advantages are needed to explain the direction of manufacturing operations and related internationalization of R&D. Corporations may move some labour-intensive activities to countries having an abundant unskilled work-force, and others (such as R&D) to countries with rich endowments of skilled labour. Still other activities may be moved towards countries with abundant energy resources.

The Evolutionary Theory

In the emerging evolutionary theory of the international firm, and contrary to the internalization-of-markets approach (which presents knowledge as a public good, and thus difficult to protect), knowledge appears to be difficult to transfer. MNCs specialize in the transfer of superior and – at least partially – tacit knowledge and expertise. It is not the risk of market failure or the potential opportunism of the technology buyer that keeps the transfer internal to the firm; rather, the advantages procured by this knowledge push firms to internalize the transfer from parent to subsidiary. The evolutionary theory, based on Richard Nelson and Sidney Winter's work (Nelson and Winter, 1982), relies mostly on the specific-asset approach (Kogut and Zander, 1993). A firm is defined by its strategy, its structure (routines), and its core capabilities (Nelson, 1994).

These capabilities are the basic process and product skills that provide the firms access to markets. They are usually difficult to imitate, and they change slowly over time. Firms transfer their competencies more efficiently than markets do, because these competencies, being at least partially composed of tacit knowledge embodied in key personnel, can more easily be conveyed within the firm than through arm's-length agreements. Also, firms prefer to keep their competencies – which constitute their competitive advantages – for themselves, rather than putting them in the market and assuming the costs of the transfer. The evolutionary theory predicts that MNCs will transfer their competence to wholly owned subsidiaries.

The Rise of Foreign R&D and Organizational Learning

Over the last ten years, new empirical literature on the internationalization of R&D has unveiled the pull and push factors that explain this process, its location determinants, and the role of government policy (Cantwell, 1992, 1995; Granstrand, Håkanson, and Sjölander, 1992; Serapio Jr, 1993; Taggart, 1993). This literature has shown wide variations in the patterns of internationalization among countries, industries, and periods. The usefulness of the PLC model was questioned, as much of the new foreign investment in R&D appeared to be aimed at the production of new knowledge.

At the same time, a more theoretical literature came to explain these new patterns. It characterized firms as learning organizations (Nonaka and Takeuchi, 1995). MNCs learn through several mechanisms, but foreign R&D is one of them and is used increasingly, particularly in high and medium-technology industries.

NSIs Are Open

In two previous articles (Niosi et al., 1993, Niosi and Bellon, 1994) we argued for a national-system approach, rather than the international perspective. We postulated that national systems are understandable in terms of systems theory: NSIs are "open," in the sense that they are exchanging matter, energy, and information with their environment. In systems theory, open systems may undergo discontinuous transitions towards states of increasing order and complexity, as they move away from the original equilibrium. Also, close to the transitions, because of the absorption of external elements, open systems undergo stochastic fluctuations, and their behaviour becomes indeterminate before they attain a new equilibrium.

It is arguable that the FTA and then NAFTA opened Canada's economy even further and provoked a series of new external stimuli. The result of this growing "openness" was an increasing flow of FDI from Canada to the United States and a related flow of R&D activities, while the reverse did not happen. Canada's NSI is thus increasingly open, and the result has been the delocalization of a growing portion of its R&D industrial units to the United States. At the same time, creation of a larger European Union attracted more Canadian firms towards western Europe, thus also increasing the "openness" of the Canadian NSI towards that region.

CANADIAN FOREIGN DIRECT INVESTMENT

Canada holds one of the largest amounts of FDI in the world and over thirty large MNCs, plus dozens of large and medium-size corporations with different degrees of internationalization of their production activities. By the end of 1994, Canadian FDI was worth $125 billion, or approximately U.S.$100 billion. More than 50 per cent of this amount was invested in the United States, 22 per cent in Europe, 2 per cent in Japan, and the balance in Asia, Latin America, and Australia. The United States and the United Kingdom had almost two-thirds of Canadian FDI; six G7 countries (other than Canada) had 70 per cent. In 1994, Canada was also the fourth-largest foreign investor in the United States, after the United Kingdom, Japan, and the Netherlands;

Germany, France, and Switzerland followed. A strong correlation exists between FDI and foreign R&D activities: the seven largest foreign investors in the United States are also the seven largest sources of foreign R&D expenditures in that country.

The differences between the large and small countries appear overwhelming when one compares their R&D expenditures in the United States with their gross domestic expenditure on R&D (GERD) and their domestic business expenditure on R&D (BERD) (see Table 7.1). Smaller industrial countries (Canada, the Netherlands, and Switzerland) show much higher R&D expenditures in the United States as a proportion of both BERD and GERD than do large industrial nations such as France, Germany, Japan, and the United Kingdom.

Canadian FDI and overseas R&D are concentrated in a small number of large MNCs in non-ferrous metal refining, paper and its products, food and beverages, aircraft and transportation equipment, machinery, shoes, textiles, and electronic products. There are of course some small and medium-sized MNCs in high-technology areas, but their total significance is small when compared to the largest firms (Niosi, 1985; Niosi and Rivard, 1990; Rugman and Verbeke, 1990).

CANADIAN PATENTING ABROAD

R&D expenditures are a valuable input measure of the expatriation of innovative activities. Patents are one of the most useful measures of output. All the usual caveats about patent statistics apply here: patents underestimate the amount of invention (many inventions are kept secret instead of being patented; others, such as software and plant design, are not usually protected by patents), and both commercially critical and negligible inventions count equally in patent statistics. In addition, product innovations tend to be more frequently patented than process innovations (Winter, 1989). Nevertheless, patents offer one of the best quantitative estimates of the industries, technologies, corporations, and inventive outputs in a given economy.

I created a list of some 170 Canadian-owned and -controlled manufacturing firms with foreign subsidiaries in 1994. I excluded from the start foreign-controlled Canadian corporations with foreign subsidiaries that have R&D activities abroad (such as Ford Motor Co. of Canada and Canadian Marconi), in order to keep only Canadian-owned and -controlled corporations.

These Canadian companies entered the U.S. and European markets through the acquisition of existing industrial firms, a strategy that contrasts with the Japanese preference for "greenfield" investments in the

Table 7.1

Foreign R&D expenditures in the United States and at home, by country, 1990

| | Expenditures (u.s.$million) | | | | |
Country	A R&D expenditure in the USA	B BERD	C GERD	D A as % of B	E A as % of C
Canada	1,955	4025	7406	48.6	26.4
United Kingdom	1,864	13810	19995	14.2	9.3
Germany	1,754	22989	32031	7.6	5.5
Switzerland	1,657	2900	4000	57.1	41.4
Japan	1,215	47450	66965	2.6	1.8
France	810	14357	23762	5.6	3.4
Netherlands	805	2713	4827	29.7	16.7

Source: OECD, 1995; NSF, 1993.
Note: Figures for Switzerland are estimates.

United States, Canada, and the European Union (Kenney and Florida, 1993). These newly acquired, wholly owned foreign subsidiaries often possessed R&D capabilities before they were absorbed by the Canadian corporation. Thus acquisition, not creation of new laboratories, was Canadian firms' preferred method for entering R&D abroad.

I analysed the U.S. patent database in order to discover the patent activity of the foreign subsidiaries of Canadian corporations. All the Canadian companies and their foreign subsidiaries were investigated in the U.S. patent database, and I attributed patents to the country of the original inventor, as registered by the U.S. patent database.

Between 1 January 1992 and 31 December 1994, seventy-two corporations (42 per cent of the 170) had obtained U.S. patents. In those years, some sixteen hundred (out of the forty-two thousand manufacturing corporations registered by Statistics Canada, or 4 per cent) conducted R&D within Canada's borders. The propensity to conduct R&D is thus ten times higher among Canadian corporations with foreign operations than among purely domestic firms. Canadian MNCs are technology-intensive firms, with ownership advantages consisting at least partly of internally created knowledge.

Forty of these internationally active manufacturing firms had patented in the United States at least one invention produced by their U.S.

subsidiaries[*]; as well, fifteen Canadian corporations had patented in the United States inventions developed by their European subsidiaries. Three Canadian corporations had patented in the United States several inventions produced by their Japanese subsidiaries; three others reported patents from their Australian subsidiaries. In all, forty-six corporations have been granted at least one patent in the United States, stemming from their expatriate corporate research, either in the United States or elsewhere. In other words, 27 per cent of the initial list (forty-six of the one hundred and seventy industrial corporations with foreign subsidiaries) had some substantial foreign R&D capability that had produced novelties worth patenting. Also, 64 per cent of the seventy-two corporations with new patents between 1992 and 1994 had obtained patents from their expatriate R&D laboratories.

More detailed results appear in Tables 7.2 to 7.7 and in Figure 7.1. The figure shows the similar geographical distribution of both FDI and patents. The "rest of the world" (essentially the developing countries) has received Canadian FDI, including some R&D investments, but has produced no patents. Table 7.2 shows the patent activity of large (over five hundred employees worldwide) Canadian-owned and -controlled enterprises in the United States. Twenty-nine large Canadian companies have received patents for inventions that they produced in their U.S. laboratories. Half of them are MNCS, and the other half have substantial operations abroad. Their U.S. R&D activities are very significant, as measured by the number of patents originally requested in the United States: for eighteen large corporations, including seven MNCS, more than 50 per cent of the U.S. patents that they were granted in the United States originated in their American R&D operations. My data showed that 91 per cent of the thirty-three large Canadian firms obtaining patents from foreign R&D are diversified, but most of them (twenty-four of the thirty-three large firms or 72 per cent) have diversified into related businesses. They produce lines of products abroad that are related to those that they manufacture in Canada. These findings are in line with the evolutionary theory of the firm, which suggests that firms acquire new technologies through a complex, slow, and path-dependent process (Kogut and Zander, 1993).

---

[*] These figures exclude one large U.S. chemical corporation in which a Canadian corporation has minority control. According to Canadian definitions, foreign control requires the parent to hold over 50 per cent of the voting shares of the foreign corporation; in the U.S. Department of Commerce's definition, minority control is assumed if no other stockholder owns another sizeable block of shares. Thus the American chemical corporation is deemed in the United States to be under Canadian control but in Canada is classified under American control (Dalton and Serapio, 1995).

Figure 7.1
Canadian direct investment abroad, 1994, and Canadian patents abroad, 1992–94

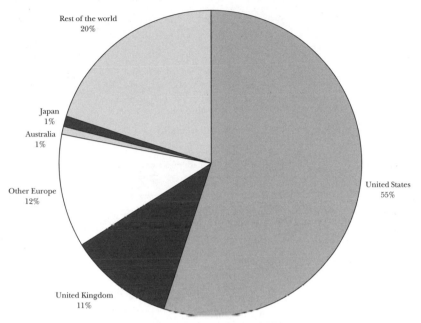

Canadian direct investment abroad, 1994

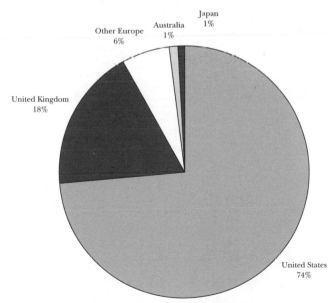

Canadian patents abroad, 1992–94

Table 7.2
U.S. patents of large Canadian MNCs, granted to their U.S. subsidiaries, 1992–94

Corporation	Product, industry	A Patents (no.) granted to U.S. subsidiaries	B A as % of total patents granted in USA
Alcan Aluminium*	Aluminium and alloys	13	12% (110)
BCE/Northern Telecom*	Telecommunication equipment	23	10% (232)
Bombardier*	Aircraft, mass transportation equipment	1	6% (17)
CAE Inc.*	Flight simulators, machinery	1	17% (6)
CCL Industries Inc.	Perfumes, cosmetics, soaps	11	73% (15)
Derlan Industries Ltd	Machinery, aircraft parts	18	78% (23)
Dominion Textiles*	Textiles	1	100% (1)
Domtar Inc.	Pulp, paper, bldg materials	2	20% (10)
Dorel Industries	Furniture	4	100% (4)
EMCO Ltd.*	Plumbing and heating equip.	9	69% (13)
Inco Ltd.*	Nickel, cooper, and alloys	21	48% (44)
Inter-City Products	Refrigeration, heating equipment	12	100% (12)
IPSCO Inc.	Steel, steel pipes	2	66% (3)
John Labbat	Alcoholic beverages	6	60% (10)
McCain Foods*	Food	3	100% (3)
Magna International*	Auto parts	2	14% (14)
Molson Companies*	Beer, chemicals, retail	3	50% (6)
Moore Corp.*	Business forms	114	91% (125)
Noranda Inc.*	Non-ferrous metals, forest products, oil, and gas	2	8% (26)
Nova Corp.	Oil, gas, chemical products	9	56% (16)
Premdor Inc.	Building materials	1	100% (1)
Repap Enterprises	Pulp and paper	1	100% (1)
Sico Inc.	Chemical products (paints)	2	100% (2)
Spar Aerospace	Satellites, robotics	3	27% (11)

Table 7.2 *(continued)*
U.S. patents of large Canadian MNCs, granted to their U.S. subsidiaries, 1992–94

Corporation	Product, industry	A Patents (no.) granted to U.S. subsidiaries	B A as % of total patents granted in USA
Torstar Corp.*	Printing	1	100% (1)
Unican*	Security electronic products	1	20% (5)
United Dominion Industries*	Building machinery, engrg., and construction	6	100% (6)
Valiant Machine & Tool	Machinery	1	25% (4)
Ventra Group Inc.	Auto parts	1	100% (1)
Total patents and weighted average		274	38% (722)

Source: U.S. Patent Database (Cassis).
* MNCs.

Table 7.3 details the figures for eleven small and medium-sized enterprises (SMEs, having fewer than five hundred employees worldwide) with R&D activities in the United States. While the number of patents and firms is smaller than that for the large corporations, some companies conduct most or all of their R&D activities in the United States. Size is a major determinant of expatriate R&D, as more than half of patent-producing foreign research is conducted by large enterprises, such as Alcan, Inco, Moore, and Northern Telecom.

Between 1992 and 1994, fifteen Canadian firms also conducted R&D in Europe and obtained patents in the United Kingdom and elsewhere. The United Kingdom was by far the most common destination of Canadian R&D in that continent, with seventy-three patents, but some original research activity by Canadian firms was also evident in Germany, France, Switzerland, Austria, Ireland, Italy, and Spain (Table 7.4).

Patents granted to Canadian-owned and -controlled corporations represent 11 per cent of all patents granted to Canadian inventors in Canada. Foreign technology was crucial to Canadian firms with foreign operations: expatriate R&D represented 82 per cent of all original inventions patented by the same enterprises in Canada and 31 per cent of all patents obtained in the United States by these firms from all locations. The number of foreign patents obtained by Canadian firms is in line with their large foreign expenditures on R&D. For a majority of

Table 7.3
U.S. patents of Canadian SMEs, granted to their U.S. subsidiaries, 1992–94

Corporation	Industry	A Patents (no.) granted to U.S. subsidiaries	B A as % of total patents granted in USA
Bionaire Inc.	Other manufacturing (humidifiers)	3	100% (3)
Consolidated Mercantile	Furniture, packaging	1	100% (1)
Davstar Industries	Medical products	5	100% (5)
Deprenyl Research	Human biotechnology	1	25% (4)
Dyment Ltd	Signals and advertising	1	100% (1)
Frannan Holdings	Electronics, auto parts	2	29% (7)
Innopac	Packaging materials	1	100% (1)
JWI Ltd	Paper machinery	3	75% (4)
ODC International	Machinery	1	50% (2)
SBN Systems Ltd	Electronic products	1	100% (1)
TecSyn International	Telecommunication equipment	1	100% (1)
Total patents and weighted average		20	66% (30)

Source: U.S. Patent Database (Cassis).

Canadian MNCs, one-third of their patented novelties came from their expatriate laboratories (Table 7.5).

Table 7.6 shows that more than one-third (eight of twenty-two) of the largest Canadian MNCs conducted all their research activities abroad, as judged by the origins of the patents that they obtained between 1992 and 1994. One other MNC conducts all its R&D in Canada (Cascades), and two (Bata and Cominco) had no patents abroad in this period.

Finally, Table 7.7 tests comparative advantage in the eclectic theory of the firm. It shows the relationship between the industrial distribution of foreign patents obtained 1992–94, and the revealed technological advantage (RTA) of these industries. The RTA is the share of patents attributable to domestic patents in a given industry, normalized by all foreign patents of the country and all foreign patents

Table 7.4
U.S. patents of Canadian firms, granted to their European subsidiaries, 1992–94

Corporation	Countries where subsidiaries located	Industry	European patents (no.)	European patents as % of total U.S. patents
Alcan Aluminium*	Germany, UK	Aluminium	24	22% (110)
BCE/Northern Telecom*	UK	Telecommun. equipment	40	17% (232)
Bombardier*	Ireland, UK	Aircraft	7	41% (17)
CCL Industries	UK	Metal products	1	7% (15)
Canstar Group	Switzerland	Other mftg	1	25% (4)
EMCO Ltd*	Austria	Metal products	4	31% (13)
Husky Injection Molding Systems*	Germany, Luxembourg	Machinery	3	9% (33)
Magna International*	Germany	Auto parts	1	7% (14)
Mitel	UK	Telecommun. equipment	1	6% (18)
Molson Companies*	Spain, UK	Chemicals	3	50% (6)
Moore Corp.*	France, UK	Business forms	7	6% (125)
Seagram*	France	Alcoholic beverages	1	100% (1)
Unican Security Systems*	Ireland, Italy	Electronics	3	60% (5)
Velan Inc.	France	Machinery	1	50% (2)
Total patents and weighted average			97	16% (595)

Source: U.S. Patent Database (Cassis).
* MNCs.

granted in the United States in the same industry. The test shows a strong negative association between the two rankings: some industries that are strong in foreign patenting (such as printing, organic chemicals, metal alloys and composites, and electronic components) are at a disadvantage in terms of domestic RTA. Conversely, several industries that are high in the RTA ranking (such as shipyards, rail transportation

Table 7.5
Patents granted in the United States to Canadian-owned and -controlled corporations operating abroad, and patents granted to Canadian inventors resident in Canada, 1992–94

Variable	No. of patents
Patents granted in Canada to resident inventors (1)	3,564
Patents granted in the USA to Canadian-owned and -controlled corporations with foreign operations, resulting from their Canadian R&D activities (2)	494
Patents granted in the USA to Canadian-owned and -controlled corporations, resulting from their R&D in the US (3)	294
Patents granted in the USA to Canadian-owned and -controlled corporations, resulting from their R&D in Europe (4)	97
Patents granted in the USA to Canadian-owned and -controlled corporations, resulting from their R&D in Japan or Australia (5)	8
Patents granted in the USA to Canadian-owned and -controlled corporations operating abroad, resulting from their foreign R&D activities, as percentage of their total U.S. patents (3)+(4)+(5)* 100/ (2)+(3)+(4)+(5)	399*100/893 = 45%
Patents granted in the USA to Canadian-owned and -controlled corporations operating abroad, resulting from their foreign R&D activities, as percentage of patents granted in Canada to Canadian residents: (3)+(4)+(5)* 100/(1)	399*100/3564 = 11%

Source: Canada, Intellectual Property Office, special compilation; U.S. Patent database (Cassis)

equipment, ammunition and explosives, water treatment, and inorganic chemicals) have no foreign patents. This finding provides evidence against one dimension of the eclectic theory – foreign activities (including R&D) do not always directly represent national comparative advantage. Firm strategies and firm-specific advantages appear key. A few companies have built competence on the basis of their national technological advantages but had built new competences beyond the original ones. This result is essentially in line with the evolutionary theory of the MNC.

CANADIAN DOMESTIC AND FOREIGN R&D ACTIVITIES COMPARED

In 1990, Canada spent some U.S.$7.400 billion on R&D inside its frontiers. This figure Canada's GERD represent the total size of Canada's domestic innovation system. Some 18 per cent of it – or

Table 7.6
Patents from foreign R&D obtained by Canadian MNCs, 1992–94

Corporation	Patents from expatriate R&D as % of total U.S. patents
Alcan Aluminium	32
BCE/Northern Telecom	27
Bata Corp.	0
Bombardier Inc.	46
CAE Inc.	17
Cascades Inc.	0
Cominco Inc.	0
Dominion Textiles	100
EMCO Ltd	100
Husky Injection Molding Systems	9
Inco Ltd.	49
McCain Foods	100
Magna International	21
Molson Companies	100
Moore Corp.	100
Noranda Inc.	8
Seagram	100
Torstar	100
Unican Security Systems	20
United Dominion Industries	100
Weston	100

Source: U.S. Patent Database (Cassis).

U.S.\$1.300 billion – was conducted by foreign companies within Canadian borders, including U.S.\$1.159 billion by American companies (National Science Foundation, 1993). In the meantime, by 1995 Canadian corporations were spending U.S.\$1.4 billion on R&D in the United States. If the ratio of 3 to 1 that we found in patents applies to foreign expenditures, Canadian companies were spending U.S.\$500

Table 7.7
Rank correlation between foreign patents and RTA of Canadian firms

Patents (1992–94)			RTA (1988–91)	
Rank	Number	Industry	Rank	Value
1	123	Printing and publishing	28	0
2	72	Telecommunication equipment	17	1.03
3	50	Machinery and metal products	9	1.35
4	39	Metal alloys and composites	21	0.71
5	27	Organic chemicals	24	0.43
6	23	Metallurgy	14	1.18
7	14	Building materials	1	3.15
8	13	Food and beverages	13	1.27
9	11	Other manufacturing	12	1.28
10	8	Aircraft and parts	18	1.02
11	5	Electronic components	27	0.26
12	5	Electronic equipment	16	1.11
13	4	Motor vehicles and parts	11	1.30
17	1	Textiles	26	0.35
17	1	Paper and cellulose	4	2.09
17	1	Biotechnology	8	1.44
17	1	Furniture	28	0
27	0	Shipyards	2	2.66
27	0	Railtransportation equipment	3	2.14
27	0	Ammunition and explosives	5	1.65
27	0	Water treatment	6	1.61
27	0	Inorganic chemicals	7	1.51
27	0	Mines	10	1.31
27	0	Pharmaceutical products	20	0.77
27	0	Electrical equipment	20	0.77
27	0	Nuclear reactors and systems	23	0.52
27	0	Computers	25	0.41

Source: U.S. Patent Database (Cassis).
Spearman's rank correlation coefficient = – 0.605.

million in overseas R&D elsewhere, mainly in western Europe and Japan. The total size of the Canadian NSI (R&D conducted anywhere in the world by Canadian factors) would then be closer to U.S.$8.000 million.

Location within the United States

Canadian FDI in the United States has historically tended to be located closer to the U.S.–Canadian frontier (McFetridge, 1994). This is less the case for the subset of Canadian-owned and -controlled innovative corporations operating in that country. The forty Canadian firms conducting R&D and obtaining patents in the United States are scattered across thirty-five states. Between 1992 and 1994, they produced patented novelties in thirteen of the sixteen border states and in twenty-two others. These thirteen border states were hosts to Canadian subsidiaries that received 134 patents between 1992 and 1994, or 45 per cent of the total. New York, Pennsylvania, Illinois, New Hampshire, West Virginia, Massachusetts, Tennessee, and South Carolina concentrated 67 per cent of the Canadian patents obtained by expatriate R&D between 1992 and 1994. The correlation coefficient between the propensity to patent in 1992–94 in a given state and the fact that the state has borders with Canada is weak ($r = 0.21$).

I have tested some variables measuring high skills and high R&D expenditures, such as total R&D expenditures by state, total patents by state, and R&D expenditures by population within each state. I also tested total state population, as a proxy for market size. All these variables (for 1991) were statistically significant as predictors of Canadian location of R&D. The best statistical relationship was between total number of patents by state and total population of the state (in each case $r = 0.51$); less significant, but still a major factor, was a state's total R&D expenditures ($r = 0.42$). These findings indicate that Canadian subsidiaries with R&D operations move closer to inventive activities, R&D funds, and larger markets. Geographical proximity to their Canadian headquarters does not seem to be a major factor.

Three of the independent variables are strongly correlated – namely, the fact of having borders with Canada, total expenditures on R&D, and total population of the state. A factorial analysis among these three variables and the dependent variable (patents), excluding one atypical observation, gives a strong $R2 = 0.35$, confirming that Canadian companies in the United States chose to situate their laboratories in large markets and innovative environments.

Table 7.8
Correlation coefficients and factorial analysis for location determinants of Canadian
R&D in the United States

Correlation coefficients

Variable	Y1	X1	X2	X3	X4
Y1	1.0000	0.2102	0.5099	0.5117	0.4221
X1	0.2102	1.0000	0.1473	0.683	0.0612
X2	0.5099	0.1473	1.0000	0.9460	0.9577
X3	0.5117	0.0683	0.9460	1.0000	0.8894
X4	0.4221	0.0612	0.9577	0.8894	1.0000

Factorial analysis
Extraction: 1 for analysis 1, principal components analysis (PC)

Variable	Initial statistics				
	Communality	Factor	Eigen value	% of var.	Cum. %
X2	1.0000	1	2.86207	95.4	95.4
X3	1.0000	2	0.11107	3.7	99.1
X4	1.0000	3	0.02687	0.9	100

Factor matrix: Factor 1
X2   0.99098
X3   0.96751
X4   0.97157

Variable	Final statistics				
	Communality	Factor	Eigen value	% of var.	Cum. %
X2	0.98204	1	2.86207	95.4	95.4
X3	0.93608				
X4	0.94395				

Varimax rotation: 1 for extraction   1 in analysis   1- Kaiser normalization
Variables:
X1 = border with Canada.
X2 = total patent of the state.
X3 = total population of the state.
X4 = total R&D expenditure of the state.
Y1 = number of patents.

Four Case Studies

Four case studies illustrate the international expansion of R&D within Canadian MNCs. The first two (Alcan Aluminum and Inco Ltd) show (Inset 11) the initial wave of Canadian multinationals, centred on natural resources and static comparative advantages. New Canadian MNCs with R&D capabilities include firms in telecommunications equipment, aircraft and aerospace, software, and biotechnology. The two largest and best known are Northern Telecom (Inset 12) and Bombardier (Inset 13).

Inset 11   Primary Metals: Alcan Aluminum and Inco Ltd

The foreign R&D activities of large Canadian MNCs started in the late 1930s with Alcan Aluminum and International Nickel (now Inco Ltd). These companies are the world's second-largest producer of aluminum and the world's largest producer of nickel, respectively. In the 1920s and 1930s both acquired subsidiaries in the United States and the United Kingdom to manufacture products and alloys from the metals that they refined in Canada; these products were thus best fitted to the main overseas markets of both companies. Foreign output included both finished products (consumer and industrial goods) and aluminum and nickel alloys. Alcan built its first laboratory in Banbury, England, in 1937 and two others in Canada during the Second World War. Before that war both companies had manufacturing subsidiaries in the United States and the United Kingdom, together with R&D laboratories. Today, these two countries are still the most important hosts of the foreign research units of both corporations. Advanced materials and specialized downstream products are the main fields of expatriate R&D in both enterprises.

Inset 12   Northern Telecom

Northern Telecom was founded in 1882 as the Canadian subsidiary of Western Electric, the manufacturing arm of AT&T. In 1956, it became a Canadian-owned and -controlled corporation, a subsidiary of Bell Canada, which supplied telephone services to 80 per cent of the Canadian market.

In 1958, Northern started conducting R&D in Canada, and from 1975 onward it did so also in the United States, through acquisition of R&D-active U.S. firms or through creation of new labs by its subsidiary BNR Inc. In 1987, it bought an interest in STC plc., and in 1992 it acquired total control, absorbing STC's plants and research laboratories in England and improving its capabilities in fibre optics and opto-electronics. By 1998, it acquired Bay Networks in the United States, for $2.4 billion. Northern had then manufacturing subsidiaries in Brazil, China, France, Ireland, Turkey, the United Kingdom, the United States, and elsewhere and re-

search facilities in Australia, Austria, Canada, China, France, Germany, India, Ireland, Japan, the United Kingdom, the United States, and Vietnam. In 1997, it was the world's fourth-largest producer of telecommunication equipment, with sales of over U.S.$18 billion. Its total expenditure on R&D in 1997 was over U.S.$2.1 billion (13.9 per cent of its total revenues). Its 80,000 employees worldwide included some 20,000 conducting R&D.
Sources: NorTel website; *Research Money*.

Inset 13   Bombardier
Bombardier invented the snowmobile in the 1930s. The company was officially founded in 1942 and launched a whole range of specialized transportation vehicles in the 1940s and 1950s. In the late 1960s, it initiated a vertical integration that led to acquisition of Rotax, the Austrian manufacturer of snowmobile engines. In the 1970s, Bombardier started making rolling equipment for railways and subways. Since 1970, it has been operating a tramway manufacturing plant in Vienna; later it started producing rolling equipment in Canada. In the 1980s, it ventured into aircraft: it took control in 1986 of Canadair, the largest Canadian manufacturer of aircraft, and later of Short Brothers (with plants in the United Kingdom and Ireland, 1989), Learjet (with U.S. plants 1990), and finally De Havilland (in 1992), the second Canadian manufacturer of aircraft.

With sales of nearly $8 billion in 1996 (50 per cent in aircraft), and some 40,000 employees, Bombardier is now one of the world's largest producers of mass-transportation equipment and the third-largest manufacturer of aircraft. It also produces advanced railway equipment for the Eurotunnel through its subsidiaries in the EU. Its Recreational Vehicle Group produces snowmobiles, personal watercraft, and other small vehicles and boats. Bombardier owns plants in Austria, Belgium, Canada, Finland, France, Germany, Ireland, Mexico, Sweden, the United Kingdom, and the United States, and it conducts innovative research in Ireland, the United Kingdom, and the United States (for aircraft) and in Canada and the United States (for other transportation equipment).
Sources: M.A. Baghai et al., *The Growth Philosophy of Bombardier*; McKinsey Report, 1997; U.S. Patent Database.

These four cases show a pattern of internationalization that is different from the Japanese. Instead of starting greenfield subsidiaries and new laboratories, Canadian companies have acquired foreign firms that already possessed in-house R&D capabilities. Most often these new subsidiaries produce complementary or downstream products related to the original Canadian goods that the expanding firm manufactures at home. Also, Canadian firms with foreign R&D capabilities are not concentrated in one area of the technological spectrum (such as high technology or natural resources) but are widely distributed across industries.

CONCLUSION

Patents granted to Canadian-owned and -controlled corporations from their expatriate R&D represent 31 per cent of all patents obtained in the United States by these firms from all sources. This figure shows a significant degree of internationalization of Canadian R&D. Most of it occurred through acquisition of foreign, wholly owned subsidiaries operating in related products.

These results confirm most of the research on Canadian MNCs (Niosi, 1985; Rugman and Verbeke, 1990; Solocha, Soskin, and Kasoff, 1990; Solocha and Soskin, 1994). Canadian MNCs tend to enter foreign production by means of acquisitions, and firm-specific advantages seem key to their success. This study shows that R&D patterns of Canadian MNCs abroad are consistent with other characteristics of Canadian FDI.

Foreign R&D activities of Canadian firms and patents originally granted to these firms abroad suggest that foreign research laboratories are not simply technology transfer units. If they were, they would be conducting minor, not patentable transformations of their basic technologies. In Walter Kuemmerle's (1997) classification, they would be knowledge-exploiting facilities. Conversely, foreign laboratories are crucial, knowledge-acquiring assets in the international competition of firms, and they bring to Canadian MNCs many valuable patented technologies.

Most of the Canadian firms conducting R&D abroad are MNCs owning proprietary technology. Their propensity to conduct R&D is much higher than that of purely domestic firms. But, contrary to the specific-assets approach, many of their specific advantages derive from their foreign operations.

Expatriate R&D activities tend to move towards large markets, large pools of talent, and friendly environments. Nevertheless, firm strategy mediates between national comparative advantage and foreign activities: only some firms have transferred abroad a typical Canadian expertise, close to national RTA; most firms that are producing patents abroad are diversifying on the basis of, but beyond, their nationally acquired competence.

The emerging evolutionary theory of the MNC goes a step further. These Canadian firms are acquiring competitors (and their R&D facilities) in areas close to their core competencies and knowledge. This strategy allows for related diversification, which tends to increase these capabilities in a gradual, progressive (thus feasible) way. This approach permits them to use efficiently their existing competencies, composed largely of expertise and tacit knowledge, and to enhance it by the acquisition of new, related knowledge. Evolutionary theory would predict that the international firm grows not only through the transfer abroad of some existing competencies but also through acquisition of related activities and competencies, in the operation of which the firm can use and enhance its accumulated capabilities.

Finally, the open-systems approach to NSIs is supported by the rapid increase of Canadian FDI in the United States and a concomitant rise of Canadian industrial R&D in that country. The following chapter sets some of the limits of this "openness," by showing that the international technology transfers between both countries are limited.

8 Canadian R&D Abroad: Management Practices

In the last ten years, the internationalization of industrial research and development has increased very rapidly. Foreign-affiliated corporations operating in the United States undertook some 9.3 per cent of all company-funded R&D in that country in 1987, and close to 18 per cent in 1995 (Dalton and Serapio, 1999). Similarly, foreign R&D expenditures by U.S.-affiliated companies abroad have more than tripled.

Canadian industrial R&D abroad has grown at a similar pace. It now includes over one hundred research facilities owned by some sixty Canadian corporations, through subsidiaries in the United States, western Europe, Japan, Australia, and several developing countries (Brazil, China, India, Mexico, and Turkey). However, little is known about the characteristics of this foreign R&D: missions, managerial practices, budgets, or innovative activity. This study is the first to present original data from a survey of these facilities, complemented by secondary material from annual reports and the financial and technical press. It follows the previous study on Canadian patents abroad (see chapter 7), which concluded that overseas diversification into related activities was the strategy of Canadian multinational corporations (MNCs) with foreign R&D activities. Like the previous one, it is based on the open system approach to NSIs, an idea that was developed jointly in the early 1990s by Niosi and other researchers (Niosi et al., 1993; Niosi and Bellon, 1994).

This chapter presents, first, a short summary of some relevant literature on the management of foreign R&D; second, the design of the study; third, the results; and fourth, a test of theories with Canadian data. It offers conclusions about the existence of three distinctive types of internationalization in Canadian R&D, each with different strategies and outcomes.

THE MANAGEMENT OF INTERNATIONAL R&D

In spite of neglect before the 1990s (Cheng and Bolon, 1993), the literature on the internationalization of R&D and the management challenges that it creates is growing quickly. This increase in writing follows the rapid expansion of foreign R&D by MNCs. This section summarizes some of the main issues in the literature.

Determinants of Centralization and Decentralization

Technology production has usually been centralized in the host country MNCs (Patel and Pavitt, 1991). Many factors dictate this pattern of behaviour: desire to reduce costs of communication and control, economies of scale in R&D, better coordination between productive facilities and R&D units, better protection of strategic technical knowledge, easier access to governments at home than in host, foreign nations, and more experience with domestic than with overseas markets in the launching of new products (Terpstra, 1977).

However, more and more corporations are creating or acquiring foreign laboratories and conducting expatriate R&D. The many reasons for this growing decentralization of R&D can be classified into three main groups – demand-side, supply-side, and environmental factors (Granstrand, Håkanson, and Sjölander, 1992). Demand-side factors include increasing the subsidiary's competitiveness through transfer of technology from the parent company (which requires at least some adaptive R&D capabilities in the former), the subsidiary's pressures to enhance its status within the corporation, greater access and sensitivity to local markets, and proximity to customers. Supply-side factors include hiring foreign highly skilled labour (usually barely mobile), increasing the inflow of ideas from dynamic markets and innovative milieux, and monitoring development of technological fields abroad. Environmental factors include a friendly regulatory legislation for intellectual property (which is key in industries such as pharmaceuticals and electronics), tax advantages, subsidies for R&D, and government pressures to improve the subsidiary's capabilities beyond the simple assembly of proven products and into innovative activities.

Classifying R&D Activities

The analysis of the functions of expatriate R&D activity has evolved, following a parallel evolution in the foreign technological activities of MNCs. The first writings emphasized adaptive R&D and technology transfer from the parent company to the subsidiary. In a landmark study on U.S. R&D overseas, Mansfield, Teece, and Romeo (1979) concluded that "the principal purpose in most, but not all, firms has been to help transfer technology abroad." At the same time, Ronstadt (1977, 1984) arrived at a similar conclusion: U.S. MNCs had established foreign R&D units to transfer and adapt their home technology to foreign markets. He found, however, an evolution of some of these technology-transfer units (TTUs) towards indigenous technology units (ITUs), developing new products for local markets. In time, however, some of these ITUs would move into more advanced activities – design of products for global markets (global-technology units, or GTUs) and generation of new ideas for the corporate parent (corporate-technology units, or CTUs). Similarly, Hewitt (1980) found that foreign R&D could be classified into three main types – adaptive, local-market oriented, and global. Like Mansfield, Ronstadt, and others, Hewitt found the first type predominant.

More recent studies emphasize the increasing role of innovation in foreign subsidiaries. Pearce (1992) insisted on the significance of locally relevant innovation: support for local manufacturing was found to be the major activity of expatriate R&D establishments. In his study of the world pharmaceutical industry, Taggart (1991, 1993) suggested that pharmaceutical MNCs are increasingly creating knowledge abroad, through what Ronstadt has called GTUs and CTUs. In the same direction, Casson and Singh (1993) have pointed out that large MNCs have in some industries, such as pharmaceutical, computers, and telecommunication equipment, created global networks of laboratories. Similarly, on the basis of an in-depth study of a sample of MNCs in four industries (chemicals, petrochemicals, telecommunications, and electronics), Chiesa (1996: 21) found increasing division of labour among central and foreign technology units, with each type "making distinctive contributions to centrally coordinated programs."

In the late 1990s, several new classifications sought to explain the activities of foreign firms (Niosi, 1999a). Most reflect increasing perception of the MNC as a learning organization more than simply a vehicle for technology transfer. Among these classifications, it is worth mentioning the dichotomy elaborated by Walter Kuemmerle (1997, 1999), who suggests that expatriate R&D activities are either knowledge-exploiting or knowledge-augmenting. His point is that the second type is on the rise, to the detriment of the former. Of course, both may overlap and coexist; his accent, however, is on the increasing importance of knowledge-creating expatriate R&D laboratories. For the purposes of an NSI, knowledge-exploiting activities are cross-border technology-transfer operations, while knowledge-augmenting activities often keep within the frontiers of the corporation, and usually abroad and away from the home country, the new knowledge produced at the expatriate laboratory.

Similarly, Ivo Zander (1999) suggested the dichotomy international duplication–international diversification. The first type of R&D is based on technology transfer; the second, on technology acquisition. Again, Zander's point is that the second type is gaining ground against the first, which involves of course some kind of knowledge transfer across borders, but where the emphasis is on foreign exploitation of foreign-acquired knowledge.

Subsidiary Autonomy versus Parent Control

Linked to these issues is the degree of autonomy of the expatriate R&D facility. Both TTUs and GTUs require some coordination and support of the expatriate laboratory from the parent company. In addition, the TTU stage requires that these be some home-country personnel in the foreign R&D establishment to monitor adaptation of technology borrowed from the parent, while the GTUs need only some expatriate top-level personnel to improve coordination with headquarters. Conversely, the corporate parents are inclined to grant more autonomy to overseas ITUs: local marketing units and expatriate production managers have a decisive say in the ideas and the choice of R&D projects when the lab's mission is to design products for foreign markets. Similarly, the unit's autonomy is greater when the overseas lab is exploring new basic ideas for future products. Also, the proportion of expatriate personnel in these two types of foreign R&D facility is expected to be smaller than in the TTU and GTU types.

National Differences in Corporate R&D Strategies

For many decades, countries have differed in the scale of their expatriate R&D (Cantwell, 1995). Large firms based in several smaller industrial countries, such as Canada, the Netherlands, Sweden, and Switzerland, conduct a large share of their total R&D abroad. The search for larger markets and larger pools of talent has probably spurred many national firms of several smaller industrial nations to develop overseas operations, including those related to technological innovation. This pattern is not general – Denmark, for example, displays much less internationalization of manufacturing and R&D than countries such as Sweden or Switzerland.

Large industrial countries have on average a smaller overseas commitment to R&D, but their propensity to conduct foreign R&D is also variable. British MNCs have major foreign R&D activities: over 50 per cent of recent patents of British firms are the result of research located abroad; conversely, Italian and Japanese firms conduct a larger share of their technological innovation at home. American, French, and German MNCs find themselves somewhere between these two poles.

These different national trajectories have been interpreted in diverse ways. Håkanson (1992) found that the heavy and early involvement of Swedish MNCs in foreign R&D was pulled by demand factors, such as market potential and market adaptation, more than by supply-related factors associated with high host-country R&D intensity or sizeable pools of highly skilled scientists and engineers. In 1988, Swedish MNCs performed most of their foreign R&D in the larger EU countries. Geographical proximity and larger markets seem major determinants for their overseas R&D activities. Similarly, Pearce (1992) found that demand factors – for both adaptation of existing products and development of new ones – were crucial in explaining foreign R&D by the world's largest MNCs. Supply-side factors (aspects of host-country technological capacity) ranked second.

An evolutionary model was suggested for the development of foreign R&D in Swedish enterprises (Håkanson, 1990). The first stage was that of the centralized hub of laboratories, with a central unit producing all the major innovations and a network of small, foreign, auxiliary R&D labs providing technical assistance in the adaptation and transfer of that technology from the parent company to the subsidiary. A second, "polycentric" stage would be that of the decentralized federation of laboratories, with a group of R&D units performing different tasks, including innovative research abroad. The final stage involves a globalized approach, with more communication and coordination organized by the parent company's labs, but more autonomy in the overseas R&D establishments.

Japanese MNCs are very different from the Swedish in terms of foreign R&D. Up to the 1980s, they were slowly expanding their overseas R&D, and they still lag behind those of other Western countries as a proportion of total R&D (Graham, 1992; Sakakibara and Westney, 1992; Okimoto and Nishi, 1994; Papanastassiou and Pierce, 1994; Odagiri and Yasuda, 1996). However, by the mid-1990s, they were rapidly increasing their overseas R&D commitments, both in absolute terms and as a share of their total R&D effort. Even if product development and product adaptation were their most important missions, Japanese labs abroad were relatively more committed to basic research than those of other countries. Japan's catching-up period is now over, and its corporations need to produce their own radical innovations in order to compete in Western markets. Interaction with Western science is now essential for their long-term competitiveness. In this direction, Sakakibara and Westney (1992) suggested that Japanese R&D abroad has evolved through five stages: first, technology scanning (by small units collecting scientific and technical information abroad for usc by the corporate parent in Japan); second, technology-transfer units; third, technical cooperation units for adaptation of products with host-country suppliers and customers; fourth, local product-development units; and fifth, basic-research units (or addition of basic-research missions to existing foreign R&D facilities).

DESIGN OF THE STUDY

Fragmentary evidence showed that Canadian R&D abroad was substantial (Dalton and Serapio, Jr, 1995). By 1995, in the United States alone, affiliates of Canadian corporations spent some U.S.$1.4 billion and employed over six thousand persons in R&D (Dalton and Serapio Jr., forthcoming). Some well-known Canadian MNCs, such as Alcan, Inco, Moore, Northern Telecom, and Seagram, also conducted R&D in western Europe, Australia, and/or Japan. In the 1992–94 period, nearly 40 per cent of the patents of Canadian MNCs were obtained as a result of their expatriate R&D (chapter 7). The management practices of these research activities were, however, totally unknown by Canadian scholars.

At the end of 1995, I established the population of Canadian subsidiaries with foreign R&D capabilities through several sources. I included all foreign subsidiaries patenting abroad the results of their own research; there were forty-six of these. Also included were the overseas subsidiaries of Canadian companies listed in the *Directory of American Research and Technology 1995* (Bowkker, 1995) – there were twenty-one firms with thirty-nine research labs. Among these twenty-one companies, fourteen were already identified as having patented in the United States in 1992 or later; this source thus added seven new firms. Finally, some eight other corporations with subsidiaries abroad were identified through other sources, such as the financial press, annual reports, and technical publications.

The population of Canadian firms with foreign subsidiaries conducting R&D is changing constantly. In early 1996, Ottawa-based telecommunications-equipment producer Mitel bought the integrated circuit maker ABB Hafo A.B., based in Sweden, from Asea Brown Boveri. In 1995, the world leader of flight simulators, Montreal-based CAE Inc., sold its American subsidiary Link Corp., with substantial R&D activities in the United States. Several new subsidiaries could not be included in the study, as the future organization of their R&D activities was probably still undecided and their present R&D layout depended on their previous owner. Also, several R&D facilities of Canadian companies that were recently sold to foreign interests had to be left out.

I sent questionnaires to the research-active subsidiaries of some sixty Canadian corporations, mostly in the United States (fifty-six), but some in western Europe (fifteen, but twelve of them also active in the United States), Japan (three, all of them active in the United States), and Australia (three, including two already active in the United States). Some of these subsidiaries responded that they had recently been sold to firms of other nationalities. Six explicitly declined to participate, and a few questionnaires were returned because of addresses having changed. In all, twenty-two questionnaires were returned fully completed (including a few filled out personally by the principal investigator), representing eighteen different corporations. (The R&D-active foreign subsidiaries of a large Canadian corporation filled out four questionnaires, and the foreign R&D units of another one completed two).

Most (forty-eight) of these sixty corporations were large, including almost all the large Canadian MNCs. The other twelve were small and medium-sized enterprises (SMEs). Our sample included the foreign R&D units of sixteen large and two medium-sized corporations (with fewer than five hundred employees, but over two hundred and fifty worldwide).

The questionnaire included twenty-four questions (with some sixty variables) covering personnel, budgets (amounts and origins), areas of R&D, circumstances under which R&D activities started, missions, reasons for overseas activities, origins of R&D projects, difficulties and role and importance of Canadian parent companies and expatriate managers.

The final sample included twenty-two questionnaires from eighteen Canadian-owned and -controlled firms, including thirteen laboratories from the United States, five from the United Kingdom, three from Germany, and one from China. This small sample represents the underlying population approximately in terms of both geographical distribution of expatriate R&D units and size of corporations with overseas R&D.

The eighteen Canadian enterprises included six active in the production of electronic hardware and software, three machinery manufacturers and metal producers, two chemical companies, one biotechnology producer, one printing firm, one pulp and paper company, and two other manufacturing industries.

CANADIAN LABORATORIES ABROAD

This section presents some of the most important results of the survey, with an emphasis on the similarities of the twenty-two Canadian-owned R&D facilities abroad.

Origins

A majority of the foreign subsidiaries had been acquired by the Canadian corporation while they were already in operation, confirming the Canadian tendency to conduct foreign direct investment via acquisition instead of greenfield investments (Solocha, Soskin, and Kasoff, 1990; Solocha and Soskin, 1994). In five cases out of twenty-two (23 per cent), the foreign subsidiaries had been founded by the Canadian parent firm.

Most often, the R&D activities of the foreign subsidiaries had started before Canadian acquisition. This was the case in twelve subsidiaries (55 per cent). In five other cases, R&D activities started after acquisition. In the five remaining cases, R&D started with the founding of the subsidiary by the Canadian firm.

Position within MNCs

Seven of eighteen Canadian corporations (or 39 per cent) had their central R&D laboratories abroad. In four cases, the enterprises had no R&D activity whatsoever in Canada. In three others, the corporation conducted R&D abroad for a specific type of product or process, while they undertook parallel R&D in Canada on a separate list of products or processes. Two of the four companies conducting R&D exclusively in the United States – and not in Canada – were medium-sized firms (fewer than five hundred employees worldwide). For the remaining eleven companies (50 per cent), foreign laboratories were divisional units with specific local and/or global mandates for the line of products developed overseas. Their main R&D activities were, however, located in Canada.

Number of Countries

On average, each corporation performed R&D in three countries, but when a large MNC with research facilities in eight nations was subtracted, the result boiled down to 2.5 countries, including Canada.

Fourteen corporations (of eighteen) conducted R&D in Canada; also, fourteen did so in the United States, and ten in one or more countries of western Europe – seven in the United Kingdom, four in Germany, two in France, and one each in Ireland, Italy, Luxembourg, and Switzerland. Also, R&D was conducted in Japan (by two Canadian corporations) and Australia (by another one).

There were also a few R&D establishments in several developing countries – two in India and one each in Brazil, China, Mexico, and Turkey (see Table 8.1). In all, the corporations in our sample were active in sixteen countries (five developing and eleven developed), including Canada.

Organization

A majority (twelve of twenty-two) of the foreign R&D facilities were conducting permanent in-house research programs, and three were undertaking R&D programs with outside partners in the laboratories of the latter. Another 25 per cent (six of twenty-two) were regularly conducting R&D, but on an ad hoc basis; they started R&D activities to develop a new product (for example, a new machine) or to improve an existing one and substantially reduced them once the product was in the market. Adaptation of the product to different customers or product improvement and refinement sustained a permanent but variable level of R&D. One Canadian corporation had an independent R&D subsidiary abroad, devoted entirely to R&D, but in all the other cases manufacturing accompanied research. This evidence points again to foreign R&D as being closely related to overseas manufacturing.

Size of Foreign R&D Establishments

In 1992, the average total number of personnel employed in the R&D overseas facility was 112; in 1995 it was 126. By 1995, the R&D facilities in the sample represented in all close to twenty-eight hundred R&D employees, of whom over twenty-two hundred were scientists and engineers. Few changes occurred within the sample in the 1992–95 period. four corporations increased and two decreased the number of employees in their foreign R&D, and in 1994, one smaller firm started R&D in the United States, and one larger corporation launched R&D activities in China.

In 1995, the ad hoc R&D units employed on average eight persons; in the more permanent facilities, the average was 170. However, in companies with ad hoc R&D, all staff members were devoted to this

Table 8.1
Geographical distribution of foreign R&D activities in the sample

Countries where R&D conducted	No. of labs
Canada	14
United States	14
Western Europe	
United Kingdom	7
Germany	4
France	2
Ireland	1
Italy	1
Luxembourg	1
Switzerland	1
Total	(17)
Japan	2
Australia	1
Developing countries	
India	2
Brazil	1
China	1
Mexico	1
Turkey	1
Total	(6)

activity, while in the permanent facilities, the average number of scientific and technical personnel was only 128; the remaining 25 per cent of employees consisted of supporting, mostly clerical staff.

MANAGERIAL PRACTICES

Missions

The conduct of commercial and pre-commercial R&D and product development were the most important activities of the foreign subsidiaries. Commercial applied R&D was the most frequent endeavour: twelve companies designated it as the single most important R&D activity, and all but three of the twenty-two R&D units were active in this area. Product development in the same industries as in Canada was the second choice: nine companies mentioned it as being the most important, and eight as an important, activity. Pre-commercial applied research followed – fourteen subsidiaries conducted it, including two that had it as their most important mission, and seven cited it as important.

Other notable activities were support to the parent company's marketing efforts in the host country (important or the most important for eleven companies), development into new or related industries (six firms), providing technical assistance to the parent company (five), and supporting the parent company's technology transfer from Canada to the host country (five). The less crucial missions were those of providing technological assistance to external firms and organizations (two) or to governments (two), basic research (one), and other (one) (see Table 8.2). Only four subsidiaries were transferring any technology back to Canada, and five were transferring it to other local subsidiaries of the Canadian company.

In sum, Canadian R&D units abroad are supporting local manufacturing in the host countries through innovative activities such as commercial and pre-commercial R&D, together with product and process development. This finding supports the demand-side explanations and tends to contradict the older hypothesis of technology transfer and adaptation of home technology to the host country as principal activities of the expatriate R&D laboratory.

In the same vein, foreign subsidiaries were targeting both global and local markets for those new or improved products. Most (82 per cent) expatriate laboratories were targeting the world market, and eighteen (77 per cent) were also aiming at the local market. A group of ten subsidiaries (46 per cent) designed products to be manufactured abroad and sold in the Canadian market. In Ronstadt's classification, Canadian R&D abroad is composed mostly of units with both local and global mandates.

Reasons

The reasons given for the establishment, acquisition, or continuation of foreign R&D operations were many and were consistent with the above-mentioned missions, as well as with the patent study. The questionnaire presented a list with multiple choices, with four main groups of determinants proposed – demand (D), supply (S), technology transfer from home country (TT), and environmental (i.e., public policy), factors (E) (see Table 8.3).

First, demand-side (D) determinants *stricto sensu* appeared to be the most important. Also, they were linked with one another: the Canadian corporation was moving closer to customers and markets, responding to the demands of its foreign subsidiary, and/or support-

Table 8.2
Missions of overseas R&D laboratories

Mission	Most important	Important	Of little importance	Not a mission
1 Commercial applied R&D	12	5	2	3
2 Development in same industry as in Canada	9	8	1	4
3 Pre-commercial applied research	2	7	5	8
4 Support parent company's marketing efforts in host country	3	8	0	11
5 Development into new or related industries	0	6	5	11
6 Technical assistance to parent company	1	4	3	14
7 Support parent company's technology transfer from Canada	1	4	3	14
8 Technical assistance to industry	0	2	3	17
9 Technology transfer to government	1	1	2	18
10 Basic research	1	0	2	19
11 Technology transfer to industry	0	0	4	18
12 Other	1	0	0	21

Note: Multiple-choice question.

ing local manufacturing. All these reasons indicate that R&D was re-lated above all to the productive operations of the Canadian company abroad.

Second, other factors point towards the supply of technology (s) and are also inter-related – increasing the inflow of new ideas, re-cruiting highly skilled personnel, and monitoring technical fields abroad. They indicate that corporations seek innovative milieux in order to learn – another conclusion of the preceding chapter con-cerning location factors in the United States. Also, some 50 per cent of the Canadian firms conducting R&D in western Europe and over 60 per cent of those active in the United States pointed to these sup-ply-related reasons.

Table 8.3
Reasons for establishing R&D abroad

Reason	Average score*	No. of times mentioned as important †
Proximity to customers, makets (D)	3.8	18
Responding to demands of foreign subsidiary (D)	3.3	15
Supporting local manufacturing (D)	3.0	14
Recruiting highly skilled personnel (S)	2.1	11
Monitoring technical fields abroad (S)	2.1	11
Increasing inflow of new ideas (S)	2.0	10
Adaptation of Canadian products to local market (TT)	2.0	9
Facilitating technology transfer to host country (TT)	2.0	9
Responding to the demands of host governments (E)	1.8	11
Cost factors (wages, taxes, etc.) (S/E)	1.8	8
Proximity to suppliers (S)	1.6	8
Cooperation in local R&D projects (S)	1.3	5
Tax advantages/subsidies for R&D (E)	1	4
Difficulties in closing down R&D in acquired firms (F)	0.9	3
Other	0.7	1

* Scores: 5 = extremely important; 4 = very important; 3 = important; 2 = somewhat important;
1 = of little importance; 0 = unimportant.
† Scores of 3 and over.

Third, the next group of reasons related to technology transfer (TT) from Canada. Six of the eight R&D facilities in Europe (75 per cent) pointed to them as important, as well as one in the United States (8 per cent) and one in China – our only response from a developing country. Canadian companies, particularly in high technology, seem to benefit from some kind of technology gap vis-à-vis western Europe, which does not manifest itself vis-à-vis the United States. Technology transfer appears important then in the European questionnaires, but not in those originating from the United States did so.

Western European governments seemed more eager to request local R&D from Canadian corporations: 75 per cent (six of eight) of the R&D units operating in Europe considered the demands of their host governments as major location factors, but only 38 per cent (five of thirteen) of Canadian R&D facilities in the United States did so.

Fourth, environmental cost factors (E) followed, including wages, taxes, and subsidies for R&D. However, they were less significant determinants for establishing foreign R&D facilities; some executives even indicated that Canada was, in terms of R&D costs, more convenient than the United States or western Europe. Also, there was no difference between western Europe and the United States in terms of R&D costs.

These findings fit with a major result of the previous chapter: Canadian subsidiaries tend to locate themselves in the most populous U.S. states, in large countries, and in those with most substantial innovative infrastructure. The main goals of their foreign operations are markets and sales; R&D supports these sales. Technically based supply factors are second: ideas and highly skilled personnel attract Canadian firms to the United States and western Europe.

Host governments are less significant, both as demanders of R&D activities in foreign subsidiaries and, of course, as purveyors of the tax advantages and subsidies that a majority of the companies consider major incentives to conducting R&D. If the first group of factors points to market factors, this group relates to (less critical) public policy determinants.

Inputs

The average budget of the foreign R&D facility was constantly increasing, from $13 million in 1992 to $25 million in 1995. Except in two cases, it was growing in every R&D unit. However, the dispersion was considerable: 1995 budgets, for instance, ranged between $120 million (highest value) and $0.3 million (lowest). The medians were $1 million in 1992 and $2 million in 1995. R&D budgets represented, on average, some 4.2 percent of sales, reflecting the role of high-tech industries among those with expatriate R&D labs.

Most often, these budgets came from the internal resources of the subsidiary: in eighteen cases this was the first and usually the only source of funds for R&D. Transfer for the parent company in Canada was the second largest source: in two instances it was the principal origin of funds, and in one it provided 50 per cent of R&D money. In one case, R&D contracts from external firms provided 50 per cent of the funds. Local or home-country governments, fellow companies within the MNC, and other sources were not important.

Budgets corresponded to the explicit missions of the labs. They were allocated most often to commercially applied R&D (seventeen labs), development (seventeen), technical assistance to the subsidiary (thirteen), and pre-commercial applied research (eleven). For the whole sample, these four missions received over 90 per cent of budget allocations. All other destinations were by far less important (Table 8.4).

Table 8.4
Budget allocation in laboratories, by mission

Mission	Number of firms allocating funds	Average budget devoted to mission (%)
Commercial applied R&D	17	38
Development	17	39
Technical assistance to local subsidiary	13	9
Pre-commercial applied research	11	8
Basic research	5	4
Technical assistance to outside organizations	5	1
Technology transfer to government or firms	5	1
Other	1	n*
Total		100

* n = negligible.

Table 8.5
Types of R&D establishment and main R&D activity, as perbudget

	Mean	Standard deviation	Cases
*Commercially applied research**			
Permanent in-house R&D laboratories	26.25	26.72	12
Other R&D organizations	51.00	42.02	10
Within group total	37.5	34.46	22
Development†			
Permanent in-house R&D laboratories	53.50	29.27	12
Other R&D organizations	22.00	31.55	10
Within groups total	39.18	30.32	22

* $F = 2.8141$; d.f. = 1; significance = 0.1090.
† $F = 5.8871$; d.f. = 1; significance = 0.0248.

However, the two most important missions were unequally supported among the permanent in-house R&D labs versus the other types of R&D units (ad hoc R&D groups, R&D subsidiaries, and the like). The former devoted, on average, 53.5 per cent of their budgets to development, and other types of units, only 22 per cent; conversely, permanent in-house R&D labs devoted only 26.3 per cent of budgets to commercially applied R&D, as against other types of units, at 51 per cent (Table 8.5).

Outputs

These foreign R&D activities were producing different types of outputs. On the whole, the products were consistent with missions and reasons for going abroad, as well as budget-allocation figures (Table 8.6). Prototype devices, pilot plants, and materials were the principal output in a majority of overseas R&D facilities (82 per cent of them were producing them, and nearly half of the budgets was spent in this area); algorithms and software were second in terms of budgets (20 per cent), but only ten companies (mainly in electronics and machinery) were producing them; internal reports (55 per cent of the foreign units, consuming 15 per cent of the budgets) and other outputs followed.

Patents did not represent a major type of output for any R&D unit. In fact, during the four years for which patent information was requested, four units obtained none at all. For the remainder, the average number of patents per year was 1.7. The R&D unit with the most patents had been granted some twenty of them, for the period 1992–94; on the opposite side of the distribution, four companies had obtained only one patent in four years. The subsidiaries with the most patenting were active in chemical and composite materials R&D; those with none operated in machinery and telecommunication equipment. This finding confirms a well-known finding by Winter (1989): industries differ in their use of patents to protect intellectual property.

Patents were, more often than not, the property of the foreign subsidiary: in thirteen cases out of twenty-two (59 per cent) intellectual property stemming from expatriate R&D was granted to the overseas affiliate: intellectual property was so closely connected to the other assets of the subsidiary that it had little value for the Canadian parent company. In only three cases was the controlling corporation in Canada the owner; in two other instances, the owner of the patents was a foreign affiliate of the MNC (not incorporated in Canada). The remaining subsidiaries had requested no patents.

Finally, licences were almost non-existent: only two companies had licensed any technology to outside organizations. One company mentioned using patents as a "war chest," in order to obtain other companies' technologies through cross-licensing. On the whole, however, these foreign R&D units (like the Canadian laboratories studied in chapter 4) produced technology for their own use in manufacturing, not for sale or licensing as such.

Table 8.6
Outputs of foreign R&D

Output	Units mentioning (% of total)	Average share of outputs (%)
Prototype devices and materials	18 (82%)	47
Internal reports	12 (55%)	11
Algorithms and software	10 (45%)	22
Patents and licences	9 (41%)	4
Papers for presentations	11 (50%)	4
Demonstration of devices	10 (45%)	5
Publication	4 (18%)	1
Other	2 (9%)	3
Total	22 (100%)	100

Note: Multiple-choice question.

All these figures are consistent with a picture of fairly independent Canadian subsidiaries abroad conducting R&D to support local manufacturing, including locating technological activities closer to markets, customers, and suppliers. As a result of this R&D's being beneficial to the subsidiaries (and exploited by them), intellectual property in them was also allocated to the foreign affiliate.

Links with the Parent Company

Foreign R&D units of Canadian corporations were quite autonomous from their Canadian headquarters. First, local personnel run them. Canadian citizens represented only 4 per cent, on average, of R&D managers; twelve of the R&D facilities (55 per cent) had no Canadian manager at all, and only one had 30 per cent (highest figure) of Canadian citizens among its top R&D officers. These figures contradict the hypothesis of foreign laboratories being used for technology transfer.

Second, the foreign units also enjoyed a high level of autonomy vis-à-vis the Canadian parents in project approval and selection (Table 8.7). The most common situation (fourteen of twenty-two cases. or 64 per cent) was that they submitted only major R&D projects for approval to the Canadian parent company. In only two cases did the Canadian head office exclusively determine the R&D projects of the affiliate, but in some instances no project was ever submitted to the overseas parent.

Table 8.7
How R&D projects are determined

Determination of R&D projects	R&D units using practice	R&D units using this practice exclusively
Only major projects are submitted to Canadian headquarters for approval.	14	5
R&D projects are designed by subsidiary and submitted for approval to Canadian headquarters.	11	4
No project is submitted to the Canadian parent company.	8	4
R&D projects are determined by the Canadian parent company.	5	2
Other	1	1

Note: Multiple-choice question.

Third, ideas and initiatives for R&D projects came most often from local customers, and from local production and marketing units, as well as from foreign customers' production and marketing units (Table 8.8). This finding is consistent with Canadian subsidiaries' conducting R&D for local and world markets. Parent companies were seldom a major source of projects.

Initiatives sometimes came from local collaborative firms, and less frequently from local universities or public laboratories and from production units located in third countries. Looking for foreign skills and university ideas seems a minor consideration for Canadian companies conducting R&D abroad. Conversely, the data confirm the picture of local subsidiaries solidly linked to the local and world customers and markets that they serve, from which they gather useful ideas and initiatives for R&D projects.

Most subsidiaries experienced difficulties. Only five declared no problems in operations (Table 8.9). Most difficulties were of the "transaction cost" type; coordination with Canadian headquarters and technology transfer from Canada were the most important. The small size of the expatriate R&D unit was the most widespread problem.

These findings are consistent with the existing literature on Canadian MNCs and with the previous chapter on overseas R&D by Canadian firms. Acquisition was the preferred mode of entry into foreign markets and usually into foreign R&D. Often the acquired firm already possessed R&D facilities. The mission of these foreign laboratories was

Table 8.8
Origin of R&D initiatives

Origin of initiatives	R&D units using source	R&D units using as major source
Local customers	21	20
Local marketing units	17	14
Foreign customers	19	10
Local production units	18	13
Foreign marketing units	13	9
Foreign production units	13	6
Parent company	11	3
Local collaborative research with firms	11	4
Local university, public laboratory	7	1
Other (market intelligence)	2	2

Note: Multiple-choice question.

Table 8.9
Difficulties of foreign R&D units

Difficulty	Times mentioned (% of units)	Average importance (all firms)	Average importance*
Small size of R&D unit	14 (64%)	2,5	3,8
Coordination with Canadian parent	10 (45%)	2,1	4,7
Technology transfer from Canada	8 (36%)	1,5	4,1
Other	2 (9%)	0,3	3,5

* Among units having indicated the difficulty.

commercial R&D and development either in the same industry as in Canada or in related ones. Demand factors were key to explaining foreign R&D – the need to be closer to larger local and international markets and customers and responding to the demands of the overseas subsidiary. As in the Swedish case, supply factors came second, with the recruitment of host-country, highly skilled personnel crucial. Environmental factors were much less important, Canada being a competitive country in terms of R&D costs, tax credits, and other advantages. Six companies had central labs abroad. Four had no R&D in Canada at all. The median company had R&D facilities in 2.5 countries, typically the United States and Canada, but in some cases the United States and the United Kingdom or another western European country.

These expatriate R&D units were fairly autonomous: their budgets came most often from internal revenues of the subsidiary, their managers were most commonly local residents and most research initiatives and decisions were local. They had received mandates to develop products for both the local and the global markets.

THREE MODELS

The section above has emphasized the similarities among Canadian laboratories abroad. In the present section, I differentiate among three types of expatriate laboratories. The first group corresponds to the strategy of related diversification (Table 8.10). Typically, these manufacture specialized machinery, transportation equipment, or metal products and own R&D facilities for different types of related products. Thirteen MNCs can be classified under this model. More than half of them use ad hoc R&D groups that are constantly being renewed, with the others using either permanent R&D labs or R&D subsidiaries. Their average size is around twenty-eight full-time employees. Each facility has a global mandate and creates new or improved products in its specific line of business. These overseas R&D units develop products for both the local and the global (including the Canadian) markets, and they thus exhibit some of the characteristics of both the ITUs and the GTUs of Ronstadt's typology. Their mission does not include assisting foreign governments, supporting technology transfer from Canada, or assisting the Canadian parent in marketing. Their autonomy, from a technological point of view, is great, in terms of personnel (almost no Canadian managers) and project management: typically, Canadian parents were never behind the initiative or the determination of R&D projects. Also, the R&D budgets came entirely from the revenues of the subsidiary. The units' most important outputs are prototype devices and materials.

The second type of overseas R&D is that of the internationally vertically integrated firm (Table 8.11). These MNCs were typically metal producers and forest products and chemical companies conducting primary-metals or basic-chemicals process R&D in Canada and R&D on advanced materials abroad, closer to the main markets for these types of products. The R&D establishments have typically been acquired with the subsidiary. Autonomy was substantial, but somewhat less than in the previous group: the Canadian parent initiated or determined some R&D projects, some budgets came from parent or sister companies,

Table 8.10
Related diversifiers

Characteristic	Pearson correlation
They most often conduct R&D on an ad hoc basis.	0.10746
R&D existed in subsidiary before acquisition.	0.07543
Technology transfer to government is not a mission,	0.05206
nor is supporting parent marketing activities,	0.00705
nor is supporting technology transfer from Canada.	0.01460
They develop products for the local markets,	0.10648
but seldom for the Canadian markets.	0.02018
Initiatives for R&D seldom come from parent,	0.04908
from local universities or public labs in host country,	0.02708
but sometimes from foreign marketing units.	0.06728
They typically have fewer than thirty full-time R&D employees.	0.01245
No R&D funding comes from parent company,	0.08380
but 99% of R&D budget comes from internal resources of the subsidiary (sales).	0.01240
Their most important output is prototype devices and materials (66%).	0.00930
Canadian managers represent only 2% of R&D staff.	0.00280

and, on average, 2 per cent of their R&D managers were Canadian expatriates. Their main source of R&D funds was sales by the subsidiary (where 72 per cent of budgets originated). Outputs were typically internal reports and prototypes.

Finally, there was only one case of a truly global R&D strategy (close to Ronstadt's GTU), where the company conducted R&D in different countries on various related and compatible types of electronic equipment (Table 8.12). Missions included technology transfer from Canada and supporting export marketing by the Canadian parent. Here, international coordination and communication were key, with the parent more closely supervising activities of the network of foreign labs. A larger proportion of the R&D budget (close to 38 per cent) came from parent or sister companies. Over 13 per cent of R&D managers were Canadian citizens. The Canadian parent was usually a major source of ideas and initiatives for R&D projects. These affiliates had typically been founded by the parent company, instead of being acquired from third parties while already in operation. They were large R&D laboratories, with hundreds of employees. Algorithms and software were major outputs.

Table 8.11
Vertically integrated firms

Characteristic	Pearson correlation
They more often have R&D laboratories than other R&D units.	0.10746
R&D existed in subsidiary before acquisition.	0.07543
Technology transfer to government has little importance,	0.05206
but supporting parent's marketing efforts is key,	0.00705
and they support technology transfer from Canada.	0.01460
They develop products for the local markets	0.10648
and for Canadian markets.	0.02018
Initiatives for R&D sometimes come from parent	0.04908
and from local universities and public labs in host,	0.02708
but often from foreign marketing units.	0.06728
They typically have over 45 employees in R&D.	0.01245
On average 20% of their budget comes from parent company,	0.08380
but 72% of budget comes from internal resources of subsidiary (sales).	0.01240
Their most important output are technical reports (34%) and prototypes (32%).	0.00930
Canadian managers represent only 1% of R&D staff	0.00280

Compared to the industrial research facilities of other countries, Canadian overseas R&D seems less global and more bi-national (typically oriented to the United Kingdom, the United States, or both). Few corporations have research subsidiaries in other countries. This observation recalls the "cultural proximity" factor that has appeared in some literature on overseas R&D: corporations tend to locate their foreign R&D facilities in countries with some cultural – basically linguistic and/or legal – affinity. Geographical and cultural proximity thus seems important in explaining the location of Canadian R&D abroad.

Also, Canadian R&D abroad centres more on commercial R&D and development for local and world markets, and less on basic research or technology transfer from Canada or towards Canada. The literature on foreign R&D units as listening posts for transferring back to the home country ideas produced abroad does not apply to the Canadian MNCs.

Table 8.12
The global corporation

Characteristic	Pearson correlation
They only type of R&D organization abroad is R&D labs.	0.10746
R&D is created with foreign subsidiary.	0.07543
Technology transfer to governments has little importance,	0.05206
but supporting parent's marketing efforts is key,	0.00705
and it supports technology transfer from Canada.	0.01460
It develops products for local markets	0.10648
and for Canadian markets.	0.02018
Initiatives for R&D often come from parent,	0.04908
occasionally from local universities and public labs in host countries,	0.02708
and often from foreign marketing units.	0.06728
Labs typically have over 100 employees in R&D.	0.01245
Close to 38% of budget comes from parent,	0.08380
and only 44% comes from internal resources of the subsidiary (sales).	0.01240
The most important output (68%) is algorithms and software.	0.00070
Canadian managers represent over 13% of staff.	0.00280

CONCLUSION

There are some sixty Canadian-owned and -controlled firms conduct
ing foreign R&D. Their subsidiaries are fairly decentralized and autonomous, and they are looking for dynamic markets and innovative
milieux. These milieux are not often universities or public laboratories, but more usually innovative private customers and suppliers.
This study confirms some aspects of the existing literature on Canadian MNCs – the role of acquisition as a method for conducting FDI,
and for starting foreign R&D. This chapter also adds new dimensions
to our knowledge of Canadian MNCs. Expatriate R&D facilities of
Canadian-owned and -controlled corporations differed markedly
from Japanese foreign labs, in that they were conducting principally
commercial and pre-commercial applied R&D, and seldom any basic
research. Technology transfer to Canada was a minor mission of a few
labs, and only one-third of them received any technology from the
Canadian parent.

This chapter finds some similarities between Canadian and Swedish MNCs. In both countries expatriate R&D by large MNCs is important, and demand-side factors are key: the search for larger markets and customers and pressures from the local subsidiaries are the main explanatory factors. Supply-side factors (recruitment of skilled personnel, monitoring of technical development abroad, and inflow of new ideas into the company) came second. The MNCs of both countries also follow a strategy of related diversification and are seldom full-fledged conglomerates. Both Canada and Sweden are smaller industrial nations with restricted internal markets, similar resource endowments, and a highly skilled population. Both countries belong to the same historical wave of industrialization, in the last decades of the nineteenth century. However, Canadian R&D abroad started later than Swedish, mostly after 1945. Also, this study confirms Pearce's findings about the relative importance of demand factors over supply-side ones in expatriate R&D (Pearce, 1992).

Our study shows some differences from Ronstadt's evolutionary model: TTUs with adaptive missions, and corporate technology units with a strong basic-research mandate, were non-existent, except for a Chinese TTU. Canadian foreign subsidiaries with R&D capabilities had product mandates for both the local and the global markets, making them akin to both indigenous and global technology units in Ronstadt's classification. However, global mandates arrive early in the evolution of the expatriate R&D units of Canadian MNCs, not as the result of a long process with several stages, as suggested by Ronstadt.

These large MNCs show less central coordination and control than were found in previous studies (Chiesa, 1996). Foreign R&D by Canadian corporations is fairly autonomous. Only one large Canadian MNC shows a similar degree of internal coordination to that found by these studies within a global R&D program orchestrated by the parent company. There is, however, a marked division of labour between the Canadian central laboratory and the foreign R&D units. Compared to Chiesa's vertically integrated firms, Canadian ones are, on average, less hierarchical, with major influences coming from overseas subsidiaries and markets.

Users and customers are major sources of R&D ideas and initiatives in international corporations. Foreign markets and foreign customers may well increasingly be the initiators of new products and processes. Some of the ideas on customers as suppliers of ideas (von Hippel, 1988) and on learning by using (Rosenberg, 1982) may well prove useful in the analysis of international R&D operations of national firms.

In the previous chapter, I found that Canadian companies with foreign R&D were following a strategy of related diversification. We can now split them into three groups, according to the degree of techno-logical autonomy of their subsidiaries. First, companies with a strategy of related diversification are in the majority. They allow the highest level of autonomy to their subsidiaries: managers in these are local residents, R&D budgets originate in internal revenues, and project ini-tiatives are locally made, inspired by local and foreign markets. From this decentralized model, problems of R&D coordination and commu-nication between the Canadian parent and the foreign subsidiary were absent. This looks pretty much like the decentralized federation (stage II) in Håkanson's (1990) evolutionary model.

Second, the vertically integrated MNCs are somewhere in the mid-dle: some of their research managers are Canadians, and some initia-tives for R&D projects come from the Canadian parent, which provides some funds for R&D to the foreign subsidiary. A few coordination and communication problems surfaced between the parent and the R&D unit. This type of international network does not resemble any type of structure that other studies have found.

Third and finally, only one truly global MNC appeared, with a coor-dinated world R&D program. In this MNC, the parent company often contributed to the research budgets of the subsidiaries and usually had a say in the initiative and the final determination of R&D projects. Canadian managers were more numerous in the top layer of the sub-sidiary's R&D organization. Many of the problems and characteristics ascribed to global networks within MNCs in the earlier literature (Håkanson, 1990; Chiesa, 1996) appeared in this case.

The degree of autonomy of expatriate R&D units thus depends on the allocation of corporate activities across countries. Related diversi-fication with different products located in various countries results in R&D establishments abroad that are fairly autonomous. Vertical inte-gration through borders requires a somewhat higher degree of coor-dination and technology transfer among units. A global network of R&D labs is much more constraining, requiring higher levels of coor-dination and international flows of R&D personnel, budgets, technol-ogy, and initiatives from the parent company to its foreign R&D laboratories.

This study tends also to validate the dichotomies produced by both Kuemmerle and Zander: international diversification and knowledge-augmenting activities are on the rise, while pure international duplica-tion and knowledge-exploiting expatriate R&D seems less important.

Canadian "knowledge borders" do not seem to be strongly affected by large inward or outward transfers of technology by these MNCs, which acquire foreign subsidiaries in order to exploit foreign markets in related areas and produce abroad most of the technology needed by their foreign affiliates. Again, this chapter tends to confirm the open-system approach to NSIs, based on general systems theory, rather than the existence of a North American system of innovation. Canadian MNCs are looking for larger markets and innovative ideas from foreign suppliers and customers, but they are not often modifying their Canadian activities because of these inputs. Rather, they are exploiting new opportunities abroad, through incorporation of new lines of products.

9 Conclusion: Canada's NSI Today

In the postwar period, Canada, on the basis of its vast natural resources, and despite its small domestic market, has built a national system of innovation (NSI) borrowing institutions and policies from both the United States and western Europe and importing basic technology from the same places. This mix of institutional imitation and a specific economic and political restructuring has endowed Canada's NSI with its own particular characteristics. More interesting and relevant for developing countries in the future, Canada created its NSI while keeping its economy open, both to trade and to investment, and maintaining a stable macroeconomic foundation, thus building institutions without violating the rules of what is usually considered good government policy today.

A period of governmental trial and error and public learning started with the Second World War, about how to stimulate innovation. During five decades (1940–90), the Canadian government increased its involvement in innovation, adding horizontal policies nurturing the development of private R&D and evaluating and redirecting some of them when it considered that the attended results were not attained. At the same time, it targeted a few specific sectors – emerging industries such as nuclear energy, aerospace, telecommunication, biotechnology, and software – and launched a set of specific policies, including creation of government laboratories and parallel, specialized programs, to foster their growth. Finally, by the 1990s, the NSI was established and its present contours were in place. Under budgetary and international trade policy restrictions, Ottawa's efforts receded somewhat, and the NSI operated alone, like a plane flying on automatic pilot after an energy-intensive take-off. The new routines were now well entrenched in industry, government laboratories, and universities, and these needed only horizontal policies to keep incentives operative, while more direct technology policies almost disappeared.

THE RISE OF CANADA'S NSI

In chapter 2, it appeared that the first set of government measures, evolving from Confederation to 1939, aimed essentially at complementing weak private R&D with government laboratories and university research. These were providing public-good knowledge for farmers, mining companies, and other private firms, mostly transforming natural resources (such as oil and gas, chemicals, pulp and paper, and metals). During the 1930s, the federal government slowly adopted a more active approach in science and technology. At the end of the decade, government laboratories (both federal and provincial) consumed only one-quarter of Canada's very modest R&D expenditures. University research, mostly funded by the National Research Council, represented some one-eighth of Canada's total R&D expenditures. Industrial R&D was confined to adaptation, technology transfer, and imitation of foreign technology. Emblematically, the major industrial laboratories were those of Imperial Oil and the Pulp and Paper Research Institute of Canada. No major breakthrough innovation stemmed from domestic pre-1939 industrial activity. Despite the increasing technological efforts of the 1930s, Canada lagged behind other advanced nations, in private and public innovation, with just 0.1 per cent of its GDP devoted to R&D.

During the Second World War and in the immediate aftermath, Ottawa increased its activities, mainly through creation of new public, mostly defence-related laboratories. This was mostly mission-oriented, vertical technology policy, aimed at developing a few specific emerging defence industrial activities, such as nuclear research, telecommunication, aircraft, and aerospace. After the war, some of these R&D labs were either privatized (as in turbine research) or spun off from the NRC towards the Department of National Defence or to crown corporations (as in nuclear research). Slow, but increasing federal involvement in promotion of science and technology occurred during the 1950s.

The real take-off of Canada's NSI occurred in the 1960s, with the development of horizontal technology policies, such as R&D tax credits, tax deductions, and the Industrial Research Assistance Program (IRAP), and it proceeded slowly to the early 1990s (Table 9.1)[2].

NEW R&D ROUTINES IN INDUSTRY

If the first and major goal was to create new R&D routines in private firms, the programs succeeded. Between 1960 and 1970, national R&D expenditures increased three-fold, from $300 million to over $1 billion (in current dollars) and by 2.5 times (in constant dollars). Government-performed R&D expenditures doubled, industrial R&D multiplied by 4.5, and university R&D multiplied by six, from $52 million to over $300 million (in current dollars) (Cordell and Gilmour, 1976: 41).

By 1984, the number of companies claiming investment tax credits for R&D had increased to nearly thirteen hundred, from only seventy-five in 1977. Also, the number of firms carrying out R&D activities, though not necessarily in-house, grew continuously from less than four hundred in 1955 to over one thousand in 1969, over three thousand in 1989, and more than sixty-six hundred in 1995. The industrial sector, which spent only 29 per cent of Canada's GERD in 1960, finally responded to the many incentives offered by the federal and late, the provincial governments. Its share of Canada's R&D expenditures, by performing sector, increased continuously to 39 per cent in 1970, 44 per cent in 1980, 54 per cent in 1990 and 65 per cent in 1997 (Canada, Statistics Canada, 1997).

The Rise of University Research

With creation of the Medical Research Council, the Natural Sciences and Engineering Research Council, and the Social Sciences and Humanities Research Council in the 1960s and 1970s, university research came of age and became comparable to U.S. university research in per capita terms. University-performed R&D multiplied ten-fold between 1957 and

2 Several factors can explain differences between the number of R&D-active firms (as collected by Statistics Canada) and the R&D tax claimants (produced by Revenue Canada). R&D-active companies are those that actually conduct R&D, while some tax claimants may not perform R&D but rather subcontract it to other companies, government laboratories, or universities. Also, some tax claimants may not be in Statistics Canada's lists or may not respond to its questionnaires. Finally, some cheating by tax claimants is also possible.

Table 9.1
The evolution of Canada's NSI, 1955–97

Year	GERD/GDP (%)	No. of R&D-active firms	No. of R&D tax claimants	BERD by funding sector (current $million)	Total GERD (current $million)
1955	N/A	377	N/A	66	305*
1960	0.9	N.D.	N/A	146	458
1970	1.3	1,010†	N/A	336	1,069
1971	1.32	N.D.	N/A	348	1,287
1972	1.25	N.D.	N/A	373	1,357
1973	1.14	N.D.	N/A	409	1,450
1974	1.10	N.D.	N/A	511	1,666
1975	1.09	N.D.	N/A	582	1,876
1976	1.03	N.D.	N/A	625	2,043
1977	1.05	N.D.	75	702	2,290
1978	1.07	N.D.	143	839	2,576
1979	1.09	N.D.	290	1,104	3,009
1980	1.14	N.D.	290	1,392	3,529
1981	1.22	N.D.	726	1,800	4,358
1982	1.37	1,296	845	1,971	5,128
1983	1.34	1,435	932	1,912	5,441
1984	1.38	1,526	1,239	2,194	6,118
1985	1.43	1,784	N.D.	2,762	6,815
1986	1.48	3,414	3,700	3,091	7,373
1987	1.43	3,498	N.D.	3,228	7,764
1988	1.38	3,560	4,992	3,422	8,266
1989	1.37	3,311	5,458	3,709	8,839
1990	1.46	3,459	6,973	4,045	9,755
1991	1.48	3,556	8,146	4,218	10,203
1992	1.52	N.D.	8,725	N.D.	10,704
1993	1.57	4,485	N.D.	4,954	11,499
1994	1.57	N.D.	N.D.	5,229	12,015

Table 9.1 *(continued)*
The evolution of Canada's NSI, 1955–97

Year	GERD/GDP (%)	No. of R&D-active firms	No. of R&D tax claimants	BERD by funding sector (current $million)	Total GERD (current $million)
1995	1.56	6,628	N.D.	5,418	12,356
1996	1.57	N.D.	N.D.	6,309	12,654
1997	1.58	N.D.	11,300	6,666	13,400

Sources: Information from Statistics Canada, Revenue Canada.
* 1957 estimates; † 1969 estimates.

1968, from $26 million to $262 million. In the 1990s, links between industrial and university research increased, when the same councils increased their requests for industrial partnerships and new legislation encouraged industrial funding of university research. By 1995, well over 10 per cent of university research funds came from industrial firms, and the many links between industry and academe were growing.

Government Laboratories More Linked to the NSI

In 1990, the federal government changed the rules on intellectual property under which its public laboratories operated. First, it disbanded Canada Patent and Development Ltd. Since that year, as our survey has shown, government cooperation has increased. As a result, not all research conducted in federal labs necessarily belonged to the labs, government units were free to sign any type of agreement with private firms concerning intellectual property, and they were encouraged to collaborate with industry. The consequence, as we saw in chapters 3–5, was growth in cooperation, but not yet a large increase in revenues stemming from that cooperation. Nevertheless, government units moved closer to the private sector and became more devoted to industrial work and technology transfer. Emerging new routines in these public laboratories allowed them to conduct R&D in collaboration with industry.

The Rise of the Knowledge-based Economy

In the 1980s, in response to new sector-specific policies (including the new NRC national laboratories for biotechnology, the federal Strategic Technologies Programs, federal and provincial centres of excellence, the Canadian Space Agency, and increasing patent protection for pharma-

Table 9.2
Share of patent applications in manufacturing in Canada, by industrial sector,
1975 and 1990

Industrial sector	1975 (%)	1990 (%)
Science-based*	32.92	35.64
Product-differentiated	31.49	28.05
Scale-based	20.35	20.13
Natural resources	5.18	8.58
Labour-intensive	10.07	7.60
Number of applications (%)	100	100
Number of applications (no.)	13,879	28,854

Source: M. Raffiquzamman and L. Wheeler (1999).
* Includes aircraft and parts manufacturing, communication equipment, electrical industrial
equipment, pharmaceuticals and medicines, paints and varnishes, soap and cleaning compounds,
chemical industries, instruments and related products, clock and watches, ophthalmic goods, and
radio and TV receivers.

ceutical products), industrial R&D changed, moving further towards a
knowledge-based economy. While in the 1950s aircraft, electrical equipment, and chemical products represented over half of industrial R&D expenditures (followed by oil and coal, non-ferrous metals, and pulp and
paper), in the 1990s the knowledge industries – telecommunication
equipment, aircraft and aerospace, engineering and scientific services including biotechnology, business machines and other electronic equipment and computer and related services, and pharmaceutical products –
carried more than half of industrial R&D in Canada. In the 1990s, because of governmental technology policy, knowledge-intensive industries
have become the core of Canada's NSI (see Figure 9.1 and Table 9.2).

Simultaneously, industrial involvement in R&D increased, and it has
become the main element in Canada's NSI (Figure 9.2). Even if corporate concentration of industrial R&D remains high, thousands of new,
domestically owned firms started conducting industrial R&D. Many
were created recently in the new activities of biotechnology, software
production and computer services, manufacture of, telecommunication equipment, design of semiconductors, and research and production in advanced materials. Others were more traditional firms
diversifying into these new technologies and activities, such as printers
and editors entering software production, agricultural firms diversifying into biotechnology, and traditional materials manufacturers moving into production of composites and alloys.

Figure 9.1
Main high-tech industries in Canada, as % of BERD, 1977–97

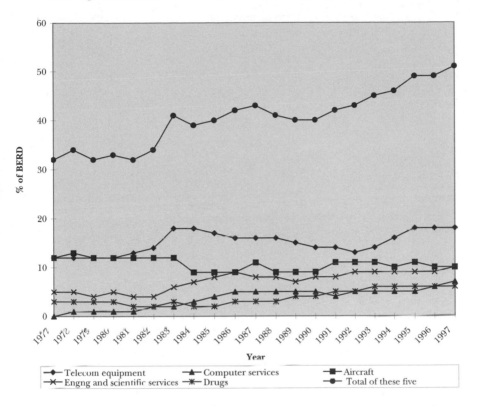

CANADA'S DOMESTIC R&D SYSTEM IN THE 1990S

Chapters 3–5 show that in the early 1990s Canada's R&D system was heavily concentrated in every sense of the word. Fewer than six hundred large laboratories (two hundred of which belonged to industry, one hundred to governments, and two hundred to universities) undertook most of the innovative activities of the country. Most industrial and government large laboratories were in Ontario, and the majority of university labs in Quebec. Government R&D units were on average the largest by any possible measure, followed by industry and university research centres.

These three types of units diverged on many accounts other than size. The main missions of industrial R&D units were commercial applied research and development. Industrial R&D was funded mostly by the labs' own resources and by parent companies. It produced

Figure 9.2
Canada's NSI: money flows

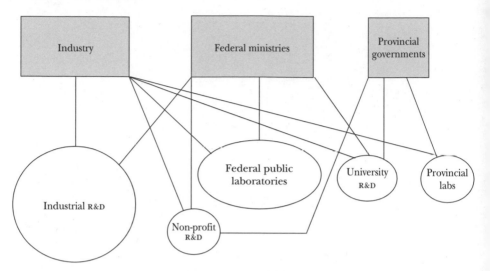

Note: Based on OECD, *Working Group on Technology and Innovation Policy. National Innovation Systems* (Paris, 1997).

prototypes and devices, algorithms and software, and internal reports. When it transferred technology (only a minority of units did), it did so in the framework of cooperation, either with other industrial firms or through participation in university or government research centres. Industry transferred technology with commercial and profit motives. In any case, only a minority of industrial labs licensed technologies, but over 50 per cent of them cooperated with outside organizations, mostly in order to obtain new technology. Most of the labs involved in technology transfer – usually the largest ones – experienced no major difficulty in this activity. For industrial labs, producing commercially useful knowledge was by far the main criterion of effectiveness – management decision that helped clarify operating routines. Also, their managers estimated that technology transfer had a very good or an excellent commercial impact on the unit.

The situation was rather different in government laboratories. At least five different missions were very important for a majority of these units: pre-commercial research, commercial applied research, assistance to government, assistance to private organizations, and transfer to private organizations. Conversely, government contracts and appropriations represented 85 per cent of their funds, and industrial grants only 13 per cent. As for their outputs, they were producing mostly published articles and internal reports. Technology transfer reflected those missions. Even if almost all government labs conducted technology transfer, their motives ranged from legislative requirements, through economic development, to cooperative R&D. Profits or budgetary considerations were marginal, and commercial impact was not always high. Three-quarters of government labs cooperated with external units, mostly with industry, but also with other public research institutions and foreign corporations. Effectiveness criteria reflect allegiances: meeting the needs of constituencies, producing commercially useful knowledge, and contributing to basic knowledge all were important in varying degrees.

Finally, university research centres had basic and pre-commercial research, together with technology transfer to private organizations, as their main missions. Funded mostly by government contracts and research grants, and only marginally (16 per cent) by industry, their research outputs were biased towards articles and reports. Slightly over half transferred technology, pushed by the growth of cooperation or in the framework of industry–university or government–university research centres. Their benefits in technology transfer consisted of visibility, knowledge, approval by government officials, a more "real world" approach for personnel, and the drawing together of researchers from different institutions, rather than commercial profits. A minority of university labs were licensing technology, but slightly over half of them were cooperating with outside units, mostly in search of new knowledge. Not unexpectedly, their effectiveness was measured by their contribution to scientific knowledge and their training of students, over and above commercially useful knowledge or the bringing of resources to the unit.

Our picture shows a well-developed network of transfers and cooperation, stimulated by government regulations and funds (or by the curtailment of those funds), confirming and shedding new light on the links between the units of the NSI.

INTERNATIONALIZATION OF THE NSI

When one moves from regional to national to international R&D, the scope of alliances and networks increases, together with the budgets and the commercial goals of the cooperative R&D projects. As I argued above, several dozen among the largest Canadian firms are now involved in foreign R&D; several hundred of them also participate in international alliances. For the vast majority of the seven thousand Canadian companies conducting R&D, however, innovative activities take place within Canadian borders.

There is no North American supranational system of innovation emerging, as I showed in chapter 6. First, even if Canadian expatriate industrial R&D has chosen the United States as its preferred destination, Canada is not the main host of U.S. R&D abroad, and it is not the main investor in the U.S. (or Mexican) R&D systems, even if it has substantially increased its participation in American industrial R&D since 1980, as have most industrialized nations. Also, Canadian international alliances, because they are based on technological complementarity, are organized more often with European firms than with American ones. Finally, little technology moves across Canadian borders through Canadian-owned and -controlled multinationals: as we saw in chapter 8, most foreign subsidiaries are free to choose and conduct R&D without even submitting their projects to the Canadian parent.

The internationalization of Canadian industrial R&D in the postwar period, particularly in the 1980s and 1990s, appears to represent a search for larger markets and growth avenues. Most large Canadian-owned and -controlled MNCs now have some expatriate R&D units. The United States, the United Kingdom, and continental Europe have become the main destination of Canadian R&D abroad. Through foreign acquisitions and related R&D activities in the largest regional U.S. and European markets, Canadian firms try to overcome the obstacles to growth created by small domestic markets and associated reduced pools of research talent. Canada has become more porous through the international operations of its own MNCs, but its system of innovation remains essentially national.

INNOVATION, TECHNOLOGY POLICY, AND TRADE

The building of an NSI in Canada has affected the country's patterns of international trade. A few of the new industries, such as telecommunication equipment and aerospace products, are now major exporters. They are also major contributors to the "receipts" column in the technological balance of Canadian international payments. In other new industries, including biotechnology and software, Canada's increasing R&D expenditures and revealed technological advantage have not yet produced major exports or a positive trade balance. The commercial results, however, may become visible in the near future.

Other, more mature, new knowledge-intensive industries have failed to produce major exports but have probably had an import-substituting effect, including the development of indigenous nuclear energy reactors.

CONCLUSION

The general conclusion of this study is that the building of an NSI in late industrialization needs the active intervention of the state – an idea that appeared in classic authors such as Alexander Gerschenkron (1962) and Douglass North (1984). Recently, authors such as Wade (1990) and – in a milder form – even the World Bank (1993) have endorsed the idea that public policy and institutions are key. A variety of inducements to stimulate private industry to conduct R&D, rapid formation of human capital and government laboratories to reduce costs, and risks involved in development of new technology appear in every case.

National governments are able not just to launch new industries or create university R&D or public laboratories. Our domestic and international surveys have shown that they can also modify these labs' functioning, missions, and performance. They can do so by implementing funding rules and regulations concerning intellectual property results or, more simply, through budgetary measures, by forcing public and quasi-public institutions to look for private R&D funds and create links with industry and by giving incentives to industry to cooperate with academe and public R&D labs.

The surveys have shown also that federal regulations in Canada have a major influence on innovative units within the national borders, but only indirectly on Canadian units operating abroad. Domestic policies have promoted special industries in a given period, and over time the companies that embody these national technological capabilities become MNCs and absorb new types of competencies through acquisitions in foreign nations. National policies thus have an impact, though indirect and in the long term, on the type of industry that internationalizes R&D.

Finally, our surveys show that policies have varying effects on different units, according to the units' own type of knowledge and organization. Policies looking for more industry–university collaboration seem to affect specific university departments and faculties, such as engineering, medicine, pharmacology, and natural sciences, but less so the social sciences and other "softer" disciplines, such as humanities. Also, some public laboratories, more engineering-oriented, are better able to turn themselves towards private industry, while the more scientific labs will have difficulties in linking themselves with industry.

More research is needed on the ability of higher education to supply labour markets with adequate personnel, as well as on failures of public policy (as in advanced materials). Also, the new knowledge-based intensive industries deserve more in-depth comparative examination.

Yet this study of a national system of innovation, while incomplete, shows that the NSI perspective is enormously useful in the analysis of national policies, management of individual units, and links among them. The systemic perspective, particularly within an evolutionary framework, thus brings something new, particularly more coherence, to the detailed analysis of specific policies, laboratories, and industries than any competing perspective offered in the past.

References

Abo, Tetsuo. *Hybrid Factory.* New York: Oxford University Press 1994.

Abramovitz, Moses. *Thinking about Growth.* Cambridge: Cambridge University Press 1988.

Abramovitz, Moses, and David, P. "Convergence and Deferred Catch Up." In M. Abramovitz et al., eds., *The Mosaic of Economic Growth,* 21–62. Stanford, Calif.: Stanford University Press 1996.

Amesse, Fernand, Lamy, P., and Tahmi, A. "L'Axe 40–401: notre 'Silicon Valley' du nord" *Gestion* 14 no. 1: 15–22, 1989.

Amesse, Fernand, Séguin-Dulude, L., and Stanley, G. "Northern Telecom: A Case Study in the Management of Technology." In S. Globerman, ed., *Canadian-based Multinationals,* 421–53. Calgary: University of Calgary Press 1994.

Aoki, Masahiko. "Towards an Economic Model of the Japanese Firm." *Journal of Economic Literature* 28: 1–27, 1990.

– "The Firm as a System of Attributes." In M. Aoki and R. Dore, eds., *The Japanese Firm,* 11–40. New York: Oxford University Press 1994.

Archibugi, Daniele, and Michie, J. "The Globalization of Technology: A New Taxonomy." *Cambridge Journal of Economics* 19 no. 1: 121–40, 1995.

Archibugi, Daniele, and Pianta, M. *The Technological Specialization of Advanced Countries.* Boston: Kluwer 1992.

Arrow, Kenneth. "The Economic Implications of Learning by Doing." *Review of Economic Studies* 29: 155–73, 1962.

Arthur, W. Brian. "Competing Technologies, Increasing Returns and Lock-in by Historical Small Events." *Economic Journal* 99: 116–31, 1989.

– *Increasing Returns and Path Dependency in the Economy.* Ann Arbor: University of Michigan Press 1994.

Baghai, M.A., et al. *The Growth Philosophy of Bombardier.* New York: McKinrey 1997.

Balcet, Giovanni. *L'économie de l'Italie.* Paris: La découverte 1995.

Barney, Jay. "Firm Resources and Sustained Competitive Advantage." *Journal of Management* 17 no. 1: 99–120, 1991.

Baumol, William J., Nelson, R.R., and Wolff, E.N. *Convergence of Productivity,* New York: Oxford Universiy Press 1994.

Best, Andrea, and Mitra, D. "The Venture Capital Industry in Canada." *Journal of Small Business Management* 35 no. 2: 105–10, 1997.

Bonelli, Franco. "The State and the Economy in the Industrialization of Italy from Its Origins to the Welfare State." In G. Federico, ed., *The Economic Development of Italy since 1870,* 626–33. Aldershot: Elgar 1994.

Bones, Herman P. "Are Foreign Subsidiaries More Innovative?" *Canadian Business Review* 6 no. 2: 15–18, 1979.

Botham, Richard, and Giguère, Michel. "The Industrial Research Infrastructure." In Paul Dufour and John de la Mothe, eds., *Science and Technology in Canada,* 68–99. Harlow: Longman 1993.

Bothwell, Robert. *Nucleus: The History of the Atomic Energy of Canada Limited.* Toronto: University of Toronto Press 1988.

Bound, John, Cummins, C., Griliches, Z., Hall, B., and Jaffe, A. "Who Does R&D and Who Patents?" In Z. Griliches, ed., *R&D, Patents and Productivity,* 21–54. Chicago: University of Chicago Press 1984.

Bowkker, R.R. *Directory of American Research and Technology 1995.* New Providence, NJ: R.R. Bowker Inc. 1995.

Bozeman, Barry, Papadakis, M., and Cohen, K. *Industry Perspectives on Commercial Interactions with Federal Laboratories.* Atlanta: Georgia Institute of Technology, School of Public Policy 1995.

Branscomb, Lewis, ed. *Empowering Technology.* Cambridge, Mass.: MIT Press 1993.

Breheny, M., Cheshire, P., and Langridge, R. "The Anatomy of Job Creation? Industrial Change in Britain's M4 Corridor." In P. Hall and A. Markusen, eds., *Silicon Landscapes,* 118–33. Winchester, Mass: Allen & Unwin 1985.

Britton, John N.H., and Gilmour, J. *The Weakest Link: A Technological Perspective on Canadian Industrial Underdevelopment.* Science Council Background Study No. 43. Ottawa: Supply and Services Canada 1978.

Buckley, Peter J., and Casson, M. *The Future of the Multinational Enterprise.* New York: Holmes and Meier 1976.

Bunge, Mario. *Scientific Research.* 2 vols. Dordrecht: Springer Verlag 1967.

Canada, Advisory Council for Scientific and Industrial Research. *A Plan for the Development of Industrial Research in Canada.* Ottawa: Privy Council 1921.

Canada. *Canadian Yearbook.* Several editions. Ottawa: Supply and Services.

Canada, Department of Industry. *Highlights of Departmental S&T Action Plans in Response to Science and Technology for the New Century*. Ottawa: Supply and Services 1996a.

— *Science and Technology for the New Century: A Federal Strategy*. Ottawa: Supply and Services 1996b.

Canada, Department of Industry, Trade and Commerce. *Directory of Scientific Research and Development Establishments in Canada*. Ottawa: DITC 1969.

Canada, Dominion Bureau of Statistics. *Survey of Scientific and Industrial Laboratories in Canada*. Ottawa: DBS 1941.

— *Industrial Research-Development Expenditures in Canada 1955*. Reference Paper No. 75. Ottawa: DBS 1955.

— *Federal Government Expenditures on Scientific Activities. Fiscal Year 1967–68*. Cat. No. 13–202. Annual. Ottawa 1970.

Canada, Foreign Affairs and International Trade. *NAFTA: A Partnership at Work* Ottawa 1997.

Canada, House of Commons. *Proceedings,* Vol. 55, Appendix 5, 1919.

Canada, *Industry Canada.* "Research in Canadian Industries." 30: 171–80, 1930.

Canada, Royal Commission on Government Organization (Glassco Commission). *Report.* Vol. IV: *Special Areas of Administration.* Ottawa: Queen's Printer 1963.

Canada, Science Council. *Towards a National Science Policy for Canada*, Report No. 4. Ottawa 1968.

Canada, Special Committee on Science Policy (Lamontagne Commission). *A Science Policy for Canada.* Ottawa, Queen's Printer 1971–77.

Canada, Statistics Canada. *Industrial Research and Development. 1997 Intentions,* Cat. No. 88–202. Annual. Ottawa 1997.

Canadian Biotech News Service. *Biotech News.* Weekly. Nepean, Ont.

Canadian Venture Capital Association (CVCA). *Venture Capital in Canada.* Ottawa: CVCA 1997.

— *Statistics.* Ottawa. CVCA website 1999.

Cantwell, John. "The Globalization of Technology: What Remains of the Product Cycle Model?" *Cambridge Journal of Economics.* 19 no. 1: 155–74, 1995.

— "The Internationalization of Technological Activity and Its Implications for Competitiveness." In O. Granstrand, L. Håkanson, and S. Sjölander, eds., *Technology Management and International Business,* 75–96. Chichester: Wiley 1992.

Cantwell, John, and Hodson, C. "Global R&D and UK Competitiveness." In Mark C. Casson, ed., *Global Research Strategy and International Competitiveness,* 133–82. Oxford: Basil Blackwell 1991.

Caracostas, Paraskevas, and Soete, Luc. "The Building of Cross-Border Institutions in Europe: Towards a European System of Innovation," in C. Edquist, ed., *Systems of Innovation,* 395–419. London: Pinter 1997.

Carlsson, Bo, and Jacobsson, Staffan. "Diversity Creation and Technological Systems: A Technology Policy Perspective." In Charles Edquist, ed., *Systems of Innovation*, 266–94. London: Pinter 1997.

Casson, Mark. *The Firm and the Market.* Cambridg, Mass.: MIT Press 1987.

– *Global Research Strategy and International Competitiveness.* Oxford: Basil Blackwell 1991.

Casson, Mark, and Singh, S. "Corporate R&D Strategies: The Influence of Firm, Industry and Country Factors on the Decentralization of R&D." *R&D Management* 23 no. 2: 91–107, 1993.

Caves, Richard. "International Corporations. The Industrial Economics of Foreign Investment." *Economica* 38: 1–27, 1971.

– *Multinational Enterprise and Economic Analysis.* Cambridge: Cambridge University Press 1982.

Chand, U.K. Randa. "Characteristics of R&D Performing Firms in Canadian Manufacturing." *Research Policy* 11 no. 3: 193–203, 1981.

Cheng, Joseph, and Bolon, D.S. "The Management of Multinational R&D: A Neglected Topic in International Business Research." *Journal of International Business Studies* 24 no. 1: 1–18, 1993.

Chesnais, François. "Les accords de coopération technique entre firmes indépendantes." *STI Revue* 4 (Dec.): 55–132, 1988.

– "National Systems of Innovation, Foreign Direct Investment and the Operations of Multinational Enterprises." In B.-A. Lundvall, ed., *National Systems of Innovation*, 265–95. London: Pinter 1992.

Chiesa, Vittorio. "Managing the Internationalization of R&D Activities." *IEEE Transactions on Engineering Management* 43 no. 1: 7–23, 1996.

Clark, W.S., et al. "Canada's R&D Tax Incentives: Recent Developments." In Canadian Tax Foundation, *Report of the Proceedings of the 44th Conference*, Ottawa 1993.

Coase, Ronald. "The Nature of the Firm." *Economica* 4: 386–405, 1937.

Cohen, Wesley M., and Kepler, S. "The Anatomy of Industry R&D Distributions." *American Economic Review* 82 no. 4: 773–9, 1992.

CONACYT/SEP. *Indicadores de actividades científicas y tecnologicas.* Mexico 1995.

Cordell, Arthur, and Gilmour, James. *The Role and Function of Government Laboratories and the Transfer of Technology to the Manufacturing Sector.* Ottawa: Science Council 1976.

Coursey, David, and Bozeman, B. "Technology Transfer in US Labs: Advantages and Disadvantages for Participating Laboratories." *IEEE Transactions on Engineering Management* 39 no. 4 (Nov.): 347–51, 1992.

Crow, Michael, and Bozeman, B. *Limited by Design: R&D Laboratories in the US National System of Innovation.* New York: Columbia University Press 1998.

Dalhman, Carl J., and Frischtak, C. "National Systems Supporting Technical Advance in Industry: The Brazilian Experience." In Richard R. Nelson, ed., *National Innovation Systems*, 414–50. New York: Oxford University Press 1993.

Dalpé, Robert. "Dimensions politiques des interventions publiques en technologie." *Recherches sociographiques* 30 no. 3: 447–64, 1989.

Dalton, Donald H., and Serapio, M. J. *Globalizing Industrial R&D.* Washington, DC: U.S. Department of Commerce, Office of Technology Policy 1995.

David, Paul. "Clio and the Economics of QWERTY." *American Economic Review.* 75 no. 2: 332–7, 1985.

David, Paul, and Abramovitz, M. "Convergence and Deferred Catch-Up: Productivity Leadership and the Waning of American Exceptionalism." In Ralph Landau, T. Taylor, and G. Wright, eds., *Growth and Development: The Economics of the 21st Century,* 21–62. Stanford, Calif.: Stanford University Press 1995.

De la Mothe, John, and Paquet, G. *Circumstancial Evidence: A Note on Science Policy in Canada,* PRIME Working Paper 94–20, University of Ottawa 1994.

– "Real Economies and National Innovation Systems." In H. Schutze, ed., *Innovation and Regional Economic Development,* 00–00. Vancouver: University of British Columbia Press 1996.

Deyo, Frederic C., ed. *The Political Economy of the New Asian Industrialism.* Ithaca, NY: Cornell University Press 1987.

Dickson, David. *The New Politics of Science.* Chicago: University of Chicago Press 1988.

Doern, G. Bruce. *Science and Politics in Canada.* Montreal: McGill-Queen's University Press 1972.

Doutriaux, Jérôme, and Barker, M. *The University–Industry Relationship in Science and Technology.* Occasional Paper No. 11. Ottawa: Industry Canada 1995.

Dufour, Paul, and de la Mothe, John, eds. *Science and Technology in Canada.* Harlow: Longman.

Dun & Bradstreet International. *Who Owns Whom? Vol. II: North America,* Bucks, England 1994.

Dunning, John H. "The Theory of International Production." In F. Khosrow, ed., *International Trade,* 114–29. New York: Taylor and Francis 1989.

Edquist, Charles, ed. *Systems of Innovation,* London: Pinter 1997.

Edquist, Charles, and Lundvall, B.-A. "Comparing the Danish and Swedish Systems of Innovation." In R.R. Nelson, ed., *National Innovation Systems,* 265–98. New York: Oxford University Press 1993.

Eggleston, Wilfred. *National Research in Canada: The NRC, 1916–1966.* Toronto: Clarke, Irwin & Co. 1978.

Evert Communications. *Research Money.* Bimonthly. Ottawa.

Fang, Rong-Jyue, and Hung-Yen Yang. "National Technology Policies in Taiwan." In Horst Mueller, Jan-Gunnar Persson, and Kenth R. Lumsden, eds., *Proceedings of the Sixth International Conference on the Management of Technology,* 986–96. Göteborg: SMR 1997.

Foss, Nicolai, and Knudsen, C. *Towards a Competence Theory of the Firm.* London: Routledge 1996.

Freedman, Ron, and Crelinsten, Jeffrey. "Canada in Space." In Paul Dufour and John de la Mothe, eds., *Science and Technology in Canada*, 181–209. London: Longman 1993.

Freeman, Christopher. *Technology Policy and Economic Performance: Lessons from Japan.* London: Pinter 1987.

– "Japan: A New National System of Innovation?" In G. Dosi et al., eds., *Technical Change and Economic Theory*, 330–48. London: Pinter 1988.

– "Networks of Innovators: A Synthesis of Research Issues." *Research Policy* 20 no. 5 (Oct.): 499–514, 1991.

– "The National System of Innovation in Historical Perspective." *Cambridge Journal of Economics* 19 no. 1: 5–24, 1995.

Gerschenkron, Alexander. *Economic Backwardness in Historical Perspective.* New York: Praeger 1962.

Ghiselin, Michael T. *The Triumph of the Darwinian Method.* Chicago: University of Chicago Press 1969.

Godin, Benoît, and Trépanier, M. "La politique scientifique et technologique québécoise: la mise en place d'un nouveau système national d'innovation." *Recherches sociographiques* 36 no. 3: 445–78, 1995.

Graham, Edward M. "Japanese Control of R&D Activities in the US: Is This a Cause for Concern?" In Thomas S. Arrison, C. Fred Bergsten, Edward M. Graham, and Martha Caldwell Harris, eds., *Japan's Growing Technological Capabilities*, 189–206. Washington, DC: National Academy Press 1992.

Granstrand, Ove, Håkanson, L., and Sjölander, S., eds. *Technology Management and International Business*, Chichester: Wiley 1992.

Green, J.J. *Aeronautics, Highway to the Future: A Study of Aeronautical R&D in Canada.* Ottawa: Science Council, Queen's Printer 1970.

Green, Milford, ed. *Venture Capital: International Comparisons.* London: Routledge 1991.

Haber, I.F. *The Chemical Industry, 1900–1930.* Oxford: Clarendon Press 1971.

Håkanson, Lars. "International Decentralization of R&D: The Organizational Challenges." In C.A. Bartlett, Y. Doz, and G. Hedlund, eds., *Managing the Global Firm.* London: Routledge 1990.

– "Location Determinants of Foreign R&D in Swedish Multinationals." In O. Granstrand, L. Håkanson, and S. Skolander, eds., *Technology Management and International Business.* Chichester: Wiley 1992.

Hall, Peter, and Markusen, A., ed. *Silicon Landscapes.* Winchester, Mass.: Allen & Unwin 1985.

Hamel, Gary, and Prahalad, C.K. *Competing for the Future.* Boston: Harvard Business School Press 1994.

Hartz, Theodore, and Paghis, I. *Spacebound.* Ottawa: Supply and Services 1982.

Hewitt, G. "Research and Development Performed Abroad by US Manufacturing Multinationals." *Kyklos* 33 no. 2: 308–27, 1980.

Holland, Stuart, ed. *The State as Entrepreneur: New Dimensions for Public Enterprise, the IRI State Shareholding Formula* White Plains, NY: IASP Press 1972.

Hull, James P., and Enros, P.C. "Demythologizing Canadian Science and Technology: The History of Industrial R&D." *Canadian Studies* 10 no. 3: 1–22, 1988.

Hymer, Stephen. *The International Operations of National Firms.* Cambridge, Mass.: MIT Press 1976.

Kaldor, Nicholas. "The Role of Increasing Returns, Technical Progress and Cumulative Causation in the Theory of International Trade," in *Economie appliquée* 34 no. 4, 1981.

Katz, Jorge, and Bercovich, N.A. "National Systems of Innovation Supporting Technical Advance in Industry: The Case of Argentina." In Richard R. Nelson, ed., *National Innovation Systems*, 451–75. New York: Oxford University Press 1993.

Kelly, Guillaume. "Les avantages technologiques révélés du Canada." MBA thesis, UQAM, Montreal 1993.

Kenney, Martin, and Florida, R. *Beyond Mass Production: The Japanese System and Its Transfer to the US.* New York: Oxford University Press 1993.

Kenney, Martin, and Florida, R. "The Globalization of Japanese R&D." *Economic Geography* 70 no. 4: 344–69, 1994.

Kim, Linsu. *Imitation to Innovation: The Dynamics of Korean Technological Learning.* Boston, Mass.: Harvard Business School Press 1997.

Kindleberger, Charles. *American Business Abroad* New Haven, Conn.: Yale University Press 1969.

Kogut, Bruce, and Zander, U. "Knowledge of the Firm and the Evolutionary Theory of the MNC." *Journal of International Business Studies* 24 no. 4: 625–45, 1993.

Kojima. K. *Direct Foreign Investment.* New York: Praeger 1978.

Krugman, Paul. *Geography and Trade.* Cambridge, Mass.: MIT Press 1993

– ed. *Strategic Trade Policy and the New International Economics.* Cambridge, Mass.: MIT Press 1986.

Kuemmerle, Walter. "Building Effective Capabilities Abroad." *Harvard Business Review* Jan.–Feb.: 61–70, 1997.

– "Foreign Direct Investment in Industrial Research in the Pharmaceutical and Electronics Industries." *Research Policy* 28 nos. 2–3: 179–94, 1999.

Lall, Sanjaya. *Learning from the Asian Tigers: Studies in Technology and Industrial Policy.* London: Macmillan and St Martin's Press 1996.

Lazonick, William. *Business Organization and the Myth of the Market Economy.* New York: Cambridge University Press 1991.

Leibenstein, Harvey. *Beyond Economic Man.* Cambridge, Mass.: Harvard University Press 1976.

Lipsett, Morris S., and Lipsey, R. *Benchmarks, Yardsticks and New Places to Look for Industrial Innovation and Growth.* CPROST Report 94–7, Vancouver 1994.

Lithwick, N.H. *Canada's Science Policy and the Economy.* Toronto: Methuen 1969.

Lundvall, Bengt-A. "Innovation as an Interactive Process: From User/Producer Interaction to the National System of Innovation." In G. Dosi, C. Freeman, R.R. Nelson, G. Silverberg, and L. Soete, eds.,. *Technical Change and Economic Theory* 349–69. London: Pinter 1988.

– ed. *National Systems of Innovation.* London: Pinter 1992.

– *The Social Dimensions of the Learning Economy.* DRUID Working Paper No. 96–1, Aalborg University, Denmark 1996.

– "Why Study National Systems and National Styles of Innovation?" *Technology Analysis and Strategic Management* 10 no. 4: 407–21, 1998.

Macdonald, Mary E. "Private Venture Capital Finding." In Daniel R. Bereskin, ed., *Research and Development in Canada,* 137–58. Toronto: Butterworths 1987.

Mackintosh, Jeffrey G. "Venture Capital Exits in Canada and the United States." In Paul J.N. Halpern, ed., *Financing Growth in Canada,* 279–358. Calgary: University of Calgary Press 1987.

Maddison, Angus. "Explaining the Economic Performance of Nations." In W.J. Baumol, R.R. Nelson, and E.N. Wolff, eds., *Convergence of Productivity,* 20–61. New York: Oxford University Press 1994.

Malerba, Franco. "R&D Growth in Itallian Industry in an International Perspective." In G. Dosi, R. Giannetti, and P.A. Toninelli, eds., *Technology and Enterprise in a Historical Perpective,* 314–50. Oxford: Clarendon Press 1992.

Malerba, Franco. "The National System of Innovation: Italy." In R.R. Nelson, ed., *National Systems of Innovation,* 230–60. New York: Oxford University Press 1993.

Mansfield, Edwin, Teece, D.J., and Romeo, A. "Overseas R&D by US-Based Firms." *Economica* 46: 187–196, 1979.

McFetridge, Donald. "Canadian Foreign Direct Investment, R&D and Technology Transfer." In S. Globerman, ed., *Canadian-Based Multinationals,* 151–78. Calgary: University of Calgary Press 1994.

Metcalfe, J. Stanley. "Technology Systems and Technology Policy in an Evolutionary Framework." *Cambridge Journal of Economics* 19: 25–46, 1995.

Morici, Peter, Smith, A.J.H., and Lea, S. *Canadian Industrial Policy.* Washington, DC: National Planning Association 1982.

Mowery, David, and Rosenberg, N. "The U.S. National Innovation System." In Richard R. Nelson, ed., *National Innovation Systems,* 29–75. Oxford: Oxford University Press 1993.

National Science Foundation. *Science and Engineering Indicators 1993.* Washington, DC: National Science Board 1993.

– *Science and Engineering Indicators 1996.* Washington, DC: National Science Board 1996.

Nelson, Richard R. "The Simple Economics of Basic Scientific Research." *Journal of Political Economy* 67 no. 3: 297–306, 1959.

– "Institutions Supporting Technical Change in the United States." In G. Dosi et al., eds., *Technical Change and Economic Theory*, 312–29. London: Pinter 1988.
– "National innovation Systems: A Retrospective on a Study." *Industrial and Corporate Change* 1 no. 2: 347–74, 1992.
– ed. *National Innovation Systems*. Oxford: Oxford University Press 1993.
– "The Co-evolution of Technology and Institutions." In Richard England, ed., *Evolutionary Concepts in Contemporary Economics*, 139–156. Ann Arbor: University of Michigan Press 1994.

Nelson, Richard R., and Winter, S. *An Evolutionary Theory of Economic Change*. Cambridge, Mass.: Belknap/Harvard University Press 1992.

Niosi, Jorge. *Canadian Multinationals*. Toronto: Garamond 1985.
– "Canada's National System of Innovation." *Science and Public Policy* 18 no. 2: 83–92, 1991.
– "Strategic Partnerships in Canadian Advanced Materials." *R&D Management* 23 no. 1: 17–27, 1993.
– "Technological Alliances in Canadian Industry." In J. Niosi, ed., *New Technology Policy and Social Innovations in the Firm*, 75–94. London: Pinter 1994.
– *Flexible Innovation: Technological Alliances of Canadian Industry*. Montreal: McGill-Queen's University Press 1995.
– "The Globalization of Canadian R&D." *Management International Review* 37 no. 4: 387–404, 1997.
– "The Diffusion of Organizational Innovations." *Management International* 3 no. 1: 65–73, 1998.
– "The Internationalization of Corporate R&D. From Technology Transfer to the Learning Organization." *Research Policy* 28 nos. 2–3: 107–17, 1999.
– "National Systems of Innovation Are X-Efficient." Presentation to the DRUID Conference on National Innovation Systems, Aalborg University, Denmark, June 1999b.

Niosi, Jorge, and Bellon, B. "The Global Interdependence of National Innovation Systems." *Technology in Society* 16 no. 2: 173–97, 1994.

Niosi, Jorge, and Chéron, E. "The Determinants of Canadian R&D in Software." Presentation to the Annual Meeting of the International Association for the Management of Technology, Orlando 1998.

Niosi, Jorge, and Landry, R. "Les gouvernements et les alliances technologiques." *Gestion* 18 no. 3: 32–9, 1993.

Niosi, Jorge, and Rivard, J. "Canadian Technology Transfer to Developing Countries through Small and Medium-Sized Enterprises." *World Development* 18 no. 11: 1529–42, 1990.

Niosi, Jorge, Sabourin, D. and Wolfson, M. The Determinants of R&D Propensity in Canadian Firms. Unpublished research paper, Statistics Canada, Ottawa 1994.

Niosi, Jorge, Saviotti, P., Bellon, B., and Crow, M. "National Systems of Innovation: In Search of a Workable Concept." *Technology in Society* 15 no. 2: 207–27, 1993.

Nonaka, Ikujiro, and Takeuchi, H. *The Knowledge-Creating Company*. New York: Oxford University Press 1995.

North, Douglass. "Governments and the Cost of Exchange." *Journal of Economic History* 44: 255–64, 1984.

Odagiri, Hiroyuki, and Yasuda, H. "The Determinants of Overseas R&D by Japanese Firms: An Empirical Study at the Industry and Company Levels." *Research Policy* 25: 1059–79, 1996.

OECD (Organization of Economic Cooperation and Development). *Main Science and Technology Indicators*. Bi-annual. Paris.

– *National Innovation Systems*. Paris: OECD Working Group on Technology and Innovation Policy 1997.

Okimoto, Daniel, and Nishi, Y. "R&D Organization in Japanese and American Semiconductor Firms." In Masahiko Aoki and Ronald Dore, eds., *The Japanese Firm*, 178–208. Oxford: Clarendon Press 1994.

Ontario. *Competing in the New Global Economy, Report of the Premier's Council.* 2 vols. Toronto: Premier's Office 1990.

Osborne, Duncan, and Sandler, D. "A Tax Expenditure Analysis of Labour-Sponsored Venture Capital Corporations." *Canadian Tax Journal* 46 no. 3: 499–572, 1998.

Pack, Howard. "Endogenous Growth Theory: Intellectual Appeal and Empirical Shortcomings." *Journal of Economic Perspectives* 8 no. 1: 55–72, 1994.

Palda, Kristian. *Innovation Policy and Canada's Competitiveness*. Vancouver: Fraser Institute 1993.

Papanastassiou, Maria, and Pearce, R.D. "The Internationalization of R&D by Japanese Enterprises." *R&D Management* 24 no. 2: 155–65, 1994.

Patel, Pari, and Pavitt, K. "Large Firms in the Production of World's Technology: An Important Case of Non-globalization." *Journal of International Business Studies* 22 no. 1: 1–22, 1991.

Patel, Pari, and Pavitt, K. "Europe's Technological Performance." In C. Freeman, M. Sharp, and W. Walker, eds., *Technology and the Future of Europe*, 223–51. London: Pinter 1991.

– "The Nature and Economic Importance of National Innovation Systems." *STI Review* 14: 9–32, 1994.

Pavitt, Keith. "R&D, Patenting and Innovative Activities." *Research Policy*, 11: 33–51, 1982.

– "Sectoral Patterns of Technical Change: Towards a Taxonomy and a Theory." *Research Policy* 13 no. 6: 343–74, 1984.

Pavitt, Keith, and Patel, P. "L'accumulation technologique en France: ce que les statistiques de brevets tendent à démontrer." *Revue d'économie industrielle*, 51: 10–51, 1990.

Pearce, Robert D. "Factors Influencing the Internationalization of R&D in Multinational Enterprises." In P.J. Buckley and M. Casson, eds., *Multinational Enterprises in the World Economy*, 000–00. London: Elgar 1992.

Perez, Carlota. "Structural Change and the Assimilation of New Technologies in the Economic and Social System." *Futures* 15 no. 4: 357–75, 1983.

Posner, M.V., and Woolf, S.J. *Italian Public Enterprise.* Cambridge Mass.: Harvard University Press 1967.

Quebec, Bureau de la statistique du Québec (BSQ). *La R et D au Québec. Les entreprises 1993.* Quebec City: BSQ 1993.

– *La R et D au Québec. Les entreprises 1996.* Quebec City: BSQ 1996.

Raffiquzamman, M., and Wheeler, L. *Recent Jumps in Patenting Activities.* Ottawa: Industry Canada 1999.

Romer, Paul. "Increasing Returns and Long-Run Growth." *Journal of Political Economy* 94 no. 5: 1002–38, 1986.

– "The Origins of Endogenous Growth." *Journal of Economic Perspectives* 8 no. 1: 3–22, 1994.

Ronstadt, Robert C. *R&D Abroad by US Multinationals.* Praeger: New York 1977.

– "R&D Abroad by US Multinationals." In Robert Stobaugh and Louis T. Wells Jr., eds., *Technology Crossing Borders*, 241–64. Boston: Harvard Business School Press 1984.

Rosenberg, Nathan. *Inside the Black Box: Technology and Economics.* Cambridge: Cambridge University Press 1982.

Rosenberg, Nathan. "American Universities and Technical Advance in Industry." *Research Policy* 23 no. 3: 323–48, 1994.

Rosenberg, Nathan, and Frischtak, C., eds. *International Technology Transfer.* New York: Praeger 1985.

Roussel, Philip A., Saad, K.N., and Erickson, T.J. *Third Generation R&D.* Boston: Harvard Business School Press 1991.

Rugman, Alan, and Verbeke, A. "Multinational Corporate Strategy and the Canada–US Free Trade Agreement." *Management International Review* 30 no. 3: 253–66, 1990.

Safarian, A. *Foreign Ownership of Canadian Industry.* Toronto: McGraw-Hill 1966.

Sakakibara, Kiyonori, and Westney, D.E. "Japan's Management of Technological Innovation." In N. Rosenberg, R. Landau, and D.C. Mowery, eds., *Technology and the Wealth of Nations*, 327–44. Stanford: Stanford University Press 1992.

Schatz, Christian, and Mowery, D.C. *Comparing the US and Japanese National Laboratory Systems.* CCC Working Paper 94–2. Berkeley: University of California 1994.

Scherer, Frederick. "Firm Size, Market Structure, Opportunity and the Output of Patented Inventions." *American Economic Review* 55: 1097–125, 1965.

– *Industrial Market Structure and Economic Performance.* Chicago: Rand McNally 1970.

– *Innovation and Growth*. Cambridge, Mass.: MIT Press 1984.
– "Schumpeter and Plausible Capitalism." *Journal of Economic Literature* 30: 1416–33, 1992.
Schumpeter, Joseph. *The Theory of Economic Development*. Cambridge Harvard 1934.
– *Capitalism, Socialism and Democracy*. New York: Harper 1942.
Serapio, Manuel G., Jr. "Macro-micro Analysis of Japanese Direct R&D Investments in the U.S. Auto and Electronics Industries." *Management International Review* 33 no. 2: 209–25, 1993.
Serapio, Manuel J., Jr. and Dalton, D.H. "Foreign R&D Facilities in the United States." *Research Policy* 28 nos. 2–3: 303–16, 1999.
Smith, Keith. "Innovation Policy in an Evolutionary Context." In P.P. Saviotti and J.S. Metcalfe, eds., *Evolutionary Theories of Economic and Technical Change*, 256–75. Chur: Harwood Academic Publishers 1991.
Soete, Luc. "Firm Size and Inventive Activity." *European Economic Review* 12: 319–40, 1979.
Solocha, Andrew, and Soskin, M.D. "Canadian Direct Investment, Mode of Entry and Border Location." *Management International Review* 34 no. 1: 79–95, 1994.
Solocha, Andrew, Soskin, M.D., and Kasoff, M.J. "Determinants of Foreign Direct Investment: A Case of Canadian FDI in the United States." *Management International Review* 30 no. 4: 371–86, 1990.
Statistics Canada (annual). *Industrial Research and Development Intentions*. Cat. No. 88–202. Ottawa.
– *Industrial Research & Development 1992*. Cat. No. 88–202. Ottawa 1993.
– *Federal Scientific Activities 1995–96*. Cat. No. 88–204. Ottawa 1996.
Stiglitz, Joseph. "Economic Organizations, Information and Development." In H.B. Chenery and T.N. Srinivasan, eds., *The Handbook of Development Economics*, Vol. I, 94–160. Amsterdam: North-Holland 1988.
Storper, Michael. "The Limits to Globalization: Technology Districts and International Trade." *Economic Geography* 68 no. 1: 60–93, 1992.
Sullivan, Kenneth, and Milberry, L. *Power: The Pratt & Whitney Canada Story*. Toronto: Canav 1989.
Swan, G.M. Peter, Prevezer, M., and Stout, D., eds. *The Dynamics of Industrial Clustering*. New York: Oxford University Press 1998.
Taggart, James H. "Determinants of Foreign R&D Locational Decisions in the Pharmaceutical Industry." *R&D Management* 21 no. 3: 229–40, 1991.
Taggart, John H. *The World Pharmaceutical Industry*. London: Routledge 1993.
Teece, David J. "Technology Transfer by Multinational Firms: The Resource Costs of Transferring Technological Know-How." *Economic Journal* 87: 242–61, 1977.
Terpstra, Vern. "International Product Policy: The Role of Foreign R&D." *Columbia Journal of World Business* (winter): 24–32, 1977.

Teubal, Morris. "R&D and Technology Policy in NICs as Learning Processes." *Research Policy* 24 no. 3: 449–60, 1996.

– "A Catalytic and Evolutionary Approach to Horizontal Technology Policy." *Research Policy* 25: 1161–88, 1997a.

– *Restructuring and Embeddedness of Business Enterprises: Toward an Innovation System Perspective on Diffusion Policy.* Danish Research Unit for Industrial Dynamics, Working Paper 97–6, Aalborg, Denmark 1997b.

United States Department of Commerce. *Statistical Abstract of the United States 1995.* Washington, DC: Government Printing Office 1995.

United States Patent Office (Annual). *U.S. Patent Database (Cassis).* Washington, DC.

Vernon, Raymond. "The Product Cycle Hypothesis in a New International Environment." *Oxford Bulletin of Economics and Statistics.* 41: 255–67, 1979.

Vernon, Raymond, and L.T. Wells, Jr. *Manager in the International Economy.* Englewood Cliffs, NJ: Prentice Hall 1991.

von Hippel, Eric. *The Sources of Innovation.* New York Oxford University Press 1988.

Wade, Robert. *Governing the Market: Economic Theory and the Role of Government in South East Asia.* Princeton, NJ: Princeton University Press 1990.

Walsh, Vivien, Niosi, J., and Mustar, P. "The Rise of Biotechnology: A Comparison of the UK, Canada and France." *Technovation* 15 no. 5: 303–27, 1995.

Williamson, Oliver. *The Economic Institutions of Capitalism.* New York: Free Press 1985.

Winter, Sidney. "Patents in Complex Contexts." In Vivian Weil and John W. Snapper, eds., *Owning Scientific and Technical Information,* 41–60. New Brunswick, NJ: Rutgers University Press 1989.

World Bank. *The East Asian Miracle: Economic Growth and Public Policy.* New York: Oxford University Press 1993.

Yang, Jih Chang. "ITRI and Taiwan's Industrial Development." Presentation to the Conference "Diffusion, Assimilation and the Use of Technology," Interamerican Development Bank, Washington, DC, Feb. 1998.

Zander, Ivo. "The Tortoise Evolution of the MNC: Foreign Technological Activity in Swedish Multinational Firms, 1890–1990." PhD thesis, Stockholm School of Economics 1994.

– "How Do You Mean Global? An Empirical Investigation of Innovation Networks in the Multinational Corporation." *Research Policy* 28 nos. 2–3: 195–214, 1999.

Index

Abo, Tetsuo, 16
Abramovitz, Moses, 15
Abramovitz, Moses, and P.
  David, 15
Aerodynamics Laboratory,
  44
Alberta Research Council,
  63, 126
Alcan Aluminum, 163
Amesse, Fernand, P. Lamy,
  and A. Tahmi, 21, 66
Aoki, Masahiko, 10
Archibugi, Daniele, and J.
  Michie, 20, 131, 132
Archibugi, Daniele, and M.
  Pianta, 11, 15
Argentina, 15, 33
Arrow, Kenneth, 23
Arthur, W. Brian, 23, 24
Atomic Energy of Canada
  Ltd, 40, 43, 47, 127
Australia, 10, 11, 14, 15,
  149, 153, 164, 172, 173,
  175, 176
Austria, 155, 157, 164

Balcet, Giovanni, 19
Barney, Jay, 24–5
Baumol, William J., and
  R.R. Nelson, 15

Belgium, 140, 164
Best, Andrea, and D. Mi-
  tra, 52
Biotechnology Research In-
  stitute, 51, 67
Bombardier, 164
Bonelli, Franco, 19
Bones, Herman P., 38
Bothwell, Robert, 40
Bound, John, C. Cummins,
  Z. Griliches, B. Hall, and
  A. Jaffe, 37
Bowkker, R.R. 172
Bozeman, Barry, xiv
Bozeman, Barry, M. Pa-
  padakis, and K. Cohen,
  16
Brazil, 33, 57, 163, 167,
  175, 176
Breheny, M., P. Cheshier,
  and R. Langridge, 21
British Columbia Research
  Council, 64
Britton, John N.H., and J.
  Gilmour, 38
Buckley, Peter J., and M.
  Casson, 147
Building Research Division,
  42
Bunge, Mario, 77

business expenditure on
  R&D (BERD), 19, 60, 65,
  134, 135, 150, 196–7,
  199

Canadian International De-
  velopment Agency
  (CIDA), 63
Canadian Patents and De-
  velopment Ltd (CPDL),
  40, 54, 63, 197
Canadian Space Agency,
  62, 63, 127, 197
Cantwell, John, 148, 170
Cantwell, John, and C.
  Hodson, 146
Caracostas, Paraskevas, and
  L. Soete, 132
Carlsson, Bo, and S. Jacobs-
  son. 9, 23
Casson, Mark, 147
Casson, Mark, and S. Singh,
  169
Caves, Richard, 146, 147
Centre de recherche indus-
  trielle du Québec
  (CRIQ), 63
Ceramic and Industrial
  Minerals Laboratory, 39
Chand, U.K. Randa, 38

Cheng, Joseph, and D.S. Bolon, 146, 168
Chesnais, François, 20, 100
Chiesa, Vittorio, 169, 190, 191
China, 24, 57, 163, 167, 173, 175, 176, 179
Clark, W.S., et al., 51
Coase, Ronald, 115
Cohen, Wesley, and S. Kepler, 37
Cordell, Arthur, and J. Gilmour, 195
Coursey, David, and B. Bozeman, 101, 103
Crow, Michael, xiv
Crow, Michael, and B. Bozeman, 26

Dahlmann, Carl J., and C. Frischtak, 33
Dalton, Donald, and M.J. Serapio, Jr, 146, 152n, 167, 172
David, Paul, 23
Defence Research Board, 47
Defence Research Telecommunications, 42
De la Mothe, John, and G. Paquet, 22
Denmark, 10, 12, 13, 15, 73, 74, 171
Deyo, Frederic C., 18
Doern, G. Bruce, 39, 47
Dominion Experimental Farms, 39
Dominion Grain Research Laboratory, 39
Doutriaux, Jérôme, and M. Barker, 50, 61
Dunning, John H., 147

Edquist, Charles, 131, 132
Edquist, Charles, and Bengt-Ake Lundvall, 75
Eggleston, Wilfred, 33, 41
Eldorado Mines, 40
England, 21, 163, 164
European nuclear research centre (CERN), 132

European space agency (ESRO), 132
European Union, 15, 16, 132, 142, 143, 149, 151

Fang, Rong-Jyue, and Hung-Yen Yang, 19
Finland, 10, 164
Fisheries Research Board, 39
Flight Research Laboratory, 44
Fonds d'aide aux chercheurs et d'aide à la recherche (FCAR), xiv
Foss, Nicolai, and C. Knudsen, 25
Freedman, Ron, and J. Crelinsten, 42
Freeman, Christopher, 5, 22, 99, 131
France, 10, 12, 13, 73, 74, 99, 139, 140, 144, 150, 151, 155, 157, 163, 175, 176

Germany, 10, 11, 12, 13, 73, 74, 95, 96, 139, 140, 144, 150, 151, 157, 164, 173, 175, 176
Gerschenkron, Alexander, 203
Ghiselin, Michael, 77
Graham, Edward M., 171
Granstrand, Ove, L. Hakanson, and S. Skolander, 148, 168
Green, J.J., 10, 42
gross expenditures on R&D (GERD), 11, 12, 19, 34, 54, 73, 135, 150, 158, 196–7

Haber, I.F., 11
Hakanson, Lars, 171, 191
Hall, Peter, and A. Markusen, 21
Hamel, Gary, and C.K. Prahalad, 25
Hartz, Theodore, and I. Paghis, 42
Hewitt, G., 169

Holland, Stuart, 19
Hull, James P., and P.C. Enros, 32, 112
Hymer, Stephen, 146

Inco Ltd, 127
India, 57, 164, 167, 175, 176
Industrial Materials Institute, 61
Industrial Research Assistance Program (IRAP), 49, 195
Industrial Technology Research Institute of Taiwan, 19
Institute for Biological Sciences, 51
Institute for Industrial Reconstruction of Italy, 19
Institute for Information Technologies, 61
Institute for Sensor and Control Technology, 61–2
Integrated Manufacturing Technology Institute, 62
International Business Machines (IBM), 107
International Development Research Centre (IDRC), 63
internationalization of R&D, 131–44, 145–66, 167–92, 201–2
Ireland, 140, 155, 157, 163, 175, 176
IRIS, 127
Italy, 12, 13, 15, 17, 19–20, 74, 75, 140, 144, 155, 157, 175, 176

Japan, 10, 11, 12, 13, 14, 15, 17, 24, 57, 61, 73, 74, 98, 139, 140, 142–4, 149, 150, 151, 153, 164, 172, 173, 175, 176

Kaldor, Nicholas, 24
Katz, Jorge, and Nestor Bercovich, 33
Kelly, Guillaume, 69

Kenney, Martin, and R.
  Florida, 146, 151
Kim, Linsu, 18
Kindleberger, Charles, 146
Kogut, Bruce, and U.
  Zander, 148, 152
Kojima, K., 147
Krugman, Paul, 10, 17, 24
Kuemmerle, Walter, 165,
  169, 191

laboratories: industry, 9,
  20, 32, 33, 34, 35, 38,
  42, 48, 52–3, 54, 55, 57–
  8, 59–60, 65–6, 70, 76–
  96, 98–111, 112–28,
  195, 196–7, 199; public,
  3, 7, 8, 9, 13, 19, 32, 33,
  34, 40, 41, 42, 46–7, 48,
  52, 53, 61, 62–3, 64, 65,
  66, 67, 76–96, 98–111,
  112–28, 199–200; uni-
  versity, 3, 9, 13, 32, 33,
  34–7, 45–6, 48, 52, 58,
  61, 62, 66, 76–96, 98–
  111, 112–128, 199, 201
Latin America, 149
Lazonick, William, 8
Leibenstein, Harvey, 25
Lithwick, N.H., 42, 45, 48
Lundvall, Bengt-Ake, 5, 26,
  131
Luxembourg, 157, 175, 176

Macdonald, Mary E., 71
Mackintosh, Jeffrey G., 72
Maddison, Angus, 3
Malerba, Franco, 19, 74
Mansfield, Edwin, D.J.
  Teece, and A. Romeo,
  169
Marine Biotechnology In-
  stitute, 51
Maritime Regional Labora-
  tory, 42
Medical Research Council
  (MRC), 49, 63, 125, 195
Metcalfe, J. Stanley, 23
Mexico, 33, 57, 133, 134,
  135, 137, 138, 139, 140,
  141, 144, 164, 167, 175,
  176

missions of the laborato-
  ries, 80, 81, 176–8,
  180–1, 186, 199–201
Mowery, David, and N.
  Rosenberg, 33

National Aeronautical Es-
  tablishment, 42
National Research Council
  of Canada (NRC), xiv, 39,
  40, 41, 42, 43, 45–6, 51,
  61, 62, 63, 64, 90, 95,
  194, 197
National Science Founda-
  tion, 57, 67, 68, 143,
  151, 159
national system of innovation (NSI), 3, 4, 5–27,
  31, 73, 77, 96, 99, 131,
  141, 144, 149, 193–5,
  197, 198, 204
Natural Science and Engi-
  neering Research Coun-
  cil (NSERC), 49–50, 63,
  110, 111, 124, 125, 195
Nelson, Richard R., 5, 16,
  26, 37, 131, 148
Nelson, Richard R., and S.
  Winter, 7, 148
Netherlands, 73, 74, 140,
  149, 150, 151, 170
Newbridge Networks, 97
New Zealand, 10
Norway, 133
Niosi, Jorge, 7, 16, 25, 26,
  50, 66, 112, 116, 142,
  143, 150, 165, 169
Niosi, Jorge, and B. Bellon,
  38, 131, 132, 149, 167
Niosi, Jorge, and E.
  Chéron, 57
Niosi, Jorge, and R. Landry,
  53, 66, 113, 121
Niosi, Jorge, and J. Rivard,
  150
Niosi, Jorge, D. Sabourin,
  and M. Wolfson, 38
Niosi, Jorge, P.P. Saviotti, B.
  Bellon, and M. Crow, 6,
  131, 149, 167
Nonaka, Ikujiro, and H.
  Takeuchi, 149

North, Douglass, 203
Northern Telecom, 164

Odagiri, Hiroyuki, and H.
  Yasuda, 171
Okimoto, Daniel, and Y.
  Nishi, 171
Ore Dressing and Metallur-
  gical Laboratory, 39
ORTECH, 63, 64
Osborne, Duncan, and D.
  Sandler, 52
outputs of laboratories, 82–
  3, 182–3, 199–200

Pack, Howard, 24
Papanastassiou, Maria, and
  R. Pearce, 171
PAPRICAN, 126
Patel, Parimal, and K. Pav-
  itt, 11, 14, 17, 67, 131,
  168
Pavitt, Keith, 67, 95
Pearce, Robert, 169, 171,
  190
Perez, Carlota, 5
Performance Plants Inc.,
  108
Plant Biotechnology Insti-
  tute, 51, 67, 95, 96
Posner, M.V., and S.J.
  Woolf, 19
Prairie Regional Labora-
  tory, 42
PRECARN, 127
Pulp and Paper Research
  Institute of Canada (PA-
  PRICAN), 37, 125–6, 194

Raffiquzamman, M., and L.
  Wheeler, 198
regional system of innovation, 4, 21–2, 64–7
revealed technological advantage (RTA), 67–9,
  156–8, 160, 165
Romer, Paul, 24
Ronstadt, Robert, 145, 146,
  169, 177, 190
Rosenberg, Nathan, 190
Rosenberg, Nathan, and C.
  Frischtak, 100

Rugman, Alan, and A. Ver-
beke, 150, 165
Russia, 10

Safarian, A., 38
Sakakibara, Kiyonori, and
D.E. Westney, 171, 172
Saskatchewan Research
Council, 126
Schatz, Christian, and D.C.
Mowery, 14
Scherer, Frederick, 37
Schumpeter, Joseph, 3, 37
Science Council of Canada,
54
Serapio, Manuel G., Jr, 148
Serapio, Manuel G., Jr, and
D. Dalton, 57
Singapore, 24
Smith, Keith, 23
Social Sciences and Hu-
manities Research Coun-
cil (SSHRC), xiv, 50, 63,
125, 195
Soete, Luc, 37
Solocha, Andrew, and M.D.
Soskin, 165, 174
Solocha, Andrew, M.D. Sos-
kin, and M.J. Kasoff, 165,
174
South Korea, 11, 17–18,
24, 98

Soviet Union, 16, 99
Spain, 155, 157
Stiglitz, Joseph, 24
Storper, Michel, 21
Structures, Materials and
Propulsion Laboratory,
44
supranational system of innovation, 132, 144, 202
Swan, G.M., P. Prevezer,
and D. Stout, 21
Sweden, 12, 13, 14, 73, 75,
99, 139, 164, 170–1,
173, 190
Switzerland, 12, 13, 14, 73,
139, 150, 151, 155, 157,
170–1, 175, 176

Taggart, James, 148, 169
Taiwan, 17, 18–19, 24, 98
tax incentives for R&D, 23,
50–1, 55, 56, 131, 185,
195, 196–7
Teece, David J., 147
Terpstra, Vern, 168
Turkey, 57, 163, 167, 175,
176

United Kingdom, 9, 10, 11,
12, 13, 14, 63, 73, 74,
96, 99, 139, 140, 144,
149, 150, 151, 153, 155,

157, 163, 173, 175, 176,
202
United States, 9, 10, 11, 12,
13, 14, 15, 16, 21, 26,
33, 34, 37, 54, 57, 61,
63, 71, 73, 74, 95, 96,
98, 99, 101, 103, 104,
133–9, 140–3, 149, 150–
5, 157, 161, 163–6, 167,
172, 173, 174, 175, 176,
178, 179, 180, 193, 202

venture capital, 51–2, 70–3
Vernon, Raymond, 146
Vernon, Raymond, and
L.G. Wells, Jr, 146
Vietnam, 164
Von Hippel, Eric, 190

Wade, Robert, 19
Walsh, Vivien, J. Niosi, and
P. Mustar, 51, 62
western Europe, 98, 141,
142, 167, 172, 173, 175,
176, 178, 179, 180, 193
Williamson, Oliver, 115
Winter, Sydney, 150
World Bank, 203

Yang, Jih Chang, 19

Zander, Ivo, 170, 191